ROBERT RINGER now sounds a clarion call for the personal liberty and individual freedom you cannot afford to ignore. . . .

The time has come. The citizens of this country either must draw the line and take America back from the politicians who now control it, or they must be prepared to relinquish forever their remaining claims on liberty.

The American Dream was about individualism and the opportunity to achieve success without interference from others. The heart of the American Dream is freedom: the lifeblood is free enterprise.

ROBERT J. RINGER

RESTORING THE AMERICAN DREAM

FAWCETT CREST • NEW YORK

RESTORING THE AMERICAN DREAM

THIS BOOK CONTAINS THE COMPLETE TEXT OF
THE ORIGINAL HARDCOVER EDITION.

Published by Fawcett Crest Books, a unit of CBS Publications,
the Consumer Publishing Division of CBS Inc., by arrangement
with QED

ISBN: 0-449-24314-1

Printed in the United States of America

First Fawcett Crest Printing: August 1980

10 9 8 7 6 5 4 3 2 1

Dedicated to men and women throughout the world who practice individualism and self-responsibility, who do not covet the fruits of the labor of others, who respect every person's right to sovereignty over his own life, and whose actions are consistent with the cause of human freedom.

Contents

Acknowledgments   9

Foreword: William E. Simon 11

"If They Understood the Situation" 17

1   In the Beginning 28

2   The System 45

3   How People Get the Things They Want 71

4   The Gourmet Banquet 120

5   Taking the "Free" Out of Free Enterprise . . . 177

6   "Promoting the General Welfare" 213

7   How the Bill Is Paid 238

8   Keeping It All in Place 288

9   Taking Back America 316

Notes 367

Bibliography 372

Index 379

Acknowledgments

First and foremost, I wish to express my gratitude to Sy Leon, a man whose words and actions exemplify the spirit of the American Dream. Mr. Leon not only has a knack for speaking and writing in a way that gets to the heart of complex ideas (as evidenced by the material from *None of the Above* which has been quoted in this book), but he is, above all, a man of goodwill. My numerous discussions with him over the years have been invaluable to me in both the formulation of basic concepts and in the resolution of specific questions.

I also wish to thank Manuel Klausner, Senior Editor of *Reason* magazine, who, on several occasions, discussed the manuscript with me and made many helpful suggestions, and Morgan Maxfield, economic advisor and author, who provided me with specific answers to a variety of questions in areas concerning economic matters.

On a reading level, in addition to the specific material and ideas of the many authors cited throughout this book, I would like to point out that the works of Ayn Rand, Robert LeFevre and Harry Browne have been particularly instrumental in helping me to construct the general foundation of my basic philosophy. In this respect, I would be remiss if I did not also pay tribute to the works of the late Rose Wilder Lane.

On a broader spectrum, Will Durant and Eric Hoffer stand out as giants among authors who have influenced my thinking. With their combined total of nearly one and a half centuries of reading, studying and writing, Durant, as historian, and Hoffer, as "longshoreman philosopher," make one feel humble, to say the least.

Perhaps most important of all are those who have performed various functions for me on a regular basis, either directly or indirectly contributing to the creation of this book. In this regard, I am, as always, deeply appreciative of the efforts of Lynn Michelson, Patti Zimmerman, Eldo Callico, Jack Medoff and Barbara Westlund, all of whom have demonstrated personal enthusiasm, attention to detail, and willingness to go the extra mile, as they have throughout the years of my relationships with them. The highest accolade, of course, must go to my editor, Ellen Shahan, whose brilliance, talent for organization, and ability and willingness to assume awesome responsibility would be impossible to describe in a way that does her justice. She is, quite simply, the best.

Foreword

Had I read this book prior to my experiences as a member of the government bureaucracy, I might have suspected the author of being an alarmist. Now, however, having witnessed Big Government in action from the inside, I can assure you he is not. And while I may not agree with all of his solutions and recommendations, nonetheless Mr. Ringer's book provides overall some potent medicine for the cancer currently afflicting our society.

Our country today sits at the very crossroads between freedom and totalitarian rule. If a majority of Americans do not soon understand this reality and help to turn the tide toward freedom, they ultimately will have no choice but to understand it—at a time when it will be too late to do anything about it.

Fortunately, many people today already realize that something has gone very wrong with our system. They are concerned about the accelerating evolution of our society into a collectivist state wherein government officials become rulers rather than servants.

One of these concerned people is Robert Ringer; by writing this book, he has done something about it. Mr. Ringer is a true and total libertarian, and I heartily support the basic premise of the book, wherein the author's uncompromising devotion to freedom is readily apparent.

The fundamental direction of Mr. Ringer's and my thinking is the same; our differences in opinion are a matter of degree, rather than substance, and illustrate the very dilemma of mankind as we seek freedom: how much government, how much control over our lives can we and should we tolerate? The basic conflict between the rights of individuals and the rights and needs of society as a whole will never be completely resolved. Political system after political system has sought to reconcile these conflicting rights—and they *are* conflicting—in some meaningful way.

In my view, the best potential for achieving the proper balance between these two basic needs for a stable society lies in our two-hundred-year-old experiment called democracy; but from anarchy to fascism, from military rule to Marxist socialism, the battle has raged and there has never been a totally satisfactory solution. It is the very challenge of this ancient and global dilemma that makes this outstanding author's analysis so compelling.

The book is appropriately named, for it was indeed the American Dream which led to our nation's becoming the freest, strongest and most prosperous country on earth. Unfortunately, liberal, vote-conscious politicians have been destroying that dream at an ever-increasing pace for the past fifty years. (*Liberal,* as used here, refers to today's misdefinition, that once noble term having been appropriated by a group who now uses it to mean *restriction* of liberty.) Robert Ringer makes his greatest contribution to the cause of freedom by exposing this destruction in a detailed, straightforward manner, demystifying government by removing the shroud of complexity that has protected it from the average citizen.

Through this book, I believe that millions of Americans will begin to understand, for the first time, the true causes of such menaces as inflation, unemployment, excessive taxation, and many other government-engendered problems that are provoking the decay of our economy and civilization. I believe they will experience the same shock and concern that I did when these realities first became apparent to me during my tenure in government.

If this should be the case, then our chances of returning to the individualism that made our country the most advanced civilization in history will be greatly increased. We must make the American people aware that the fundamental guiding principles of American life have been reversed and that we are careening with frightening speed toward collectivism and away from individual sovereignty, toward coercive centralized planning and away from free individual choices.

I also believe it to be crucial that people learn that the bond between personal and political freedom and economic freedom is an indissoluble one. Our forefathers recognized this vital connnection and took great care to protect it from those who might aspire to destroy it. The fact throughout history is that whenever government dominates the economic affairs of its citizenry, a free society is eroded, then destroyed, and a minority government ensues. Personal liberty without economic liberty is an absolute contradiction; the one cannot exist without the other, a cardinal point that Mr. Ringer very successfully illustrates.

An exceptional aspect of this book—exceptional because of today's unthinking acceptance of the welfare state as a way of life—is that the so-called functions of government are challenged on a moral basis. This is certainly a most refreshing and exciting view in an age in which people have come to believe that to violate the rights of some individuals is justified so long as the objectives for which such transgressions are committed are deemed to be worthy in the eyes of certain politicians or special-interest groups.

We all must realize, however, that the United States today is not an FDR-type welfare state, a state in which those who are reasonably prosperous are asked to lend a hand to the helpless. That was our system once, but it has changed drastically, and we need books like *Restoring the American Dream* to alert and enlighten our citizens.

Today, our state is simply a redistributionist machine run amok, one in which a relatively small group of people keeps taking the wealth out of everyone's pockets and redistributing it for a variety of purposes that they alone deem important. Yes, sadly, we have become so preoccupied with redistributing the wealth that we seem to have forgotten how to create it. Allegedly, this redistribution process serves humanitarian goals, but actually it simply gives this small group of people the power to run the lives of their countrymen.

As Mr. Ringer points out, this redistribution process is really an attempt to level all people. It is coercive egalitarianism, which is the political curse of our era. It pretends to draw its moral force from the Constitution, which speaks of equality, but it is not the equality of the Constitution which is being sought.

Constitutional equality means that every man in liberty is entitled to go as far in life as his wit, effort and ability will take him: it is equality of opportunity. Egalitarianism is the precise opposite. It punishes the hard-working and ambitious and rewards those who are not; it seeks equality of results regardless of individual differences. One of the most serious falsehoods that is being told the American people is that our present system represents the Constitutional vision of equality. They are being duped.

Restoring the American Dream asks that we begin to reevaluate government functions on a moral basis; that we begin to reevaluate the problems facing our nation in a new light; that we begin to reevaluate our own behavior to determine if we are contributors to the decay that has beset our country. To help us in these reevaluations, Robert Ringer has taken a bold stance on many fronts, unwavering in his belief that government has no right to interfere in the lives of individuals who themselves do not violate the rights of others.

I am in total agreement with the author that our greatest hope for the future lies in teaching the facts to our younger generations. If every high school and college student were to read this book, America's presently beclouded future would begin to shine brightly once more. It is essential that the young people of this country learn to respect the right of every man and woman to seek his or her happiness with minimal interference from the government. The notion that Big Government is omnipotent and omnibenevolent must be invalidated on the basis of fact and logic.

While the author goes farther in specific instances of government reduction than might be best in my judgment, his facts and logic, set forth in a manner that makes them easy to relate to one's everyday life, lead us indisputably in the right direction to restore the American Dream. People throughout the world who believe in the cause of human freedom, who have a common belief in the liberty of man, will surely share in the spirit of this book, and I urge each one of them to spread the word to as many others as possible so that the restoration of the American Dream can become a reality.

If enough people take immediate and positive action of this kind, it is possible that our children will not live under the totalitarian rule that now surely awaits them. Instead, they will live under a government—actually, above a government—that does very little ruling. Perhaps, with our help, government of the future truly will be government "of the people, by the people, and for the people."

—WILLIAM E. SIMON

It may be true . . . that "you can't fool all
the people all the time," but you can fool
enough of them to rule a large country.

—WILL AND ARIEL DURANT

"If They Understood the Situation"

When you first realize that you, and all men and women, possess the innate ability to reason, you have an inkling of what slaves throughout history must have felt when finally released from their shackles. Not that you think you're free. In fact, for the first time in your life you realize just how unfree you really are. But your mind is free—free from the enslavement of confusion, of doubt, of irrational rhetoric.

"The noblest pleasure," said Leonardo, "is the joy of understanding." The pleasure of understanding produces a high which no artificial stimulant could provide. An indescribable exhilaration comes over you. You're so excited that you want to spread the word. For the first time, morality and ethics and virtue and love have meaning to you.

Then it begins: the frustration, the utter and absolute frustration. When you try to share your newfound ability to think rationally, people either stare blankly back at you or return your words with abstract clichés.

You talk about liberty; they answer with incoherencies about "the good of society." You enthusiastically explain why everyone benefits from the virtues of individualism; they retort that your ideas are antiquated. You persist with the beauty inherent in the concept of value for value; they shake their heads patronizingly and mumble something about "the need to control man's greed."

After a while, they wear you down. Your excitement fades; you get back to the reality of everyday life. Then the depression sets in as you realize that *Atlas Shrugged* is everyday life. The world is strangling at the hands of a man-created monster—government—which grows more out of control each day. Civil rights are routinely violated by the irrepressible behemoth that slowly reaches into every area of our lives. Freedom is only a "convenience" word used to justify a thousand different *violations* of freedom. Ayn Rand's warnings about the future are no longer applicable to the future; they are applicable to the present. The future has arrived! Men do not tell their government what to do. Government tells men what to do—and backs it up with force.

After reality sets in, you begin a long period (in some cases a lifetime) of vacillation among despair, excitement, and to-hell-with-itism. Just when you're sure there is no hope for mankind, you run smack into a libertarian in the least likely place. You can't believe it: he knows all about Natural Law and natural rights. He understands the difference between equality and freedom. He understands why laissez-faire capitalism improves the well-being of every honest person in a society. You pinch yourself and find, to your amazement, that you aren't dreaming. Reluctantly you admit it: you're hooked again. You're excited.

These moments of enthusiasm come and go over the years as you bump into other "oddballs" who believe in man's right to be free, in his right to own his own life and pursue his own objectives without violating the rights of others.

But it becomes harder and harder to get you stimulated. And each time that the intoxication of a rational discussion with a rational individual wears off, your mind settles into a state of either despair or to-hell-with-itism. Fortunately, time, experience and rational thinking have a way of persuading you to lean more toward to-hell-with-itism than despair.

To-hell-with-itism is the result of acknowledging both negative and positive realities. First, the negative realities: that government is here to stay; that government will continue to grow bigger and will increasingly restrict man's freedom; that the majority of people in this world either cannot, or will not, think rationally and therefore will continue to be led down the cradle-to-grave-security path to enslavement; that "the system" is so firmly entrenched that neither I nor anyone else can do anything about it.

Then the positive realities: that I am alive; that I live in a country which still allows more freedom than most; that my life is worth living; that if I direct my energies toward my well-being, I will experience much more happiness than I could if I were to dwell on the depressing state of the world.

To-hell-with-itism is not apathy. Quite the opposite. To-hell-with-itism is based on one's belief that life is worth living and on one's intention to live it to the fullest, even if every other person in the world insists on choosing a course of self-destruction.

To-hell-with-itism means that you place a high value on your life as an individual. It means that you refuse to let Big Government get you down. It means that you are unwilling to sacrifice your life trying to save people who do not want to be saved. It means that you refuse to debate people whose arsenals are filled only with mysticism, abstract phrases and meaningless slogans. It means that you realize it is not your function in life to be a flyswatter.

Reading, discussion and the experiences of life all have their effects. Reading, in particular, causes you to vacillate. You read *Nineteen Eighty-four:* despair. Henry Hazlitt: excitement again. *The True Believer:* back to your private world of happiness. *Brave New World:* a new plunge into the depths of despair. Murray Rothbard:

a return to excitement. Will Durant: a retreat again into your own world.

And so it goes for most libertarians: concentration on the pursuit of happiness and goodwill, mixed with occasional fits of excitement and scattered moments of despair.

In what state do I now find myself? While mainly pursuing my own happiness, I find myself experiencing both more excitement and more frustration (an offshoot of despair) than usual. Though history suggests one should be cautious and skeptical, I must acknowledge that bits and pieces of glitter have begun, ever so slightly, to appear on the dreary picture of government. For example:

The recent formation of the Libertarian Party represents a bold attempt to bring together people who may once have thought of themselves as liberals or conservatives, but who have found that what they really believe in is total freedom.

Nonvoting has reached all-time highs, meaning not that people are apathetic, but that they are becomimg harder to fool with mere slogans.

The passage of Proposition 13 in California, drastically reducing property taxes, is a dramatic sign that people are beginning to revolt against excessive taxation.

The "deregulation" of airlines, while a misnomer in the context of free enterprise, makes one wonder if politicians aren't beginning to grow desperate enough to try anything.

And then there is the matter of a book entitled *A Time for Truth,* by William E. Simon, former Secretary of the Treasury.

Paradoxically, this work has provided me with reason for both excitement and frustration. It is exciting because it is the first time to my knowledge that one of "them"—a true insider in Washington's carefully guarded inner sanctum—has made many of the truths about government available to the public. Certainly he is the first to do so armed with facts and figures primarily available only to those in the hierarchy of government.

We need the works of John Stuart Mill and Adam Smith. We need the works of Harry Browne and Henry Hazlitt. They educate us in the fundamentals of the philosophy of freedom and the free-enterprise system. Mill and Smith and their libertarian contemporaries were geniuses of their times; Browne and Hazlitt and their libertarian contemporaries are geniuses of our time. But Simon—he's been there.

William Simon speaks from firsthand experience. He describes the hundreds of congressional hearings he was required to attend, all of which accomplished a grand total of zero. He cites personal accounts of Richard Nixon's and Gerald Ford's rationalizing away economically disastrous decisions in the hope that such appeasement might pull in more votes at election time. He points to the real effects of government regulation on the average American.

Frankly, I would never have believed that a politician would come forward with the facts. But that's just the point—William Simon is not a politician. He virtually stumbled into his post in government and, after viewing the horrors of Washington from the perspective of a lofty position in the hierarchy, he stumbled out as fast as he could, returning to his home in New Jersey, in his words, "a very frightened man."

But it's the very facts Simon addresses—the maze of irrational government policies, the restrictions on freedom, the self-destructive regulation, the depressing economic realities—that frustrate me. The problem of Big Government is *so* big that one seriously doubts whether it can be reduced to comprehensible components in a single book, reduced sufficiently to make the causes and consequences crystal clear to everyone. As a philosopher/writer, however, these doubts represent a challenge to me. And it is this challenge I cannot resist.

Amid all the incisive material in *A Time for Truth,* there is one statement by Simon that continually flashes before me: "I am confident that the American people would demand massive reforms *if they understood the situation.*" [*Italics added.*]

There is no doubt in my mind that most people, no matter how well educated formally, do not, in fact, understand the situation—i.e., do not understand the nature, scope or significance of our common predicament. My certainty on this point is based on most of what I read, hear and see.

In undertaking this challenge, the examination of certain facts is required. Unfortunately, that is the precise point at which many people want to jump ship. Facts concerning government seem not only boring, but complicated. It is my contention, however, that these facts are made to appear complicated by design, and that this, in turn, adds an element of boredom.

People feel that "government subjects" like inflation, unemployment, regulation, capitalism and socialism are mysterious and complex topics which can be understood only by intellectuals and politicians. And from government's standpoint, that kind of attitude is ideal, since, as Montaigne noted, "Men are most apt to believe what they least understand."

Over the years I have found that the corollary to Montaigne's statement is also true; i.e., that the better one understands government, the less he is inclined to believe anything that it says. In my own case, the more I learned about the realities of government, the more I realized that I had thought it complicated only because I was accustomed to thinking in rational and logical terms. But logic and rationality are incompatible with government policies, because government policies are based on a hopeless potpourri of contradictions, illogical premises and irrational actions.

The truth is that government is not really complicated at all when reduced to its simple components. Contrary to popular belief, one does not have to have detailed knowledge of every fact of U.S. history, every piece of legislation ever passed, or every Article of the Constitution to be knowledgeable about the workings of government and the predictable results of its actions.

All that is required to understand the effects of government on one's life is the willingness to reject beliefs that cannot stand toe to toe with facts and logic. That part is up to the reader. My job is limited to cutting through the intellectual aura surrounding government and to explaining, in simple terms, topics previously thought to be complicated.

To say the least, one runs the risk of criticism when he tries to simplify subjects jealously guarded by intellectuals. There is a snobbish element that prevails not only in literature, but in philosophy and "political science" as well. Quite simply, the public is not supposed to know about these things. "Woe to him," says Will Durant, "who teaches men faster than they can learn."

It seems that the intent has been for the world of the intellectual and the world of the layman to remain safely separated for eternity. The intellectual thrives on terms like "consumer price index"; the layman wants to know why he can't purchase as much with the same dollars as last year. The intellectual "explains" the economic intricacies of the Gross National Product; the layman wants to know why he has to pay taxes to support services he neither wants nor uses. The intellectual speaks in abstracts like "the good of society"; the layman wants to know why no one seems to care about what's good for *him*.

Layman, as used here, certainly is not meant to be a patronizing term. *Layman* includes me, you, executives, factory workers, secretaries, professional athletes, housewives, and virtually everyone else involved in the *real* world. The intellectuals who supply us with "answers" we cannot understand, and which have no bearing on our day-to-day problems, are in a world all their own.

I am a believer in Occam's Razor Principle (also known as the Principle of Parsimony), which states: *Never multiply explanations or make them more complicated than necessary. An explanation should be as simple and direct as possible.* Obviously, Occam's Razor Principle is not popular with people who "earn" their livings by making simple problems appear complicated, by creating crises that either do not or need not exist, and by talking in abstracts.

My aim is not to dazzle you with revelations, but to achieve maximum inclusiveness in the briefest possible way. There are thousands of books to which you may refer for greater detail, books on inflation, the Constitution, the fundamentals of libertarianism—on virtually everything mentioned in these pages. Philosophical books on government and economics abound, and I hope that *Restoring the American Dream* will inspire you to look into some of them.

I also feel duty bound, at the outset, to remind the reader that no system or philosophy is perfect, because man himself is imperfect. That, however, does not lessen the value of knowledge and truth. This book does not pretend to be an end-all-be-all or to contain a detailed analysis of every conceivable aspect of government. My intent could be better described as giving the reader a broad insight into the evolution, operation, results and future of government. To best accomplish this, I have tried to avoid getting sidetracked by irrelevant issues and unnecessary details.

A word of caution: problems cannot be solved unless they are first identified. By the words *if they understood the situation*, William Simon seems to be saying that people do not know what the real problems are. Let's first define the problems, then consider possible solutions. Then, and only then, will the final chapter of this book be meaningful. For this reason, if you are a "last-chapter peeker," I urge you to resist the temptation.

The same caution must also be given to "chapter skippers." Due to the nature of the subject matter, strong, rational foundations must be laid in proper sequence. I believe, however, that you will find these foundations exciting if it's truth you are seeking.

I seek the truth in this book fully recognizing that history has rarely made truth and popularity bedfellows. Obviously, in order to investigate the facts, basic premises and traditional thinking must be challenged. Often we are made to feel uncomfortable by reality. Words like *totalitarianism* frighten us. We don't want to hear things that upset us. We don't like our neatly structured notions to be disturbed. But preconceived, immovable ideas are incompatible with truth. People say they love truth, but in reality they want to believe that that which they love is true.

Perhaps it is right that "he that increaseth knowledge increaseth sorrow, and in much wisdom is much grief." Perhaps it is not so much that people do not understand as that they do not *want* to understand. Perhaps this is what Aldous Huxley had in mind in *Brave New World* when Mustapha Mond, the supreme government powerholder, said to the awed and confused Savage from the Indian reservation, "The optimum population is modeled on the iceberg—eight-ninths below the water line, one-ninth above."

"And they're happy below the water line?" asked the Savage.

"Happier than above it," replied Mustapha Mond.

Although I have great concern over the possibility that Huxley may have been right, I am writing this book based on a series of assumptions, assumptions with which Huxley undoubtedly would disagree. I am assuming that most men and women, when armed with truth, will act honestly and decently. I am assuming that most men and women are basically good, but are misled, which is why an understanding of the facts is so essential. I am assuming that most men and women, once they understand the facts, will act in good faith.

The orientation of this book is not only an appeal to man's decency, but to his rationality. Coming out of the starting gate, it gives *everyone* the benefit of the doubt. It assumes that most people, regardless of how much they may presently be contributing to the problem, have good intentions. It assumes that virtually everyone—union members, union leaders, welfare recipients, businessmen, civil-service workers, environmental activists—is a victim of one of man's greatest weaknesses: expedient, short-term thinking. This human failing motivates people to group themselves together to expedite the realization of their desires, i.e., to bring about quick, short-term solutions to their problems through government intervention. And it is this action that perpetuates the cycle which has nearly destroyed the American Dream.

This book specifically rejects the short-term, irrational "us-against-them" philosophy. As long as people, in pursuit of freedom and well-being, see themselves as laborers versus businessmen, blacks versus whites, environmentalists versus polluters, or liberals versus conservatives, to list but a few examples, the destructive cycle will not only continue, but will get worse.

It may sound like a bit of corn, but the truth is that it's *all of us* against the forces of nature. It's all of us against one of man's greatest weaknesses—expedient, short-term thinking.

Isaac Asimov, the renowned science-fiction writer, recently addressed a group of businessmen to whom I also was invited to speak. Asimov made clear that the danger in demanding special favors of government is that you risk the ultimate destruction of freedom and free enterprise, which necessarily means the destruction of your own special interest as well. Asimov emphasized this reality by suggesting the following analogy: "If my right arm decided to stab my left arm to death, my right arm would die too."

The success of this book will depend on how many people, after reading it, will understand that their own special interests will be devastated *in the long run* if they think only in terms of quick gain and ignore the big picture, and on how many of them will take rational action accordingly.

Many pragmatists think we're already too far gone to reverse the trend, and the history of civilizations certainly supports them. Optimists, on the other hand, usually give it about one chance in ten. Because of some of the positive things that have occurred recently, a few of which I touched on earlier, you could call me a pessimist trying hard to be optimistic. As such, I give it about one chance in a hundred—one chance in a hundred that our march toward totalitarianism can be halted and that we can begin a slow return toward liberty.

This book is my contribution toward that end.

—ROBERT J. RINGER

1

In the Beginning

The strain of high taxes, the frustration of trying to keep pace with inflation, the fear of unemployment, and the feeling of being stifled at every turn by ever-increasing regulations are just a few of the government-related problems that confront most people today. But this handful of items receives special attention only because their effects on our lives are so obvious. In reality, however, they barely give us a glimpse of the extent to which government is involved in practically everything we do.

Government actions affect your daily life beginning with the moment you wake up in the morning. The clock radio that awakens you is subject to many manufacturing and sales regulations. The music set off by the alarm mechanism comes from a station that is able to broadcast only because it has been granted a special government license; it must comply with the government's idea of "good programming" or run the risk of having its license revoked.

After getting out of bed, you wash your face and brush your teeth with government-controlled water. The toothpaste you use has, of course, been approved by the government. The towel you dry your hands with also has met many government-imposed standards. And so it goes with your comb, your clothes, and almost everything else you use in the process of getting ready for the day.

Your breakfast, "quite naturally," is regulated by the

Food and Drug Administration. If you have a cigarette after breakfast, you not only pay government for the privilege of smoking (through cigarette taxes), but you also are reminded, whether or not you wish to be, that "smoking is dangerous to your health."

The day continues much the same: You drive to work on government-owned streets and highways, communicate with others via the government-monopolized mail service, read newspaper accounts of government-released facts and figures on the state of the economy, and, when you finally enter the privacy of your home in the evening, you take into account government's standards of morality (backed by law) regarding leisure-time activities.

While people generally recognize only the most visible and monstrous ramifications of the creeping infringements on their freedom, ironically, to whom do they look for solutions? Government.

If it is government to whom most people turn, then one of our objectives should be to find out if government is the solution to our problems or if government *is* the problem. And that question can be properly answered only if we start at the beginning.

To understand how government first came into being—how and why men initially came under the control of other men—and to appreciate what the creation of government meant in terms of human freedom, it is essential to have an understanding of "Natural Law" and the nature of man.*

NATURAL LAW

Any philosophy—political, religious or other—must begin with a premise, a foundation upon which to build

---

*The terms *man* and *men* as used in this book are meant to include both genders, except where I have specifically referred to the male or female gender.

its concepts. Therefore, inherent in every philosophy is the same type of "first-cause" problem with which one is confronted when philosophizing about the nature of the universe. No matter how self-evident a concept may seem, no matter how axiomatic a man may claim it to be, the truthful philosopher will always admit that, in the final analysis, the starting point of his philosophy is but an opinion.

The opinion which the philosopher uses as his premise may be rational or irrational, popular or unpopular, strongly supported by evidence or based on little more than mysticism. But regardless of any of these factors, the initial premise of any philosophy can never rightfully be classified as other than an opinion.

The initial premise underlying the philosophy of libertarianism (and of this book) is that each man owns his own life and therefore has the right to do anything he wishes with that life, so long as he does not forcibly interfere with the life of any other man.* This forms the basis for what we will hereafter refer to as Natural Law. Natural Law also may be properly thought of as the "law of nonaggression"; i.e., even though a man has the right of self-choice, self-choice does not include the right to commit aggression against others.

Aggression may be thought of as force or fraud or as the threat of force or fraud. Hence, from a Natural-Law standpoint, only *one* thing is against the law: aggression against others. When aggression occurs, man's rights are violated. It naturally follows that violence for any reason other than self-defense is a violation of Natural Law.

---

*For the sake of brevity, I often will leave off what I call the "libertarian tag" when referring to Natural Law, the libertarian tag being "so long as he does not forcibly interfere with the life of any other man" (or similar qualifying statements of this kind). Therefore, whenever I make a statement to the effect that "man has the right to do anything he pleases," the libertarian tag should automatically be assumed.

One of the basic tenets of this book, then, is that liberty must be given a higher value than *all* other objectives. Intellectually, one either must accept or reject the principle of Natural Law from the outset. It must stand or fall on the basis of one's power to reason and on one's moral standards. It cannot be accepted initially on the basis of reason, then be allowed to fall at some later point on an emotional whim.

In other words, Natural Law, like all basic principles, allows no room for compromise. Ayn Rand illuminates the moral impossibility of compromising on basic principles when she asks, "What would you regard as a 'compromise' between life and death? Or between truth and falsehood? Or between reason and irrationality?"

Natural Law is a no-compromise principle. If a person claims to understand human freedom, but insists on certain exceptions to freedom, he either is admitting that he advocates the violation of Natural Law or he is demonstrating that he does not really grasp the concept of Natural Law. One must remain steadfast to the moral belief that no matter how "worthy" the cause for which a man's rights are violated, the end *never* justifies the means. That is to say, no matter how moral or humane one may believe a cause to be, if its attainment requires a violation of the rights of even one man, then the end has been achieved through immoral action.

Therefore, while the needs and desires of certain individuals (whether they be the "poor" or any other vaguely defined group*) may constitute a legitimate concern to many people, they nonetheless fall outside the scope of man's natural rights. This *does not mean* that men should not be concerned about other men; it *does not mean* that men should not be sympathetic toward other men; it *does*

---

*Quotation marks have been placed around the words "rich" and "poor" throughout this text for the reason that everyone has a different estimation of what constitutes "rich" and "poor."

not mean that men should not be helpful to other men; it *does not mean* that men should not be charitable toward other men. What it *does* mean is that men do not have the right to *force* other men to be concerned, sympathetic, helpful or charitable toward others.

If Natural Law is to be meaningful, *no part of any* man's life and efforts can belong to anyone else without that man's voluntary consent. Any time that a man (or any group of men) takes authority over someone else's life without his consent, he is violating Natural Law. Therefore, the difference between Natural Law and government law is that Natural Law demands freedom, while government law demands that certain men obey other men.

Obviously, then, one man cannot grant natural rights to another man, since men already possess these rights at birth. All men are *born* with equal natural rights. And perhaps this is a good time to examine the word *equal*. Men are not born *equal;* men are born with equal *rights*. That is, men have the right to be free to live their lives as they choose. A man has a right to survival, a right to try to better his existence, a right to enjoy one hundred percent of the fruits of his labor, a right to do as he pleases—a right to "life, liberty and the pursuit of happiness."

PROPERTY RIGHTS

It is a basic tenet of libertarianism that without property rights, no other rights are possible. I am embarrassed to admit that it took me many years to understand this fundamental concept. I had viewed property only as inanimate matter, quite separate and apart from a man's life. I could not seem to make the connection between the two. In actual fact, they are so connected that one is virtually an extension of the other. A man's property is an extension of his very life.

Consider: John T. is told that he is a free man. So, free to do as he pleases, he buys a plot of land. He "mixes" his energy and creativity with the soil and manages to grow profitable crops. A group of men, calling itself the People's Protection Council, approaches John and explains that he must give them $1,000 to help bear the costs incurred by them in "protecting the people" (including him).

John thanks them, but explains that he is not interested in being protected. Unfortunately, however, the representatives of the People's Protection Council play with guns. John is told that he either must pay the $1,000 "tax," or they will have no choice but to sell his property to obtain the funds (i.e., they will take his property by force and sell it, against his will, to obtain the required $1,000).

Clearly, John's property rights have been violated, but that is not all. John's property is actually an extension of his body in that he has used his time, effort and ability to create the crops that now grow on the land he purchased. If someone takes his property from him, are they not also taking his time, effort and ability—his very life?

How can one separate this man's life from his property? If you took everything that a man owned, he would not own his own life. The next time he attempted to earn money or create something, the fruits of his labor could again be confiscated.

The same is true of property that is purchased. The money used to make a purchase presumably was earned through the purchaser's efforts. That makes the money an extension of his life, and, therefore, the same would be true of anything purchased with that money. No matter what the circumstances, when a person's property rights are violated, his freedom is violated.

A libertarian, then, believes that no one has a right to

any other person's property, which includes both his body and everything that he owns. Once this concept is understood, it would be proper to say that, in reality, all crime is based on trespassing on the property of an owner.

When people make "humanitarian" statements about human rights being more important than property rights, they are, in a sense, correct. They are correct because human rights *include* property rights, as well as all other rights of man. A man has the right to dispose of his life *and* his property in any way that he chooses, without interference from anyone else. A man has *no right* to dispose of any other man's life or property, no matter what his personal rationalizations may be.

As explained in "Fundamentals of Liberty," there really are only three possible ways in which to view property:

1) Anyone may take anyone else's property whenever he pleases.

2) Some people may take the property of other people whenever they pleased.

3) No one may ever take anyone else's property without his permission.

Later, when we address more specifically the "functions" of today's government, it will be important to keep these three alternatives in mind. It will also be important to remember that the true tests of ownership are whether or not you may do anything you desire with your own property, and whether or not anyone else may take all or any part of it from you.

Belief in Natural Law is what differentiates the libertarian from the so-called liberal and so-called conservative. We usually see the "liberal" as someone who advocates personal freedom, but who displays enormous creativity in rationalizing the restriction of economic freedom. "Conservatives" tend to favor economic freedom but begin to draw lines where personal freedom is concerned. Libertarians reject such contradictory line drawing. Libertarians believe in freedom—period!

As such, the libertarian is incapable of prejudice when it comes to human rights. All people—"rich" and "poor," "strong" and "weak," "informed" and "ignorant"—are entitled to sole dominion over their own lives and property. Custom, tradition and government law do not influence the libertarian's reasoning when it comes to freedom. Man has a right to be free, and this freedom can be taken away only by force.

HUMAN FREEDOM

Everyone seems to be in favor of freedom, but few people seem to be able to agree on just what it means.

To the laissez-faire businessman, freedom means an end to government regulation. To the communist, freedom can be achieved only when individual incentive has been crushed and "the people" own everything.

Homosexuals think they will be free when they can "come out of the closet" without fear of reprisal. Those who oppose "gay rights" apparently believe that freedom includes being free from the flaunting of homosexuality.

Some people believe that job quotas for certain minority groups promote freedom. To a person who is antidiscriminatory in the truest sense of the word, quotas and seniority considerations are a violation of freedom.

People's notions concerning freedom are limitless. Hitler literally believed that only the complete extermination of the Jews would allow men to be free. Obviously, then, just because someone is in favor of "freedom," that does not mean you should automatically consider him to be a person of high moral standards.

One person's idea of freedom can actually be devastating to the freedom of another. To one man, liberty means doing what he wants with his own life, while to another man it means doing what he wants with *other* men's lives. Therefore, each type of man says the other man's concept of freedom is tyranny.

Based on the evidence, I think we can safely conclude that throughout history men have miscommunicated on the subject of freedom. Since conservatives, liberals, bigots, fascists, communists, back-to-nature advocates, and every other kind of group imaginable all claim to want "freedom," they obviously cannot be talking about the same thing The problem stems from a phenomenon I refer to as the Definition Game—the knack people have for stretching the meaning of a word just enough to suit their particular objectives.

The dictionary defines *freedom* as "being free." In turn, *free* is defined as "not under the control or power of another." How can there be such confusion over a definition so clearly stated?

First, people have a tendency, in reference to freedom, to think in terms of freedom for *themselves*. In other words, freedom is a license to do as they please. To a nationalist, perhaps, freedom is achieved when the people of *his* country are "not under the control or power of another."

Second, throughout history utopian thinkers have insisted on confusing freedom with equality. Nothing could be more incorrect. No matter what one's moral desires, nature has made freedom and equality totally incompatible. Will and Ariel Durant picture nature "(smiling) at the union of freedom and equality in our utopias. For freedom and equality," say the Durants, "are sworn and everlasting enemies, and when one prevails the other dies."[1]

As governments step up their attempts to defy nature and bring about equality, they find it necessary to employ force. And when force enters the picture, that means some men will come "under the control of power" of others. Exit freedom.

In other words, you may be surprised, after a little probing, to find that when people espouse freedom, often they are referring to *their* freedom, not yours. Worse, you may conclude that the gaining of their freedom necessitates the *violation* of yours.

What happens when one man's freedom interferes with the freedom of another man? If freedom is to be subjectively defined by each individual, it is reduced to a meaningless abstract. As we shall see, the only way freedom can be rationally viewed is in its pure, no-compromise form: *human freedom*.

If we think in terms of human freedom, we must think in terms of *all* men being free. Quite logically, freedom then becomes an across-the-board matter. It means freedom for the "poor," the "rich," the "handicapped," the "oppressed," the "weak," the "strong." It means freedom for *everyone*.

The idea of absolute freedom raises a number of questions, because the concept of man in a state of pure freedom is foreign to us and therefore difficult to grasp. Doesn't civilization need rules? What would happen if everyone did as he pleased?

These are valid questions, and they point up the cruelest paradox of nature: that in order to preserve freedom, freedom must, because of the reality of man's nature, be restricted. Allow freedom to be absolute and you can be sure it soon would be replaced by chaos. So it becomes a question of whose freedom, if anyone's, needs to be restricted, and to what extent, if any, it needs to be restricted in order to "protect freedom."

Another thought that inevitably surfaces when one talks about across-the-board freedom is that freedom is an outdated idea. Advocates of this view dwell on the fact that the world is now far more complex and overpopulated than it was at some unspecified time in the past. Men, they believe, need to be restrained by governments for their own good and the good of their fellowmen.

But people who use the "complex-society" argument usually are among those who, at heart, really do not want a free society. Many people are unhappy and/or unable to achieve success in a free world, thus what they really yearn for is an external force (government) that can make other people conform to *their* moral standards.

Most so-called freedom fighters and political terrorists use the word *freedom* only for convenience. As history has recorded only too well, in most instances where "freedom fighters" have succeeded, freedom has become a much *less* abundant commodity after their success. Russia, China, Cuba and Ethiopia are noteworthy examples of this.

NATURE OF MAN

Since governments are not living entities in themselves, but consist of groups of men who "govern" other men, the deepest roots of government are embedded in the very nature of man. There are certain human traits that are especially important in understanding the birth of government.

—*Survival Instinct:* First and foremost, man, as he has demonstrated so well during his long stay on this planet, is a survivor. Survival does not mean merely staying alive. It includes furthering his well-being in every possible way. This trait is sometimes translated into the often misunderstood term *self-interest*.

Self-interest does not coincide with the bleeding heart's picture of an avaricious monster trampling over bodies to grasp the last ounce of whatever it is that avaricious monsters are supposed to be after. It simply means that all men have needs and desires and that it is quite natural—

and civilized—to try to fulfill those needs and desires to the best of their abilities. As a survivor, one of man's greatest desires is to be free. It is also his greatest need if he is to function as a man.

Self-interest—the survival instinct in man—is not a moral or immoral quality in itself. It is the behavior in which this instinct manifests itself in each individual that is moral or immoral.

—*Expediency Factor:* Underscore this trait in your mind, for as you will see throughout this book, the Expediency Factor in man is one of the major forces—perhaps the major force—behind the destruction of the American Dream.

By *Expediency Factor*, I am referring to the instinct to seek quick, short-term, convenient solutions to problems. This almost always entails irrational action, because any behavior that does not take into consideration the long-term effects on one's own well-being is irrational.

—*Individuality vs. Conformity:* Every person is unique—in looks, abilities, needs, desires—in all respects. As such, each person is inherently individualistic. But some people are consciously individualistic in that they "do their own thing," so to speak. These people are usually among the most creative individuals in a society.

At the same time, however, everyone has the desire to conform to one extent or another. This is an instinct that is noticeably dominant in the majority of men, and it is this drive to conform that "keeps people in line." Most people, at least subconsciously, have a great fear of standing out, especially if it means standing alone.

—*Power Lust vs. Subservience:* Finally, we get to the heart of the matter, the addictive drive in some men for power and the submissive tendency in most men to serve "leaders." It is the inevitable union of these two types that has allowed governments to restrain man since he first became "civilized."

There are many kinds of power—physical power, the power to make money, the power to persuade people—but the power I am referring to here is pure, unadulterated, raw power—*power over other people.* To some men, the power to control the lives of others is an end in itself. While there may be financial benefits to be gained by such power, these are considered mere bonuses by the genuine power seeker. His main objective is always the fulfillment of his insatiable lust for power. Ruling others is the ultimate in ego gratification for him.

Most men, however, are of an idolatrous nature and yearn to revere prominent people. Those men who longed for power and those who by nature were subservient probably were destined from earliest times to form an institutionalized system whereby one could dominate the other.

Ironically, however, the impetus which brought respectability to the concept of some men having power over others came from a most unlikely source: men who were strong individualists.

The rational individualist knew that his needs could best be served by dealing with other men as traders, meaning that all men had to be free; therefore he did not believe in interfering in the lives of his neighbors. The individualist was not inclined to make short-term, expedient decisions. but because he was human, he did at times fall into the Expediency-Factor trap . . . and, as we shall see, Nature has never forgiven him for having fallen into that trap with the power seekers of the world.

THE CATALYST

Though we know precious little about ancient history, historians seem to be in general agreement on the one phenomenon most responsible for the beginning of "civilized man." This phenomenon is referred to as the

Agrarian Revolution. When man discovered agriculture, it freed him, for the first time, from the nomadic life of hunting for his food.* He was able to "settle down" and produce his food from the land. The evolution of the family unit followed as a natural result of his having roots, of having a place called home.

For the first time. land was not a hunting stage upon which men chased wild animals. Land, when mixed with man's labor and creativity, acquired value. Land was now *property*. Men had owned other things before—crude axes, knives, the most rudimentary coverings for their bodies—but these things could be replaced with relative ease. Not only had their values been minimal but they were easily protected because of their relatively small size. But land—especially improved land—was both valuable and difficult to protect. If a man successfully combined his energy with the soil and produced plentiful crops, the "food machine" he created could be neither quickly nor easily replaced.

The type of individual most likely to succeed by cultivating the earth's crust to further his well-being was the rational individualist. He was now free of the day-to-day struggle for survival that had depended upon his catching prey. His needs and desires could now be fulfilled by staying in one place and investing time and energy in the miracle of agriculture. Having freed himself from the uncertainties of the hunter's life man had no desire to lessen that freedom. The good life having been discovered, it was more than worth fighting to protect.

But the industrious man, by nature, has neither the time nor the inclination to fight. This presented a problem, as it has throughout history, because there were always envious men who aspired to steal the food machines

*Though *man* here refers to both genders, it should be pointed out that the evidence strongly suggests that it was women who originally developed agriculture.

created by him. From the very beginning, outlaws, in their struggle to survive, managed to create irrational justifications for plundering the property of others.

Clearly, the new property owners needed a solution. And that solution was to be found in the most unlikely alliance in history, an alliance between industrious individualists who sought protection of their property and men whose chief aspirations were to achieve power over others. Thus was government born. The floodgates had been opened.

One great occurrence—the discovery of agriculture—was the catalyst.

The birth of government gave an air of respectability to a system through which some men could rule other men. It was a way of making order out of chaos, of giving structure to society. With social order established, civilization had begun.

From the beginning, of course, the alliance was a contradiction in terms—one side desiring to have its freedom protected, the other side offering to protect it in exchange for controls over that same freedom. Freedom-loving men throughout history, men who have given the highest of all values to liberty, have regretted the arrangement ever since.

The contradiction—that in order to preserve freedom, freedom must be restricted—is always with us. And the perfect solution has yet to make its appearance.

Because of this enduring contradiction, friction was inevitable. Men who desired to have their property protected obviously intended to franchise power only to the extent that it could accomplish that end. The only legitimate function of government, as granted by "the people," was to protect the individual from aggression, i.e., to protect his life and property.

Whenever government goes beyond this basic function and acts in violation of men's rights, *it* then becomes the aggressor. At that point, government itself becomes an illegal entity that is in violation of Natural Law.

The trade-off had been simple and straightforward: "We'll give you limited power to rule us in exchange for protection of our lives and property." Government had no right, nor does it now have the right, to *violate* the rights of people or to *grant* rights. Protecting rights is far removed from violating or granting them.

Nor does it seem likely that men ever intended for government to fulfill the desires of all men or to solve their problems. From history as recent as the American Revolution, we know that our "founding fathers" made it eminently clear that they did not want government interfering in their lives and property.

To power seekers, however, government became a means to an entirely different end. As Milton Friedman has said, "The power to do good is also the power to do harm." Power seekers now had a vehicle through which they could exercise their compulsion to control other men. To them, their newly acquired power was not a means to the end that had been intended by the grantors of that power. Power itself was, and always has been, the real objective of government officials, albeit sometimes not consciously acknowledged.

In *Nineteen Eighty-four*, George Orwell, through his character O'Brien, explains the true relationship between power and government:

Now tell me *why* we (the Party) cling to power? What is our motive? Why should we want power? . . . The Party seeks power entirely for its own sake. We are not interested in the good of others; we are interestd solely in power. . . . The German Nazis and the Russian Communists came very close to us in their methods, but they never had the courage to recognize their own motives. They pretended, perhaps they even believed, that they had seized power unwillingly and for a limited time, and that just round the corner there lay a paradise where human beings would be free and equal. We are not like that. We know that no one ever seizes power with the intention of relinquishing it. Power is not a means; it is an end. One does not establish a dictatorship in order to safeguard a revolution; one makes the revolution in order to establish the dictatorship. . . . The object of power is power.

With such conflicting objectives between the ruled and ruling classes, it is understandable why the history of man encompasses one tale after another of revolutions, ingenious ploys for controlling people, and conquests of one government over another.

2

The System

The chief problem for men of power (i.e., "governments") has been the same since they formed that first ill-fated partnership with individuals who desired only to have their freedom protected: What is the most practical way in which to maintain control over people? Power seekers have experimented with many approaches, using such varying ideological guises as communism, fascism and divine monarchies, to name but a few.

An institutionalized means of controlling people, then, supported by a monopoly on the use of force, is one of the two characteristics common to *all* forms of government. The second is that all governments exist off surpluses created by the people whom they rule. The ruling classes, i.e., those people who refer to themselves as "governments," do not produce wealth, thus their existence depends upon the expropriation of assets from others.

Among the various definitions of government to be found in dictionaries are: "the exercise of political *authority, direction* and *restraint* over the actions of the inhabitants of communities, societies, or states"; "a system of ruling." [*Italics added.*]

Though governments have varied in form over the centuries, virtually all have been similar in substance. All governments restrain and rule people; therefore, all governments are totalitarian and authoritarian to one extent or another. (*Totalitarianism* refers to a centralized form of government in which those in control grant neither recognition nor tolerance to parties differing in opinion. *Authoritarianism* is a system of governing that calls for unquestioning submission to authority.)

It is never a question of whether a government is totalitarian and authoritarian, but, rather, to what degree. Most governments throughout history, of course, have been outright dictatorships, under the rule of either a single dictator or an oligarchy (a small number of men).

Two obvious examples of extreme totalitarianism are today's communist Russia and the Nazi Germany of the 1930's and 40's. Though their window dressings—"ideologies"—are very different, today's Russia does not, and Hitler's Germany did not, tolerate opposition of any kind. Nazi Germany, under Hitler, was a totalitarian dictatorship, while the Soviet Union is a totalitarian oligarchy. In both cases, individual freedom was, and is, sacrificed to unquestioning submission to authority.

But what about democracy? Isn't the democracy "government by the people?" If it is possible for government to be moral, or at least useful, then surely a government with the lofty stated goal of "vesting supreme power in the people" should be its best possible example. The analysis in this book, therefore, will focus on democratic government.

Pointing out the drawbacks of a democracy does not mean that I wish to live under any other presently existing form of government. It simply means that there *are* drawbacks to the system, and that it is in one's best interest to be aware of them. When people are not aware of the realities of a political system, or, worse, when they refuse to acknowledge such realities, they are giving men of power a free rein.

The relevant question is not whether democracy works. The question is how well it works, and for whom. We know that it works very well for those in power, as do communism and other forms of dictatorship. But whether democracy is the best type of government mankind can devise to protect individual rights is a question worth investigating. As Sy Leon has observed:

> The question . . . is not whether the system works, but whether we like the *way* it works. Just because something works doesn't mean it is desirable. Concentration camps work, if your purpose is to enslave people. Stealing works, if all you care about is money. Lying works, if you don't give a damn about your personal integrity. Literally anything, no matter how monstrously immoral, will work, depending on your desires and how you define the term "work."[2]

If men were truly free, no government could force them to do anything they did not want to do. If government truly represented you, you could give *it* orders. The reality, of course, is the opposite. Quite obviously, notwithstanding what people have been taught to believe, democracy is not synonymous with freedom.

In reality, the only way men can be *completely* free is through an *absence* of government. On the other hand, to keep men totally under control, a strong totalitarian government is necessary; to try to make men equal, a totalitarian government that takes away freedom is needed; but if a mixture of equality and freedom is the purported objective, then a democracy is seemingly the type of government best suited to accomplish this. The problem is that as a democracy leans toward equality, it leans away from freedom; as it leans toward freedom, it leans away from equality.

It is an historic fact that great civilizations experience four definitive stages. They are born; they flourish; they decay; they die. This includes the few democracies that have been attempted in past centuries. It is interesting to conjecture as to why democracies, when they have endeavored to achieve both freedom and equality, have decayed and died along with all other systems of government.

Historically, democracies, in their decaying process, usually have evolved into tightly controlled totalitarian governments. Ironically, what brings about this collapse is an excess of democracy, which causes chaos and leads to totalitarian rule. When a democracy degenerates into a free-for-all stampede of citizens vying both for favors and for increasing infringements on the rights of fellow citizens, total collapse is inevitable.

And therein lies the major weakness in a democracy. The very nature of a democracy promotes that irrational, destructive human instinct—the Expediency Factor. A democratic government becomes a vehicle through which each citizen, dominated by thoughts of expedient solutions to his own problems, hopes to live at the expense of his neighbor. He accomplishes this through "majority rule"— a concept which, by its very definition, implies that it is justifiable to violate the rights of the minority so long as the majority consents to it.

But Majority Rule, as men have time and again discovered, can be far more lethal than a bullet. By use of this clever device, some men can take control over other men's lives, expropriate their wealth, and generally do as they please to them, without having to resort to physical violence. Next to "inflation," Majority Rule is the most ingenious scheme ever contrived by governments.

MAJORITY RULE

Majority Rule should be examined from three viewpoints: morality, logic and reality.

MORALITY

Assuming one accepts the premise that men need to be governed to one extent or another, the inevitable question regarding all rulers and all rules is: Who shall decide?

Shall it be God? This might be a satisfactory solution to many people, but, unfortunately, God seems to have more important things to do than to make frequent appearances on earth. And in His absence, there seem to be several million differing interpretations of His laws.

Shall it be "the minority?" Common sense dictates that minority rule would be an unjust concept.

To this date in history, Majority Rule seems to be the best method through process of elimination; i.e., it seems to be the method preferred by men who believe in government, but who seek as much individual freedom as possible. The danger lies in confusing the word *best* with *moral* or *good*. To say that a system is best is to beg the question. Being a better system has nothing whatsoever to do with being moral.

When one says that a method is best, he is not assigning it any sort of absolute rating; he is merely making a comparison. Being the "best" could mean simply being the "least immoral." As Lysander Spooner asked 100 years ago, "Suppose (the U.S.) be 'the best government on earth,' does that prove its own goodness, or only the badness of all other governments?"

It is important to test the moral validity of Majority Rule, if for no other reason than to decide whether or not it deserves the aura of sanctity that surrounds it. Most people have never dared to question that basic morality or logic in the assumption that a majority should have power over a minority.

A majority of people in the South once believed in black slavery. Did that make it moral? What laws, divine or natural, gave the majority a right to hold others in bondage? Whether or not one realizes it, if he believes in the moral validity of Majority Rule, he *does*, at least unknowingly, believe in slavery. Because a majority *can impose slavery* on a minority any time that it wishes.

The fact is that the practice of Majority Rule violates Natural Law. It interferes with an individual's right to pursue his own happiness without interference from others. It violates his inalienable right to his own property. If a man's rights are inalienable, then people are not morally entitled to violate those rights just because they happen to do so through group action.

One cannot say he believes in human freedom (i.e., Natural Law), then make an arbitrary exception when an act of aggression is taken by some unspecified number of men calling itself "the majority." If this logic were to be accepted, any small group of men would have the moral right to agree upon something, then approach a stranger and force him to go along with it. This is how a lynch mob works, and a lynch mob, too, is a majority. A lynch mob is Majority Rule stripped of its fancy trappings and its facade of respectability.

The most important person in this country is you! In your life, *you* are the majority. You have a natural right to live your life as you please, without interference from others—no matter how great their numbers. No group of people, regardless of size, has the right to take the fruits of your labor without your consent. No group of people, regardless of size, has the right to tell you what to do with your property. No group of people, regardless of size, has the right to tell you what you can smoke, drink or eat.

If you are not interfering with the life of anyone else, no group of people, regardless of size, has the right to interfere with yours. If you do not believe in interfering with your neighbors, but ten of your neighbors vote to interfere with each other's lives and with yours, you are, morally speaking, already a majority of one.

One of the great myths of the world in which we live is that the majority is inherently vested with some divine power to choose between right and wrong. The idea that the majority automatically is aligned with that which is "good" is an absurd assumption. Such an idea forces the conclusion that the minority represents that which is "evil."

In reality, Majority Rule has nothing whatsoever to do with morality, justice or truth. It means only that more people have voted one way or another on a candidate or issue, and, in actual practice, the Expediency Factor more often than not makes their choice an *immoral* one. The highest moral principles are contained in Natural Law, not in laws decreed by the majority.

From a very early age, there was something about Majority Rule that did not ring true to me. I had followed the concept through to what I believed to be its logical conclusion, and the ultimate implication seemed an atrocity to me. For years I have been describing this ultimate implication of Majority Rule as the *Black Hair/Blond Hair Theory*.

Simply stated, the Black Hair/Blond Hair Theory translates Majority Rule into "tyranny of the majority."

Consider: 51% of the people in a community have black hair and 49% have blond hair. If the members of this community believe in, and live by, the absolute sanctity of Majority Rule, then the slight minority—the 49% who have blond hair—find themselves at the mercy of those who outnumber them by only 2%. If Majority Rule is morally valid, then the black-haired people of this hypothetical community possess the moral right to do with the blond-haired people as they wish. Even a decision to execute them would be "moral" on the grounds that it is "the will of the majority."

Drawing lines on Majority Rule does not work, either. One cannot say, "Well, the majority should not be allowed to have the minority executed, but it should have the right to decide on matters that do not violate the rights of others." But *all* Majority Rule violates the rights of others if it forces them to go along with actions with which they do not agree.

In a community where homosexuals outnumber heterosexuals, should the majority have the right to outlaw sex between married partners of the *opposite* sex? In a community where atheists outnumber non-atheists, should the majority have the right to outlaw the practice of religion? In a community where people over the age of sixty-five outnumber all other ages combined, should the majority have the right to force the others to turn over 90% of their wages to them? Where does one draw the line? It always gets back to Natural Law. And if Natural Law is one's moral foundation, Majority Rule is *against* the law, because it always involves aggression.

You either believe in human rights or you do not, and Majority Rule *always* violates human rights. Those who would like to make Majority Rule apply to some situations, but not to others, are advocating that arbitrary lines be drawn, thereby giving rise to the same old question: Who shall decide? The majority? If the majority is to decide on which matters the majority should be allowed to rule, then in reality the majority is being given *absolute* rule.

The dream of Majority Rule is that it is morally virtuous. The reality of Majority Rule is that it is moral cannibalism. The bottom line of Majority Rule is that one group of people, simply by outnumbering another group of people, can do what it wishes to that group. Theoretically, Majority Rule could validate *literal* cannibalism!

In today's society, then, a free man might appropriately be defined as a person who is allowed one voice in millions in deciding what will be done to him and his property, as well as one voice in millions in deciding what will be done to other people and their property. Certainly the term *self-government* is a misnomer, because each person does not govern himself. In reality, self-government means that each person is governed by all the rest of the people.

Government "by consent of the people" means that *a certain number of people* have consented either to be governed by certain people or to be bound by certain laws. But those who do not so consent are forced to go along with it anyway. Jim Davidson describes this dilemma of the victimized minority by defining democracy as "that form of government where everybody gets what the majority deserves."

In other words, whereas a dictatorship allows only a small number of people to interfere in the rights of others, a democracy makes it possible for great numbers of people to impose their wills on others—through the force of government. Is an act of aggression any more right if carried out by the majority rather than by a dictator? Does a person feel better if he is coerced by the majority rather than by, say, a monarch?

Logic

The basic premise of Majority Rule is that "good" is defined as "that which is best for the greatest number of people." Such a premise, however, is so vague as to be meaningless. Every person in a society has a unique set of circumstances, unique needs and desires, unique personality traits, unique fears, and unique ambitions. A certain political action might be a catastrophe for person A, of no consequence to person B, and very good for person C. Another political action, however, might be wonderful for person A but very bad for person C.

In this abstract example, how can one determine which actions are "best for the greatest number of people?" Clearly, there are no such actions. Each person's uniqueness dictates which actions are best for him.

REALITY

Having examined Majority Rule from the standpoints of logic and morality, let us see how well the concept works in actual practice.

First of all, the majority, in reality, does not rule. On the contrary, it is the minority who rules the majority. Since a maximum of approximately half of the eligible voters vote in most elections, it is the nonvoters, along with those who vote against the winning candidate, who actually form the majority in an election. This means that approximately 75% of the people are ruled by officials of laws for which the remaining 25% have voted.

In truth, then, "mandate of the people" means the mandate of a small *minority* of people whose candidates are elected and whose propositions are passed. Hardly what a schoolchild envisions when he is taught about the justice of Majority Rule.

A similar myth concerning Majority Rule is the belief that "the people have chosen." What in fact takes place in an election is that two hand-picked candidates are propped up before the citizenry, each candidate having been selected by a very small group of politically active people. A *minority* of the people, erroneously described as "the majority" (as explained above), then elects one of the two hand-picked candidates to rule itself *and* the majority.

A third fallacy of Majority Rule is that not only does the majority *not* rule, but the real gut-level ruling—where the worst violations of natural rights occur—is carried out by people in regulatory agencies who are not even elected to office. What The System really boils down to is that officials, who are elected by a minority of the population, in turn dole out awesome power to nonelected bureaucrats who do not have to answer to voters and who are almost impossible to remove from their jobs.

Majority Rule, then, is incompatible with Natural Law and therefore incompatible with human freedom. But there is little doubt that it is the best system for those in power. Democracy's main attraction—Majority Rule—is ideal from government's standpoint because it gives the illusion of consent. People, through preposterous slogans and mind-twisting logic, are led to believe that government represents them, thus they feel content.

And when a "democratic" government does an efficient job of maintaining this illusion, the reward can be a power seeker's dream: the actual support of a large percentage of the people who are ruled.

THE VOTE

The vehicle through which Majority Rule supposedly asserts itself is "The Vote"—the political process known as an election. An election involves the art of "politics," the dictionary defining politics as "the plotting or scheming of those seeking personal power, glory, position, or the like." What a reassuring definition. Welcome to the wonderful world of The Vote!

One might properly describe Majority Rule as the window dressing of The System and The Vote as the machine used to do the dressing. Notwithstanding the fact that the average person's life is not affected one way or another by the outcome of elections, the outcome matters a great deal to politicians. The politician who wins a greater part of the minority vote (i.e., a majority of the votes cast) wins power! The loser must sit on the sidelines and wait until the next time around to try to capture (or recapture) the fruits of power. The Vote is therefore very important to the players of the power game in a democracy.

THE FOUR GREAT POLITICAL REALITIES

So long as a democracy proves to be the most practical method of controlling people, The Vote will remain a critical aspect of The System from the standpoint of politicians. And so long as The Vote is a critical aspect of The System, certain realities are almost unavoidable. Four of the most important of these realities are as follows:

REALITY NO. 1: No person can become a serious candidate for office without having substantial financial backing and/or important connections made available to him. It takes great naiveté to believe that IOU's, payable in favors, are not issued at the time of the disbursement of campaign "contributions," whether such contributions are in the form of money or connections.

REALITY NO. 2: It takes votes to get elected to office.

REALITY NO. 3: In order to collect enough votes to get elected, a candidate must, to put it politely, make unrealistic and contradictory promises to a wide variety of special interests throughout the citizenry. To put it not so politely, it is virtually impossible to get elected to public office without lying. You might say that it is a mandatory condition built into The System; it is the only way the politician can appeal to the Expediency Factor in most voters.

REALITY NO. 4: Once elected, a politician must violate Natural Law, i.e., he must commit aggression against both voters and nonvoters in an effort to make good on at least some campaign promises. Virtually all political action involves violating the rights of various members of society, whether such action entails redistribution-of-the-wealth programs, government intervention to help certain businesses, favors for special-interest groups, or enactment of victimless-crime laws to satisfy the moral judgments of certain individuals.

The result of The Four Great Political Realities is a relentless appeal to the Expediency Factor in every eligible voter. It stimulates people to think in terms of expedient, short-term solutions to their problems. The politician's expediency is political (attainment of power); the voter's expediency is material and moral. Though it is an absurd paradox, in reality a candidate's chances of winning are tied to his ability to convince voters that he will, if elected, commit more aggression than his opponent. What this boils down to is a description offered by Jim Davidson:

> You pool your life and property with those of other citizens and cast them into the electoral pot to be put at the disposal of politicians. Those who win the election promise to manipulate you to achieve the "common good." More often than not . . . the politicians are really promising to steal from you to reward special interests.[3]

The Vote borders on being a sport. Indeed, Thoreau saw voting as "a sort of gaming, like checkers or backgammon, with a slight moral tinge to it, a playing with right and wrong, with moral questions; and begging naturally accompanies it."

This is an example of how democracy destroys itself by "an excess of democracy." The voting game brings out the worst in people, its very nature being such that it encourages everyone to claw zealously for his piece of the plunder. Good politicians recognize this weakness and know how to use it to win the game.

Plato observed of ancient Greece, in Will Durant's words, that "the crowd so loves flattery . . . that at last the wiliest and most unscrupulous flatterer, calling himself the 'protector of the people,' rises to supreme power."[4]

Can 70 Million Americans Be Wrong?

Citizens are continually urged to vote. Media and celebrity pawns flood us with admonishing slogans like, "If you don't vote, don't gripe." Even acquaintances make perplexing statements to us to the effect that "it doesn't matter who you vote for, just so you vote." (Why doesn't it matter???)

And yet, notwithstanding this constant barrage of reasonless rhetoric, nonvoters continue to increase their standing as the true majority in every election. In 1962, John F. Kennedy initiated a movement to increase voter participation. Literacy tests and poll taxes were eliminated, residency requirements were liberalized, and voter registration was simplified. The result: the percentage of nonvoters has steadily *increased*.

In 1960, 37% of the voting-age population did not vote. In the 1976 presidential election, the figure had grown to 45%. That means that almost 70 million eligible voters did not participate in the last presidential election. It also means that Jimmy Carter was, *at best*, the choice of about one-fourth of the eligible voters (a little more than half of the 54% who voted).

As usual, nonvoters piled up a huge majority—46% to 28%—over those who voted for the "winner." Carter, in other words, was no different than all recent "winners" of U.S. presidential elections. No president in modern history has ever received a true majority—i.e., 51% of the votes of eligible voters. It is therefore absurd for an elected official to claim that he has a "mandate of the people."

Just why people do not vote has been the topic of many interesting discussions, articles and books. For quite some time it has been a popular myth that nonvoters are generally found among the less educated, poorer segment of our population. But a national survey conducted by Peter D. Hart Research Associates, prior to Jimmy Carter's 28% minority victory, uncovered some interesting facts.

The survey revealed that approximately 10 million nonvoters had previously voted, but had since given up on the voting process. It also showed that these 10 million nonvoters tended to be older, *more* educated and *more* affluent than other nonvoters. When asked what might inspire them to vote in the future, 62% checked "having a candidate worth voting for."

Other polls have shown that people have not been voting because they do not believe politicians can do anything about their problems. And they're right. Because their problems are unique, and so are those of their neighbors. Remember, Majority Rule is the meaningless concept that "good" is "that which is best for the greatest number of people." *You* can best solve your own problems because you understand them better than anyone else and because you *care* more than anyone else.

Finally, the polls show that people are at last beginning to understand that there really is no distinction between the two major parties. Doesn't every candidate urge you to vote? Doesn't every candidate urge you to pay your taxes? Doesn't every candidate talk about helping the "poor?" Doesn't every candidate endorse obeying laws, regardless of whether those laws are moral? It is rarely a matter of differing principles; it is virtually always a case of debating over the degree to which each candidate exhorts you to adhere to traditional government doctrine.

If half the people in this country are not voting, it is fairly obvious that they are trying to tell the government something. But the government, instead of being responsive to the people whom it supposedly represents, retaliates with an endless barrage of slogans, the essence of which are, "It's your *duty* to vote."

To say the least, the politician has a closed mind when it comes to the nonvoting phenomenon. He refuses to consider the possibility that people are not voting because they are not satisfied with *any* of the candidates or because they do not wish to be governed by *anyone*. That kind of thinking simply does not fit in with the politician's plan for perpetuating his power.

In reality, what the U.S. has is a one-party system—the "Demopublican Party"—masquerading as a two-party system (Democrats and Republicans). No matter who you vote for, you are voting for the Demopublican Party. Again, if one were inclined to be impolite, he might go so far as to say that the so-called two-party system in this country is a sham and a hoax.

When the lone U.S. political party feels threatened, it does not hesitate to reveal its totalitarian instincts. And it definitely feels threatened when a new party tries to get in on the action. Remember, the dictionary defines a totalitarian government, in part, as one in which "those in control grant neither recognition nor tolerance to parties differing in opinion." When was the last time you saw a Demopublican presidential candidate debate a third-party candidate on television?

Many new parties have tried hard to maneuver their way into the power game, usually without even making it to first base. And the few who have managed to slip one foot in the door have ended up limping away with a very swollen foot. The System itself is controlled by the power structure of the Demopublican Party, and so long as it can continue to perpetuate false beliefs about Majority Rule, it should be able to avoid the ugliness, expense and uncertainty that come with having to resort to violence to keep people in line.

How do the powerholders control the voting process? Basically, through two methods. First, through the hard reality of legislation. Since the Demopublicans are in control, they can pass any law that suits them—any law that makes it difficult, if not impossible, for a new party to compete. There is one law which in effect gives only Demopublican candidates access to taxpayer money to finance election campaigns. Another law refuses Secret Service protection to "outsider" candidates, with but a handful of past exceptions.

The most potent of all laws, however, are state laws which deny voters the opportunity of free choice—the right to vote for someone other than Demopublican candidates. The laws in most states make it so expensive, so time consuming, and generally so difficult to qualify as a "legitimate" party that few well-intentioned rivals have managed even to get on the ballot.

The second method for controlling The Vote is far more clever because of its subtlety. The totalitarian concept of not granting recognition to parties of differing opinion is not lost on the Demopublicans. Thus its major weapon against competition is simply to ignore it. "Great is truth," said Aldous Huxley, "but still greater, from a practical point of view, is silence about truth. By simply not mentioning certain subjects . . . totalitarian propagandists have influenced opinion much more effectively than they could have done by the most eloquent denunciations."

A good example of this was the magnificently successful silent treatment the Demopublicans gave the Libertarian Party in the 1976 presidential election. The platform of the Libertarian Party was based on across-the-board freedom for *everyone*, with clearly stated intentions to abolish a majority of regulatory agencies, to eliminate most taxes, to put an end to the most devastating enemy of the "poor"—inflation—by attacking its *real* cause (which will be explained in a later chapter), and to rid private citizens of the harassment of so-called victimless-crime laws.

Yet, through skillfully executed silence, coupled with crippling election laws, the Demopublicans managed to keep Roger MacBride, the Libertarian Party candidate, virtually unknown to the general public. Needless to say, the media, for the most part, cooperated with this scheme by giving MacBride, as well as other "outsider" candidates, little or no coverage. MacBride's requests for TV debates were, of course, ignored by all networks.

Let's give credit where credit is due. The System does work very well indeed—for those in power!

If The Vote really is a meaningless ritual, why even bother with elections? Why don't the Demopublican powerholders just vote among themselves? For one very important reason: The Vote is a process of legitimization. In reality, the mechanics of "representative government" amount to nothing more than a validation of The System by the citizenry.

Candidates make a point of telling us that "it doesn't matter who you vote for, just so you vote." Why is it so important to a politician that you vote, even if you may not vote for him? Because by casting your ballot, you cast a vote for The System—the system which can satisfy his urge for power and provide him his livelihood. By casting your ballot, you help perpetuate the illusion that "the people have chosen." The truth is that if politicians were honest, they would encourage a person to vote only if he sincerely believed in one of the candidates.

Politicians like to create the impression that a large voter turnout is a sign of a healthy political system, but this idea disintegrates rather rapidly when one is reminded that Russia has almost a 100% turnout for its "elections."

In Australia, another democracy moving rapidly toward totalitarianism, the establishment has become so nervous over the situation that it has made it *against the law* not to vote. What a comical and embarrassing government decree: Citizens are *forced* to vote in order to preserve their freedom! At present, nonvoting brings only a fine in

Australia, but it does not take great powers of prophecy to envision nonvoters of the future being jailed.

When pople say you have to participate to change The System, it sounds great until you try it—as did the 10 million voters who dropped out because they had become convinced that nothing ever changes regardless of who is elected.

Nicholas von Hoffman quotes Sy Leon as saying that "voting is like going through one of two doors. Whichever one you take you wind up in the same room." Von Hoffman goes on to say that "such talk (about having to participate to change things) has a convincing ring until one has participated, elected his man and then found out he might just as well have supported the loser for all the difference it made."

In short, the players change but the game is always the same. The powerholders give us a "choice" of two candidates, each of whom is acceptable to the general aims of the Demopublican Party. When given the opportunity to vote on issues, there are, likewise, only two alternatives, each of which falls within the framework defined by government.

The alternatives are whether to increase restrictions on the freedom of some people (or, in some cases, all people) or whether to decrease restrictions on freedom. The choice is never between *complete* freedom and restriction of freedom. Political debates, when stripped of politicalese, always boil down to discussions of whose freedom should be increased or decreased and to what extent.

The fact is that our present political system offers choice, but not *free choice*. The two are only vaguely related. A prisoner who is told by his captors that he has the right to die either by shooting or by hanging is given a choice. If he were given a *free choice*, however, you can be sure that he would choose a third alternative not presently available to him.

One might justifiably describe our democracy as a system through which everyone has the freedom to elect officials to restrict his freedom. "A man is none the less a slave," said Lysander Spooner, "because he is allowed to choose a new master once in a term of years."

"Government by the people," then, really means government by approximately one-fourth of the eligible voters who vote for the winning candidates and issues *from among those made available to them by the government.* Or, to cut through all the hocus-pocus, "government by the people" really means "government by those in power."

THE NIGHTMARE OF THE SYSTEM: EXPEDIENCY

The overall result of The System—culminating in The Vote—is a nation of Expediency Factors run rampant. And the trait seems to feed on itself. As more and more people base their decisions on the expediency of the moment, more and worse problems are created and more chaos results.

As each person sees his neighbor getting a bigger piece of the government pie, he feels he must take quick action to see to it that he is not left out. Working and minding one's own business have become outdated virtues. The name of the game is "grouping"—aligning oneself with others whose situations vaguely resemble one's own, then letting the candidates know that they either must meet your collective demands or lose your vote. Given this reality, one can see why H. L. Mencken described an election as "an advanced auction of stolen goods."

Grouping is one of the banes of man's existence. It is irrational and degrading. It robs the individual of his individuality. It encourages a moral person to rationalize the taking of immoral action in the name of "the cause." The cruel irony is that it links, under common banners, dishonest people with hardworking, honest people. It calls upon honorable men and women to do the expedient thing in order to defend "the group" against the "injustices" of society.

Politicians, who rarely base their decisions on anything *but* the expediency of the moment (which translates into that which will result in the most votes), are very aware that The Vote revs up people's expediency mechanisms. And they play this weakness to the hilt. Through The Vote, politicians pit union members against businessmen, blacks against whites, law-and-order advocates against civil-liberties supporters, "rich" against "poor," "young" against "elderly." Government represents *power*, the power to "protect" ourselves from our greedy neighbors—to help us get *our* goodies before the rest of the avaricious population takes everything there is.

This is a delightful state of affairs for powerholders, because it motivates virtually everyone to vie for government's attention. You want a lollipop? There is only one place to get it—from Uncle Sam. Only he has access to the printing presses. Only he has the legal right to use force. The bureaucratic process is completely controlled by the bureaucrats themselves, through that marvelous invention known as The Vote, an invention which plays upon that common human weakness known as the Expediency Factor.

Since the end of the rainbow is in Washington, it is not surprising that there are now 10,000 lobbyists in that city maneuvering to get the politician's attention. Also headquartered in Washington are 1,900 national groups, employing about 40,000 people, all of whom are fighting to satisfy the Expediency Factors of those whom they represent.

Whht Makes Sammy Steal?

Sammy, of course, is only a mythical character. Uncle Sam really is a compilation of an army of little Sammies called "politicians." One of the reasons that government acts in such confusing, contradictory ways is that each little Sammy, at any given time, says and does those things which he believes will gain him the broadest possible support (i.e., the most power).

Government malfunctions as a problem-solver for individuals because it consists of thousands of elected officials, each of whom tries to please a wide variety of groups whose aims are conflicting. That is why you hear the same politician espousing the merits of capitalism one day, while preaching socialism the next. Political expediency means not only that the decisions of politicians must be based on immediate results for the greatest number of people, but that these results must be *easily identifiable*. Long-term consequences are of little concern to the politician, since they are almost always too difficult for the average voter to identify.

Thoreau certainly was right; The Vote *is* a sort of gaming. Each politician has to take his best guess as to which combination of expedient demands by the public will bring him the greatest number of votes. A demographic study of the population takes much of the guesswork out of it, but even so it can sometimes be a tricky business. Furthermore, each politician's opponents have access to the same statistics. A politician's job, then—like the participant in any game—is to win.

But the fact remains that no man, winner or loser, has the competence to direct the lives of other men. That is the danger with The System—that it gives ordinary men the power to commit aggression. "The ordinary man with extraordinary power is the chief danger for mankind—not the fiend or the sadist," warned Erich Fromm.

The one "qualification" that all office holders have in common, as previously pointed out, is an excessive drive for power over the lives of others. Their expedient actions are based on this thirst for power. Their code of ethics is a simple one: that which increases or cements one's power base is good; that which lessens or threatens one's power base is bad.

Does this make all politicians evil? Evil may be a harsh word, but, in the context of Natural Law, I consider them evil to the extent that they desire to rule other men (i.e., commit aggression against others). Some politicians may be wonderful human beings in many respects. Nothing prevents a politician from being a good family man, from acting humanely toward others (outside of political matters), and from generally having good intentions. In fact, naive as it may sound, I believe that most politicians do not consciously acknowledge that their chief aim is power. Most of us are expert at making ourselves believe things which cast us in a positive light.

While there certainly are a great number of politicians around who know full well that their real objective is power, I feel certain that a large percentage of office holders probably have convinced themselves that they are missionaries of God, put on this earth to "protect" others and to keep them in line.

Unfortunately, it is this latter type, the one who deludes himself into believing that his violations of Natural Law are for "the good of society," who poses the greatest danger to freedom. A man who rationalizes aggression as the means to a self-proclaimed virtuous end has mentally positioned himself to justify the commission of virtually any kind of atrocity.

The entire election process, then, boils down to form, not substance. A politician's success depends upon his physical appearance, his personality, and his speaking ability. The man who does the best job of convincing the greatest number of people that he will give them more of everything stands the best chance of grabbing the brass ring of power. All candidates run on virtually the same platform, so what they actually say is not a factor. What is important is how good they are at saying it.

These are rather odd criteria for picking a man to rule a country, as Plato, paraphrased here by Will Durant, has pointed out: "In politics we presume that everyone who knows how to get votes knows how to administer a city or a state. When we are ill . . . we do not ask for the handsomest physician, or the most eloquent one."[5]

The more polished the politician, the more he bases his actions on the expediency of the moment. So-called Republicans normally spend their time trying to convince voters that, if given a chance, they can be just as liberal as so-called Democrats. Recently, so-called Democrats have been trying to make voters believe that they can be as fiscally responsible as so-called Republicans, notwithstanding their lethal spending policies of the past fifty years.

With Democrats trying to act like Republicans and Republicans trying to act like Democrats, it is no wonder that the Demopublican Party resembles a barnyard full of chickens scurrying about in every direction, frantically searching for worms. Over the long haul, however, the Demopublican Party has patterned itself more after the preachings of its Democratic subsidiary, with the result being that the Republican subsidiary has virtually no identity of its own.

The reason for leaning toward the Democratic line of rhetoric is to be found, of course, in the numbers. The Democratic sales pitch has a much more expedient ring to it: "Vote for us and we will give you more of everything, no matter what it costs or from whom we have to take it."

And *that* is what makes Sammy steal!

He promises billions of dollars in services and direct payments in exchange for votes, yet he has no means of producing wealth on his own. No one ever got elected by promising less. Remember, one of the two conditions common to *all* governments is that they exist off the surpluses of others. If a little Sammy, once elected, refused to steal, the least that would happen to him is that he soon would be out of office, a situation quite incompatible with his power objective. At worst, he could face a physical uprising from those to whom he had made his expedient promises.

To add to the problem, when the head Sammy ascends the throne after a presidential election, he always seems to become afflicted with a phenomenon I refer to as "kingitis." No sooner does a new president take office than he has delusions of being loved by everyone. Power breeds in him the absurd notion that he is the "protector of the people."

Each new president longs to go down in history as the benevolent leader who solved *everyone's* problems. If you have ever been puzzled (or frustrated) about why a conservative presidential candidate swings to the left after being elected and why a liberal candidate swings to the right, it is because they have been stricken with a bad case of kingitis.

Kingitis only increases Sammy's already dangerous kleptomaniacal habits. Once he puts himself in a position to believe that he not only has to deliver, but deliver to *everyone*, Sammy's only way out is to steal on a massive scale.

Sy Leon has suggested that what all politicians really are afflicted with is Politicoholism, and he offers this solution to their problem:

There seems to be but one remedy for acute Politicoholics. They should be placed in a comfortable institution, beyond the reach of dangerous weapons, where they can act out their fantasies with each other, unencumbered by the real world. They can make speeches, solicit the votes of other inmates, plan the lives of one another, levy taxes in play money, issue decrees, and start imaginary wars for the good of their institution. Clearly, this is the only humanitarian solution to the problem of acute Politicoholism.[6]

3

How People Get the Things They Want

The next logical topic to discuss, were I to adhere to proper sequence, would be the actions (i.e., "functions") of today's government, actions which are the result of the realities of The Vote.

This chapter, however, does *not* discuss government functions. If one likes things to follow in smooth sequence, which I do, this chapter may seem more like a detour than a continuation of the existing flow. Call it a necessary detour. We will return to the logical sequence of things in the next chapter, at which time we will delve into government functions.

I have decided to take this "economic detour" because I believe that without it I would fail to lay a proper foundation for a meaningful discussion of government functions. I say this because, while most of today's government functions can be invalidated on moral grounds, it nevertheless is important to understand the economic consequences of government actions. For if one understands why policies are economically diastrous, *in addition to being immoral in concept*, it becomes clear to him why a political system based on the expedient actions of 220 million people is a prescription for national suicide.

THE HEART OF THE FREEDOM ISSUE

Though most people would prefer to avoid the issue of economics, the fact is that the economic realities of government functions cannot be fully analyzed without an understanding of certain fundamentals of economics and economic systems. And economics is at the very heart of the human-freedom issue.

As I explained in an earlier chapter, for years I was unable to make the connection between human rights and property rights. I related economics to property matters, viewing property as something that was inanimate, totally separate and apart from a man's life. Economics, therefore, was of no concern to me.

Now I fully realize that if one misses the boat on economics, he misses the boat on the issue of freedom. And I am sorry to say that by far the majority of Americans (and people throughout the world) do seem to miss the boat on economics.

I was reminded recently of just how easily people overlook economics when I came across a quote by a young woman who had worked on the George McGovern presidential campaign in 1972:

"I look back now and say, 'How could I believe? Where were my senses?' But you get caught up in the enthusiasm. . . . I didn't know anything about economics. . . . I now realize that money for people programs has to come from people."

And that is the essence of the matter! There is no such thing as a government function that does not have an economic reality attached to it, because every so-called function costs *you* money.

My discussion of economics will be restricted to certain basics which I feel are crucial to analyzing the purported functions of modern-day government. The truth of the matter is that fundamental economics is relatively simple and can therefore be explained in simple language. Adding technical jargon does nothing whatsoever to change basic economic principles.

I realize that this is heresy in the jealously guarded world of intellectual economists. Many of these economists maintain an unholy alliance with government and serve it well by generating the illusion that economics is an impossibly complex subject. These economists keep people both bored and confused (much to the government's delight) by the use of "insider" jargon, by references to factors which have little bearing on the problems of individuals, and by generally becoming entangled in their own esoteric webs. Beware the economist who cannot explain matters in simple terms. Unclear expression is a sign of unclear thought.

People often wonder why supposedly brilliant professional economists so often disagree on issues of great importance. First, they are human beings. Like all human beings, they have biases, political attitudes, economic motives, and a wide variety of values and social interests. All of these may be subconscious, but they do exist. The wide disparity of opinion among economists once prompted an observer to say that if all the nation's economists were laid end to end, they would point in all directions.

Economics is defined by one dictionary as "the science that deals with the production, distribution, and consumption of wealth (goods and services)." Simple translation: economics is the study of how people get the things they want.

By "the things they want," I am referring to the material things people desire. Economics does not deal with love, religion, ethics, philosophy or emotional issues. These and many other subjects may be very significant to most people, but they simply are not related to the science of economics. It is important to remember this when thinking in economic terms.

More specifically, "things" refers to what the economist calls *wealth*. Wealth is food, clothing, TV sets, automobiles, and other products desired by individuals. To a businessman, wealth also may consist of factories and equipment, things which can be used to produce products and services desired by consumers.

Money itself is not wealth. Money is a medium of exchange, used for the purpose of acquiring products and services that the individual desires. (This very important point will be discussed in great detail in a later chapter.)

What stimulates economic growth—the production of wealth—is voluntary action on the part of individuals trying to improve their well-being. It is unfortunate that the idea of individuals' becoming wealthy bothers some people. Whatever their moral or ideological reasons, many of these people seek to interfere with the natural process of people striving to obtain what they desire on a value-for-value basis. What is more unfortunate, many of these people are economists who advocate the strong arm of government as the most effective way to interfere with the right of people to promote their well-being.

When such interference occurs, one of the most basic laws of economics—*the law of supply and demand*—is violated. It is the working of this law which creates a relationship among prices, wages and costs. For example, if prices go up, this causes demand to drop, which in turn causes employees to be laid off, which in turn causes wages to go down, which in turn causes fewer goods to be produced.

Using another example, if natural conditions create an excess supply of goods in the market, these goods will then be offered at a lower price, which in turn increases demand, which in turn pushes prices back up, which in turn attracts more entrepreneurs to that particular industry, which in turn attracts higher wages and more employees—and on and on the cycle goes. Unless, of course, government intervenes to stop the natural flow of things.

What is *good* about the creation of surplus wealth is that it leads to an increase in plants and equipment, which in turn leads to the creation of both new jobs and new products. The sale of these products to consumers leads, hopefully, to profits, a large part of which are then reinvested in still more plants and equipment or in research and development. Thus economic growth continues and everyone's well-being is improved.

But what if all profits are not reinvested? The fact is that surplus wealth must lead to growth in virtually all cases, even if it is not reinvested in the business from which it was derived. Suppose, for example, that a man builds a very successful business, then "cashes out" for $10 million. He has no desire to produce anymore; he just wants to enjoy the good life. What, then, is the result of his leading a retired life of luxury?

If he buys a car, he helps to employ auto workers and automobile salesmen. If he takes a trip, he helps to employ hotel personnel, airline employees of all kinds, luggage factory workers, and travel agency employees, to name just a few. If he builds a mansion, he again employs a wide variety of workers.

Even if this man puts his money into stocks, bonds and/or savings accounts, he stimulates the economy by making money available to other businesses. About the only way he can escape contributing to the national economy is to hide all his money in his home, a highly unlikely possibility, to say the least. Even then he would require certain products and services just to live.

One can see why Ayn Rand long ago proclaimed that money is the root of all good! Surplus wealth stimulates the economy, which is critical to the poorest people in any society. The greater the surplus wealth, the greater the chances that those at the lower end of the economic scale will begin to reap benefits.

The second fundamental law of economics, one that most expediency-oriented politicians refuse to acknowledge is: *There is no such thing as something for nothing!*

Wealth cannot be created out of thin air. Only productive effort can create TV sets, refrigerators, automobiles and houses. *Money* (today) can be created out of nothing (actually, out of paper), because, as previously mentioned, money is *not* wealth.

The simple reality is that you cannot have more without creating more. There are no magic formulas by which to create wealth, even though the public has been disastrously led to believe otherwise. Income to the people of a nation must not exceed their output (what they produce). If it does, the nation experiences what is known as "false prosperity." When output increases, *real* income (i.e., income derived from productive effort) increases. When output decreases, real income decreases—*no matter how much more "money" people receive*.

When a person finds that his higher income of today buys less than did his income of five years ago, he is living in a country that is being deluded (and destroyed) by false prosperity. He is living in a nation where the combined income of the population exceeds the total production of goods and services. He is living in a nation that is courting economic collapse.

Some economists, in what seems like a desperate attempt to justify government interference in the marketplace, argue that false prosperity is better than risking a depresssion (the polite phrase is "severe recession"). They could not be more wrong. A depression is an adjustment period in the supply-and-demand cycle which forces people and businesses to become more efficient. Like children, people are "reprimanded" for being naughty. This happens when they treat themselves to the fantasy that prosperity can be created without work. The more irresponsible their actions, the worse the reprimand—in the form of a recession or depression—hence, like children, the better they learn their lesson.

Not everything that is good for us feels good, and so it is with a depression. Long term, it is a healthy process—a financial catharsis. Prices fall to levels where merchandise can be sold, overvalued investments drop to realistic plateaus, and, when everything reaches its *natural* level once more, the market is again healthy. Just as it is in the *long-term* best interest of children to experience an occasional spanking, so it is with adults who have misbehaved.

The question is, what politician has the courage to spank 220 million people? Certainly not one who is tied to The Vote.

And now the shocker. That is the end of your lesson in economics. I can hear the screams of economists from New York to Tokyo. What about macroeconomics and microeconomics? What about the Gross National Product? What about elasticity of demand? What about the consumer price index? What about M-1 and M-2?

I'll tell you what about them—they *all* relate to supply and demand and to the fact that there is no such thing as something for nothing. One can sermonize patronizingly about oversimplification, about the world of today being much too complex to be explained away in such an elementary manner, and about a thousand-and-one factors that "must" be considered, but the reality always remains that each of these leads us right back to the two basic laws of economics just discussed.

ATTITUDES TOWARD THE "LAWS"

While the basic laws of economics never change, there are, theoretically, two different attitudes which govern-

ments may take toward these laws. They may either obey
them or they may choose to violate them, depending upon
the "economic systems" they use.

At one idealistic extreme, any government that allowed
laissez-faire capitalism would thereby show complete respect for the law of supply and demand; it would demonstrate, through its actions, that it understood that wealth
cannot be created by magic. At the other extreme is communism (in its theoretical form, as opposed to its real
form). Theoretically, communism refuses to acknowledge
the unrelenting law of supply and demand and implies
that wealth can be produced without labor.

It should be pointed out that neither of these systems
challenges the concept of "division of labor," which might
properly be referred to as industrialization. It is this division-of-labor concept that has allowed man to advance
technologically in quantum leaps. Man's vastly superior
brain first gave him the capacity to make tools, which was
the beginning of his technological climb. A tool is an object which allows men to produce more with the expen-
diture of less time and energy.

The next great advance in man's technological evolution (if one does not consider the development of agriculture a "technological" advance) was the discovery that he
could produce far more through the division of labor; i.e.,
through each man's specializing in one craft, rather than
meeting his daily needs by making every item himself.

The division-of-labor concept was further refined during the Industrial Revolution in England, when it was discovered that the multiplication of output was even greater
if large groups of men were organized to produce just one
product, with smaller groups of men within the same factory specializing in just one aspect of a given product.

Division of labor in industry is practiced by all modern
nations, though it is interesting, as we shall see, why some
succeed at it far better than others. No serious, educated

person of the twentieth century advocates the vague concept of "returning to nature," to pretechnological times when disease, poverty, suffering, and early death were horrors that awaited each newborn child. Only fools and romantic dreamers talk of returning to a pretechnological period when people were clean, well-fed, healthy and happy—indeed, a period that never existed!

Industrialization, fortunately, is not the issue. The only issue is, who will control the means of industry? If industry operates in a free environment, men can be organized by mutual consent to increase production. If industrialization takes place through coercion, men are forced to produce against their will.

RESPECTING ECONOMIC LAW

Capitalism is technically defined as "an economic system characterized by private . . . ownership of capital goods, by investments that are determined by private decision rather than by state control, and by prices, production, and the distribution of goods that are determined mainly in a free market."

In other words, capitalism is an economic system that works through the *absence* of controls, a system that works through *individuals*. The term *free enterprise* is generally synonymous with capitalism, and for purposes of this book the two will be interchangeable. So that there will be no confusion, however, over what I mean by the terms *capitalism* and *free enterprise*, let me make it clear that I will always be referring to *laissez-faire* capitalism or *laissez-faire* free enterprise (unless specifically stating otherwise).

Laissez-faire is a French term meaning "a doctrine opposing governmental interference in economic affairs beyond the minimum necessary for the maintenance of peace and property rights." Note that the definition *spe-*

cifically spells out the original intentions that led to the birth of government (protecting men's lives and property).

Obviously, capitalism of the laissez-faire variety has never been tried on this planet. When one realizes what capitalism has accomplished despite government interference of every conceivable kind, one cannot help but wonder what the well-being of mankind might be *without* government intervention. Capitalism is not a dying idea. Capitalism, in its pure form, has yet to be discovered!

The very thing that makes the free-enterprise system work is the absence of interference. Free-market competition assures the public of the widest variety of goods at the lowest possible prices. To the degree that the market is not regulated, it will respond naturally to the law of supply and demand, and both producers and consumers will be better off. To the degree that the market is regulated, the law of supply and demand will be negated, causing the market to be less efficient and more costly, and causing both producers and consumers to be worse off.

Many people have been taught that capital is the only thing rewarded in a capitalistic society and that labor is "cheated." Let us examine how capitalism works and see if there is any merit to this charge. The capitalistic cycle requires four elements: ideas, capital, labor and management.

Obviously, the idea must come first. But an idea is worthless until someone is willing to invest capital (i.e., surplus wealth) in it. So the backbone of capitalism is creativity and risk taking—the entrepreneur who has the ability to come up with a plan and the entrepreneur who is willing to risk money on the plan. These same entrepreneurs also must have the ability to organize the plan and the money into a venture. Clearly, the entrepreneur is the "first cause" in the capitalistic cycle.

But without workers and managers (who, in reality, are

also workers), ideas and capital are useless—unless the entrepreneur is willing to build his product, piece by piece, through his own efforts. Which is exactly what people did, for the most part, before the Industrial Revolution brought on a refinement of the division-of-labor concept.

Thus, the capitalistic cycle works like this: An entrepreneur comes up with an idea, risks his capital (or the capital of investors), and organizes a venture. To operate the tools in which he has invested, he must hire employees, which means job opportunities are created. The more he modernizes his facilities (i.e., invests in new equipment), the more the productivity of his operation increases (i.e., there is an increase in the output of each worker). This greater output increases the production of goods and makes them available to consumers at lower prices.

Though everyone benefits from the cycle, it may justifiably be argued that the man with the lowest income benefits most from capitalism, for several reasons: first, because he is free to take a job at any wage, and, in fact, both employment and wages increase; second, because he is free to start a small business without the necessity of obtaining a license or having to comply with costly regulations that only large companies can afford; third, because it keeps prices down, which allows him to buy things he would not ordinarily (under controlled market conditions) be able to afford.

And the entrepreneur, hopefully, will make a profit— hopefully a very *large* profit. If so, he will have more surplus capital available to invest in more and better plants and equipment, which means more employment, more products, lower prices—and so the cycle continues, unless and until it is interrupted by coercive forces.

The thing that enables capitalism to work so smoothly and to be of automatic benefit to all men of goodwill is each person's desire to improve his well-being. Adam

Smith pointed this out more than two hundred years ago in his book, *The Weath of Nations*. Smith, contrary to what many have been led to believe, had no great sympathy for the businessman. He spoke of the "invisible hand" of the marketplace that would assure the masses of gaining more than through any other system. He pointed out that even if a man were not interested in the welfare of other human beings, when he based his actions on the profit motive (in a free market, without committing aggression), those actions automatically would benefit others whether he liked it or not.

How much easier it is to rest at night, knowing that your well-being will be improved because of the desire of other people to pursue *their* well-being, rather than to depend on the highly suspect "altruism" of politicians.

The reason capitalism works so smoothly is because it is in harmony with nature—with man's natural instincts. If people have the *freedom* to engage in economic activities to improve their well-being, innovations will come about and economic growth will occur. The result is that civilization advances, meaning that more people are healthier, wealthier and happier. When such freedom is restricted, growth is slowed or, in extreme cases, halted, the result being that civilization declines.

The free market is the only freedom-of-choice voting system ever invented. In a free market, a person does not have to go along with the desires of the majority. That is, he can "vote" to buy any product *he* desires, without regard to whether others want it. The free market not only gives the individual free choice, but also offers him great diversity in products and services. As soon as government intervenes and imposes regulations, price restrictions and other controls, businesses and people are forced to conform and the individual's choices are restricted.

Common Fears about Capitalism

Capitalism, of course, has its faults, as does any system, but these are offset many times over by its merits. It is to the myths about capitalism that I wish to address myself, myths that have been perpetuated through ignorance, envy, or the desire to control the lives of others.

—Didn't the Industrial Revolution prove that business-men, when unregulated, will subject workers to inhumane working conditions, long hours and low wages?

The Industrial Revolution, which occurred in England roughly during the period 1760 to 1840, brought about the greatest improvement in the well-being of man since the Agrarian Revolution. Prior to the Industrial Revolution, the Black Death, scurvy, rickets and other diseases regularly wiped out large segments of the populations of Europe. For the average person, life was day-to-day misery.

Before the Revolution, most people knew no other life *but* work, and their work was almost always under "inhumane" conditions. Those who were lucky earned enough to keep their families alive.

In point of fact, it was the Industrial Revolution that changed all this. Industrialists did not roam the country-side with shotguns, rounding up workers for their factories. On the contrary, as word of the new opportunities spread, people invaded the cities by the thousands, aggressively competing for the "inhumane" jobs. Of course wages were low—by *today's* standards. Of course hours were long—by *today's* standards. Of course conditions were bad—by *today's* standards. But that misses the whole point!

It was not *today's* standards that the eighteenth-century laborer used as a measuring stick. What caused him to migrate to the cities to seek employment in the so-called sweatshops were the filth, sickness and inhumane conditions he left behind! The conditions in the factories, by comparison, were like the Promised Land to him. Never before had he lived so well. People do not voluntarily leave one job for another if the new job offers lower pay, longer hours and inferior working conditions.*

The bottom line is that people gladly left bad situations for the vastly improved living conditions made possible by the Industrial Revolution.

The fact that the rich may have grown richer is only one aspect of the whole affair. Just as important is the fact that industrialization lifted the living standards of the masses to a level never before dreamed of. One may properly say that it lifted them to a level that, for the first time, made the average worker conscious enough of better living conditions to complain about long hours, low wages and bad working conditions. When people are struggling just to stay alive from one day to the next, such thoughts do not occur to them.

An interesting side note to this question is the so-called illegal-alien problem in the Southwestern United States. Stories of the deplorable living conditions of these victimized aliens abound, yet they flood our borders by the thousands. Why? To live under deplorable conditions? Yes—to live under deplorable conditions which are *so much better* than those left behind in Mexico that they are willing to take great risks to attain the lifestyle of an illegal alien.

—*Didn't the "Robber Barons" prove that if big busi-*

*Anticapitalistic versions of working conditions during the Industrial Revolution have been grossly exaggerated. For a clearer view of the actual conditions which existed at that time, several excellent works are available. One especially good source is *Capitalism and the Historians,* edited and with an Introduction by F. A. Hayek, which includes a supplemental report produced during that period, a report which factually refutes most of the commonly taught exaggerations.

ness is not regulated, men will amass fortunes through unethical means?

The so-called Age of the Robber Barons occurred in the United States roughly between 1875 and 1910. In America, as in England, not only did the rich get richer, but never before had so many people lived so well. The Rockefellers, Carnegies and Fords did not accumulate wealth by printing money. They produced oil, steel and automobiles, all of which necessitated the employment of thousands of workers. And in order for workers to be able to afford to purchase their products, they had to be paid decent wages.

I do not mean to imply that all men of that era were honest capitalists. There are honest and dishonest entrepreneurs, just as there are honest and dishonest laborers. The only person I would consider to have amassed his fortune through "unethical" means would be the person who used coercion (i.e., force or the threat of force) to attain his ends. Unfortunately, then, as today, all too many businessmen did collude with government to gain special favors, protection from competitors, and other legislation that interfered with the rights of others.

In other words, it was the availability of government power—government intervention itself—which gave men the opportunity to acquire wealth unethically. To the extent that businessmen of that era used government aid to accumulate wealth, yes—I would consider them to have used "unethical means." To the extent that they amassed great fortunes by providing better products and services at prices the public voluntarily paid, I admire them and believe that the people of this country owe them a debt of gratitude.

—*Didn't the Great Depression prove that capitalism does not work without government controls?*

As is so often the case, people have been led to look at the cause as the solution. The Great Depression in this country occurred roughly between 1929 and 1940. By 1929, government intervention in the economy had become pronounced (relative to earlier standards) and had begun to disrupt the workings of the free market.

One of the worst contributions the government made to the Depression was the passage of the Federal Reserve Act in 1913. The enactment of this law put Sammy in a position to steal on a level which would have been inconceivable to our founding fathers. But I don't want to jump the gun; the mind-boggling truth about the Federal Reserve Act will be discussed in a later chapter. Let it suffice to say that it put government in a position to, among other things, arbitrarily inflate the currency and provide easy credit for unknowledgeable amateurs who thought they could get rich quick in the falsely inflated stock market.

Also in 1913, government passed the Sixteenth Amendment, which created the present-day income tax structure and opened the way for Sammy to pilfer in still greater amounts. And there was more: in the 1920's, government meddling reached into the areas of collective bargaining, national old-age insurance, and many other aspects of the economy. "Public works" were increased, employers were persuaded to "divide" time among their employees to "spread the work," and industries were "encouraged" to expand for the sake of keeping the economy from collapsing.

To make matters worse, government officials continued to assure the public that the economy was healthy and that the future of the country looked great, *just as government officials do today*. When the Federal Reserve Board did try to slow credit and inflation, people complained to their congressmen that the big operators on Wall Street were trying to cut the little man out. Political expediency being the disease it is, congressmen of course responded to these complaints by seeing to it that easy credit continued.

Once things started crumbling, government added to the deterioration of the economy by delaying necessary liquidations, lending money to shaky businesses, further inflating the currency, and artificially propping up wages and prices. In general, government, as always, made matters worse by *increasing* its intervention, rather than get out of the way and allow the free market to adjust itself as normally and rapidly as possible.

Capitalism did not fail. As always, it was *government controls* which caused the economy to fail.

One other significant feature of the era should be pointed out here, that being the way in which the Expediency Factors of the general populace contributed to the conditions leading up to the Great Depression. Like today, a something-for-nothing attitude prevailed, which is in violation of one of the two cardinal rules of economics. In those days, however, the something-for-nothing urge was satisfied through unrealistic investment in the stock market. People were appallingly irresponsible in their investments, pushing stock prices to totally unrealistic levels.

As we discussed earlier, the free market "reprimands" financially imprudent people with something called a "depression." The more the laws of economics are violated, the worse the reprimand. The indiscretions of the late 1920's were bad indeed, hence the very bad depression that followed.

—If greedy businessmen were not controlled, wouldn't they make unreasonable profits through price gouging?

Here we have a rather impressive array of anticapitalistic terms. Let us examine them one at a time.

"Greed" is a subjective term used to describe what one person believes to be excessive desire (usually for material gain) on the part of another; i.e., it is one person's *opinion* as to whether another person tries too hard to improve his well-being. But the desire to further one's well-being is a trait common to *all* men, and is not dependent upon someone else's opinion.

The difference in men's fulfilling their desires is not so much one of extent, but of the different ways in which they go about it. Clergymen may fulfill their desires by helping others. Dedicated medical researchers may fulfill their desires by discovering cures for diseases. Successful businessmen may fulfill their desires by creating better products and services at a profit. Single-issue crusaders may fulfill their desires by imposing their moral standards on others. Rapists and murders may fulfill their desires by committing aggression against their victims.

All of us, knowingly or unknowingly, attempt to further our well-being—to act in our own self-interest—but the actions of some of us do not involve aggression, while the actions of others are clearly in violation of Natural Law.

And what are "unreasonable profits?" An opinion, to be sure. How does one determine if a profit is unreasonable when every risk is different, every person's efforts are different, every situation is different? How can there be an absolute standard for determining how great profits should be? When a man invests in a venture, he has no guarantee that there will be any profit at all. If it turns out to be a losing proposition, is there such a thing as an "unreasonable loss?"

In truth, a reasonable profit is whatever profit a person can make by selling his product or service at whatever price the public is willing to pay—without the use of coercion. Profits are *never* too high. The higher the profits, the better for the economy in general, for all the reasons previously discussed.

Henry Hazlitt has put the necessity for profits in still another light: "The function of profits . . . is to put constant and unremitting pressure on the head of every competitive business to introduce further economies and efficiencies. . . . In good times he does this to increase his profits further; in normal times he does it to keep ahead of his competitors; in bad times he may have to do it to survive at all."[7]

Disregarding the fact that high profits allow for higher shareholder dividends and a greater investment in production facilities, they should be welcomed if for no other reason than because they give workers the security of knowing that the company they work for is solvent. It certainly does not give a worker peace of mind to know that his company is barely profitable.

Finally, we have "price gouging." Again, a subjective term. One could just as easily argue that an unskilled worker making $2.90 an hour as a result of government-enforced minimum-wage laws is guilty of price gouging. The same line of reasoning can be used here as was used to discuss "unreasonable profits." In the absence of coercion, there is no such thing as price gouging. A seller is entitled to the highest price that the market is willing to pay him.

But that does not mean that he will get any price he wants; there is a limiting factor. It is *competition* that determines whether someone's prices are too high. And, as we shall later see, *everyone* has competition in a free market, though, once again, the public has been misled into believing otherwise. Only government force can protect a business from the necessity to compete.

All this brings us right back to the basic law of supply and demand. People will buy a product according to how badly they want it and how high it is priced; at the same time, its price will be determined by this demand and by the existing supply of the product. It is for this reason that some professional athletes make close to $1 million a year, while the annual salary of a great scientist may not exceed $40,000. The fact that some people believe this to be unjust is irrelevant. This is merely their *opinion*.

The hard reality is that enough people apparently think

it is right, otherwise they would not be willing to pay big money to see an athlete hit a home run or dunk a basketball. At the same time, apparently not enough people place a high value on sending a man to the moon, or whatever else it is that the scientist may do. The law of supply and demand can never be wrong, because it allows people to "vote" freely for what they want. What others think they should want is of no concern to them.

Price gouging is not possible in a free market because, contrary to the collectivist mentality of government, both sides profit in a voluntary transaction. They profit in the sense that each person receives what he is willing to accept. In my financially depressed days, I sold my last pieces of furniture for ten cents on the dollar, but my action was voluntary. Those who paid me 10% of my original cost did me a favor; they were on the *high* end of the market demand for used furniture. I profited in the sense that I would have suffered a far greater loss had I not entered into the transactions at all.

Capitalism rejects the notion that one man's gain is another man's loss. When dealing on a voluntary, value-for-value basis, that is not possible; *everyone* must gain.

—If there were no government controls, wouldn't small operators be put out of business?

I am particularly sensitive to this charge, because I have had so much firsthand experience with it. In my early days, I failed in many businesses. But in each case I can trace the failure either directly to my own imprudent actions or to government intervention. *In not one instance was competition from big businesses a factor*.

In fact, I found quite the opposite to be true. I always felt as though big companies could not compete with *me*, because I was right on top of my situation at all times. I could move swiftly, without having to consult cumbersome committees, and I could afford to give my personal touch to each transaction.

It is because of this that ambitious entrepreneurs, even in the face of ever-increasing government meddling, have been able to start from scratch and build companies like Polaroid and Holiday Inns in industries that were already dominated by corporate giants. The fact is that the giants are too busy trying to keep pace with other competitive giants to watch all the tortoises creeping up behind them. And by the time they are aware of an industrious, enterprising upstart, it usually is too late.

It is true that laissez-faire capitalism helps to put some people out of business, but that is a *good* feature of capitalism, because it automatically weeds out inefficient producers who are not competitive—a process which is necessary to a healthy economy. It is efficient businesses which produce the best products at the lowest prices, employ the greatest number of people at the highest wages, and reinvest surplus profits to increase efficiency and continue the process onward and upward.

One of the effects of this process is that workers from unsuccessful companies are absorbed by successful companies. Owners of businesses who cannot keep pace, including myself in past years, have no divine right to remain in business if they cannot compete. They have a natural right to *pursue* a business venture, but not a guaranteed right to be successful at it.

I recently read an article by a bleeding-heart liberal, typically ignorant in economics, who pointed out that Thomas Edison's invention of the lightbulb indirectly destroyed the livelihoods of many owners, workers and investors in the kerosene-lamp business. As if Edison's invention did not open the doors to countless opportunities for employment and investment theretofore undreamed of! Many people simply do not understand that it is in everyone's long-term best interest for inefficient, antiquated businesses to fold as new, efficient businesses take over.

This is what keeps the economy healthy and helps to keep unemployment low.

Capitalism is *not* the dog-eat-dog system that many have decried. In a free society, men do not put other men out of business by being "ruthless" (which can only relate to forcible interference), but by providing better products and services at lower prices. A capitalistic society is one in which free men are free to trade with other free men, at their sole discretion, without interference from others.

Is Wealth Really "Evil?"

There are many other myths about capitalism which have become trademarks of free-enterprise antagonists over the years. All of them, however, can be answered with plain facts and simple logic, as were the preceding sample questions. At the root of these myths against capitalism is the fact that too many egalitarian minds are, quite simply, envious of the success of others. As a result, they try to believe that the wealth of one person impoverishes his neighbor—as though there were a fixed amount of wealth on this earth.

This, of course, is nonsense. A nation as civilized as the United States can afford rich people. As a matter of fact, it cannot afford *not* to have rich people, because it is the opportunity to become rich—the ultimate material symbol of the American Dream—that provides the best hope for the impoverished.

The billion dollar empires of the Gettys, Hugheses, Vanderbilts and others symbolized hope. Every man who started from humble beginnings and built a financial empire represented living proof that anyone who was willing to pay the price had the *opportunity* (*not* the guarantee) to go as far as his talent and energy could take him. Financial empires gave every impoverished young man and woman *hope*—hope based on living proof—that he or she also could achieve great success.

Just as important, financial empires provided a value system for the people of this and other civilized countries. There was no confusion about the moral way to achieve financial success. Men and women clearly understood that the marketplace was the arena for financial gain and that winning in the marketplace led to material well-being.

As The System slowly changed the rules of the game to include needs and desires—as defined by anyone politically active enough to bring about government intervention in the marketplace—Expediency Factors went into high gear, people began to resent those who accumulated great wealth, and, eventually, the anything-goes attitude that prevails today came to replace the concept of value for value in the marketplace.

I sincerely believe that free enterprise is a godsend for the "poor." I believe that the best insurance for having a chicken in every pot and a car in every garage—*on a permanent basis*—is for the ambitious, risk-taking entrepreneur to know that he has the opportunity to have *ten* chickens in his pot and *ten* cars in his garage—if he earns them. *The "poor" are only as secure as the "rich."*

As the super fortune becomes more and more a phenomenon of our country's past, incentive grows weaker and weaker. Government says to people, "Forget about the evils of making millions. 'Tis better to have security from the cradle to the grave." So incentive drops to new lows each year, bringing the economy down with it.

Envying successful people is a serious mistake, and one that power-hungry politicians prey upon unmercifully. Equating wealth with evil is an offshoot of such envy. William Simon has stated that "the crude linkage between wealth and evil, poverty and virtue, is false, stupid, and of value only to demagogues, parasites, and criminals—indeed, the three groups that alone have profited from the linkage." It is the production of wealth, in spite of government intervention, that has brought man to his present living standard, a living standard impossible to conceive of just a few centuries ago.

But perhaps an even greater mistake is the refusal of those who know the truth to stand up and tell it. As Eric Hoffer has repeatedly pointed out, one of the tragic curiosities of our day is the loss of courage on the part of talented and successful people, particularly those in positions of leadership. Again William Simon puts it succinctly in *A Time for Truth:*

> As is so often the case in our society, when the liberals orchestrate a nationwide uproar over good versus evil, all those defined as evil suffer an acute loss of nerve. Businessmen and bankers, who seem to value respectability more than their lives, are incapable of tolerating this moral abuse. Invariably they collapse psychologically. And whatever they may think and say in private, in public they either go mute or stumble frantically over their own feet as they rush to join the moral bandwagon.

Many modern intellectuals of the left claim that to seek one's own happiness, "without concern for the rest of society" (as defined by them), is uncivilized. On the contrary, I believe that to thwart man's basic instinct to improve his well-being is uncivilized and tyrannical. What it boils down to is that some people wish to take it upon themselves to restrict the freedom of others. Nobel-Prize winner Dr. Milton Friedman pinpointed this presumptuousness by noting that "a major source of objection to a free economy is precisely that . . . it gives people what they want instead of what a particular group thinks they ought to want. Underlying most arguments against the free market is a lack of belief in freedom itself."[8]

Those who hammer away at the "injustices" of capitalism would do well to recognize the reality that never have so many people lived so comfortably as in America, even though its capitalistic system is stifled more each year. And, as the last vestiges of laissez-faire are dissolved by omnipotent government, the threat of losing that comfortable way of life is becoming more ominous each day.

No, the "Robber Barons" were not the great industrialists who amassed huge fortunes by giving Americans the highest living standard in the history of mankind. The real robber barons are those power-hungry bureaucrats and envious collectivists who would rob you of your property, your freedom and your self-esteem. What these robber barons desire is for you to relinquish your individuality and deliver control of your life into their hands, having faith that their "superior" standard of ethics will protect you from the temptation to pursue your own well-being.

DISRESPECTING ECONOMIC LAW

Communism is technically defined as "a theory advocating elimination of private property; a system in which goods are owned in common and are available to all as needed; a totalitarian system in which a single authoritarian party controls state-owned means of production with the professed aim of establishing a stateless society; a final state of society in Marxist theory in which the state has withered away and economic goods are distributed equally."

Though the definition of communism is confusing, to say the least, there is really only one thing wrong with it: it does not work. It does not work in theory and it does not work in actual practice. When I refer to "theory" and "practice," I mean to say that theoretical communism, as described by Marx, Engels, Lenin and other historically prominent communists, bears virtually no resemblance to *real* communism, i.e., communism as it is actually practiced in so-called communist countries.

Theoretical Communism

Can we make any sense of the dictionary definition of communism? How are goods "owned in common?" Does this refer to some sort of utopian partnership among individuals? And what is meant by "available to all as needed?" Who determines who is in need? Who determines what it is that they need? Who determines how much they need? The same question stalks us relentlessly: Who shall decide?

Several years ago I had occasion to ponder this muddled concept of the way communists believe men should live. It happened during a visit to a friend's beach home. While viewing the beach from the balcony, I became engaged in a discussion with a woman and her husband. During the course of our conversation, the woman offered her opinion that it was not right for people to build private homes on the beach. I asked why, and she answered that "all the ocean frontage should belong to 'the people.' " Her statement genuinely interested me, because I felt she sincerely believed her viewpoint to be morally valid.

Pursuing my curiosity, I began asking her questions. "Who is it you are referring to when you use the term *the people*?"

"Everyone," she answered.

"Do you mean that you and I should be joint owners, along with millions of other people, of every square inch of this beach?"

"Of course," she replied with certainty.

It seemed to me that such an involuntary partnership held the potential for enormous practical problems.

"What happens if both you and I want to sit on the same four square feet of beach at the same time?"

"That's getting overly technical," she protested. "It would be highly unlikely to occur."

In my mind, I silently translated the real meaning of her response to be: "I can't answer that."

In reality, common sense told me that it was just this sort of problem that would, in fact, continually occur in a "common-ownership" society. Worse, it would occur on a much larger scale.

What would stop a gang of people from getting up early each morning and staking out fifty yards of the most desirable beachfront in a given area? After all, since they would own every square inch of the beach in common with everyone else, it would be their right to do so. Is this what the original communist theoreticians had in mind—a chaotic society that would operate on a first-come-first-served basis?

But wait a minute. Why should the gang have to arise early each morning to lay claim to the preferred area of the beach? Does communism provide for a time limit on the use of commonly owned property? Why not just have a couple of gang members guard the property at night? Technically, they would merely be exercising their right to use "common property"; it's just that their use, in this particular case, would be continuous. To carry this line of reasoning to its ultimate conclusion, why not just live on that particular area of beach on a permanent basis? And *that* would be the precise point at which "the people" would be engaged in something called *private ownership of property*.

It seemed very clear to me that the vague concepts of "elimination of private property" and "goods owned in common" could only mean, in real life, that land and other wealth should be taken from their rightful owners and made available to the strongest person or group to come along and claim them. In that case, it is theoretical communism, not capitalism, that is a dog-eat-dog system.

The only meaningful way in which to think of property is that someone either owns it or he does not. And, as was discussed in Chapter 1, the true tests of ownership are whether or not you may do anything you desire with your own property and whether or not anyone else may take all or any part of it from you. You might also recall the listing of only three possible ways in which property can be viewed. Theoretical communism seems to favor the first of those three views: that anyone may take anyone else's property whenever he pleases.

Another aspect of theoretical communism is the notion that the individual is unimportant and that it is therefore moral to sacrifice him for "the good of society." But since "society" is nothing more than a term for a large number of individuals, this means that every person is subject to sacrifice, at any time, and that such sacrifice is subject to the whims of any group of individuals strong enough to enforce its will.

This is precisely the kind of society that existed in pre-civilized times. Men lived communal lives to protect themselves from beasts and the hazards of nature. Cannibalism was considered moral, because only one individual needed to be sacrificed to feed the group. This is especially interesting since one of the standard "arguments" of free enterprise antagonists is that capitalism is outdated. Advocates of freedom are labeled as old-fashioned thinkers. In truth, it is communism that has been outdated since man first discovered the miracle of agriculture and began his climb toward civilization.

A final aspect of theoretical communism which should be mentioned is the so-called Labor Theory. This is the rather vague concept which calls for a laborer to "receive all the fruits of his labor" or which insists upon "the right of a laborer to the products of his labor." But in a division-of-labor society (which, as previously noted, exists in *all* civilized countries today), how does one determine how much labor (in terms of money) each laborer puts into a particular product?

Theoretically, the Marxist believes that if a man puts $100 worth of labor into the making of a product (and assuming he makes every aspect of the product himself, which is almost never the case), he is being exploited if someone buys it from him for $100 and resells it for $125. The Marxist would argue that the additional $25 belongs to the laborer who made the product. Of course, the Marxist does not explain what happens if the next person sells the product for only $75. Should the laborer then refund the $25 loss?

And how does one keep track of each laborer from whom he has bought a product, so that, say, ten years later, he can send him the profit realized from selling the product at a higher price? It is obvious that the Labor Theory, aside from the aspects of forcible interference involved, is unrealistic to the point of having no real-life meaning. It is an unintelligible notion that has no way of being explained in the real world—or in any other world.

And yet these kinds of abstract notions, such as "the laborer should not be exploited for profit," persist, particularly among the young and uneducated. It is sad—and very dangerous—that young people of our times are being brought up to believe in such utter nonsense.

I recall that a certain professional athlete, noted for his collectivist sentiments, once made a statement to the press to the effect that "only those who do the actual *physical* work should receive the profits from that labor." Here was a young man, barely out of college, publicly waving the Labor-Theory banner as though it had some concrete meaning. I wondered what kind of education this fellow had received in college that had led him to make such a nonsensical statement.

Had he ever stopped to analyze what constituted "physical labor?" Is writing a book, for example, physical labor? Or should an author's profits go to the laborers who do the typesetting, printing, shipping and other physical tasks relating to the manufacture and distribution of his book?

Obviously, no college professor had explained to this man-child the connection between freedom and free enterprise. No one had ever explained to him that before there can be physical labor to perform, someone must come up with an idea, someone must invest capital, and someone must organize men together for productive purposes. In the meantime, this young giant goes on earning his several-hundred-thousand dollars a year by throwing a basketball through a metal hoop. And I go on wondering if he considers such playful activity to be "labor."

Even if it were possible to define the Labor Theory in an intelligible way, it still would overlook the fact that, in the real world, cost, price and value are three distinctly different considerations. Cost relates to how much capital (including that invested in labor) it takes to produce a product. Price is what is being asked for the product. Value is what any particular person at any given time thinks the product is worth. You and I may buy the same item at the same time for the same price, but you may value it more than I. You may have been willing to pay a higher price for the item, had it been asked, but I may not have been willing to do so.

The Labor Theory is just another example of the government-mentality belief that in every transaction one person must win and another must lose. This, of course, is nonsense, for the same reason that every person in a voluntary transaction theoretically profits because he exercises free choice. The only way the Labor Theory can make any sense (although it would be impossible, as well as undesirable, to apply) is if every person were an individual entrepreneur producing each item in its entirety. And a society of entrepreneurs is hardly compatible with the goals of hard-line communists.

Like laissez-faire capitalism, theoretical communism

has never existed anywhere in civilized times. The difference, however, is that capitalism is very simple in concept and is in harmony with Natural Law and man's natural instincts. Theoretical communism, on the other hand, is not only unintelligible, it violates every canon of ethics concerned with human freedom.

Real Communism

Real communism is quite another story. Though it violates human freedom, it certainly is easy to understand. Whereas communist leaders would like to have the gullible masses believe that "the people" own everything, the reality is that *real* communism turns out to be a dictatorship in which the dictators, unlike most other dictators, own everything. Everything includes not only all land and material wealth, but people's lives as well. Every citizen of a twentieth-century communist country is a literal slave, unless he is part of the power structure.

In truth, communism (as it is theoretically proposed) is myth. While it purports to have as one of its main objectives "common ownership of all property," in reality no one (except the dictators) owns *anything*. An owner, as we have discussed, has absolute say-so over what will be done with his property.

The people of Russia, China, Cuba and other communist countries have *no* say-so whatsoever about what will be done with *any* property, including their own lives. They are told what jobs they will perform. They are told where they will perform them. They are told what hours they will work. They are told how much they will be paid for the work they do (hardly in accordance with the vague notion of the Labor Theory). And, not only may they not quit their jobs like workers in capitalist countries, they may be imprisoned for even daring to challenge any of these commands.

The notion that people in communist countries own everything "in common" is preposterous in light of the facts. Afer sixty years, Russia's iron-fisted totalitarian government still exploits its workers unmercifully. The tools of industry, like everything else in communist countries, are owned by a small group of men who control the government. These men are the actual owners, because an owner is someone who can say what will be done with his property, without interference from others. And you can be sure that when the Soviet dictators wish to do something with any property held within Russia's borders, no citizen interferes with them.

Earlier I said that freedom and equality are incompatible goals and that this incompatibility is one of the things at the heart of democracy's problems. Democracy strives for balance, but has difficulty keeping the scales tipped away from equality and toward freedom. Under communism, however, there is *no* freedom and glaring *inequality*. It is true that there is some degree of *equal misery* among the masses (in whose name revolutions are always carried out), but you can be sure that government leaders do not live like the rest of the population.

There is one aspect of *theoretical* communism that is also a grim reality of *real* communism. That is the belief that the individual is nothing and that the only thing that matters is the State. And that is one of the main reasons why communism does not work, because, as pointed out, the State is nothing more than millions of *individuals*. How can the individual be nothing and the State be everything when the State *is* individuals? Rose Wilder Lane, in her evolution from communism to libertarianism, described the precise moment when this incongruity first struck her:

"When the capitalist is gone," she asked, "who will manage production? The State. And what is the State? The State will be the mass of toiling workers.

"It was at this point," said Rose Wilder Lane, "that the first doubt pierced my Communist faith."[9]

If you will recall our earlier discussion of the capitalistic cycle, the impetus for the productive process is the investment of surplus wealth. How, then, does a communist country carry out an industrial venture?

First, by investing whatever wealth has been accumulated by the government through the efforts of the people. Second, by utilizing the country's huge pool of slave labor, which represents a vast reservoir of "surplus wealth" for the dictatorship. The government merely invests slave labor in its projects, along with whatever surplus wealth it amasses through the efforts of these same slaves. This is precisely how Lenin, Stalin, Khrushchev and other Russian leaders built subways, factories, dams, railroads, and virtually all other large-scale projects constructed by the Soviet Union.

If Karl Marx were alive today, he no doubt would be horrified by the realities of communism. Marx naively predicted that the dictatorship established by the communists would be a temporary thing, that it would eventually be dissolved because there would be no need for it. He believed that people, after seeing how wonderfully communism worked, would be happy to work for "the good of society."

Needless to say, the hundreds of millions of people enslaved in Russia, China, Cuba, Ethiopia, and other communist countries around the globe are *not* happy to work for "the good of society." That is why awesome security forces must be maintained to keep the people from escaping. If collectivism is such a wonderful way of life, I wonder why people, particularly those in Western nations who praise the cultures of communist countries like Russia, are not storming their borders trying to get *into* those countries? The flight is most decidedly in the other direction.

And, needless to say, no communist dictatorship has intentionally dissolved itself. Recalling George Orwell's words once again, "One does not establish a dictatorship in order to safeguard a revolution; one makes the revolution in order to establish the dictatorship." More than sixty years after Lenin first took power in Russia, the dictatorship still exists. The excuse for a revolution is always to "free the people" or to give "all power to the people." But revolutionary heroes almost always turn out to be as bad as, and usually worse than, the oppressive governments they overthrow.

After Lenin overthrew the existing Russian government in 1917, one of his first moves was to set up a bloody and efficient network of secret police to stalk enemies of "the people." Lenin has long since died, but the secret-police force, now called the KGB, remains—except that it is much larger, much stronger, and much more oppressive. Years after the "all-power-to-the-people" ether of revolutionary heroes wears off, the people find themselves still enslaved. "The people" to whom "all power" goes always turns out to be the small group of people who led the revolution (and their successors). Napoleon admitted quite bluntly, "Vanity made the revolution; liberty was only a pretext."

The horrible truth is that those leaders who have cried the loudest for equality, particularly equality via the collectivist route, have been the bloodiest and most inhumane of all dictators. Stalin may qualify as the world's all-time mass murderer, making Hitler's destruction of human life look small by comparison. It is estimated that Lenin and Stalin combined murdered some 60 million of their own countrymen in an effort to accomplish their aims.

Have the 60 million lives been worth it? Has communism succeeded? It has succeeded only in the sense that perhaps never before in history has the enslavement of a people been carried out so efficiently. Its brutal methods, which include its incredibly effective secret-police force, have prevented serious threats of uprisings against it. In other words, as with democracies, communism works very well for those in power. Its leaders, because of the realities of communism, must simply direct more of their energies toward crushing dissent, whereas U.S. politicians are obliged to direct their energies toward The Vote.

But from the standpoint of the masses, communism has been a colossal failure. The cruel irony is that the greatest technological advances made by the Soviet Union have come from Western capitalist nations. Within a matter of a few years after Lenin took power, conditions were so bad in Russia that he was on the verge of being confronted with another revolution. As a result, he threw open the doors to despicable Western capitalists, inviting them to help industrialize Russia.

Just as they are doing today in China, major U.S. corporations scurried off to Russia to help save the country from its own system. And to this day, the help continues; Russia relies heavily on Western technology.

Meanwhile, Russia is able to use its slave-labor force to concentrate on the production of armaments, while American farmers and manufacturers ease its domestic difficulties. Because of this, as Eric Hoffer has noted, though "communism is a failure as an economic system (it) may triumph as a military instrument."

Alexander Solzhenitsyn, *who has been there*, assures us from firsthand experience that without the help of the United States, Russia's communism would almost certainly collapse:

It is American trade that allows the Soviet economy to concentrate its resources on armaments and preparations for war. Remove that trade, and the Soviet economy would be obliged to feed and clothe and house the Russian people, something it has never been able to do. Let the socialists among you allow this socialist economy to prove the superiority that its ideology claims. *Stop sending them goods.* Let them stand on their own feet, and then see what happens.[10]

The reality is that the communist has been allowed the luxury of keeping his collectivist cake, while eating off the fruits of capitalism. When college students suddenly "see the light" (read about communism for the first time) and run about preaching the beauty of collectivism and the evils of capitalism, they should be reminded that, after more than thirty years in China and sixty years in Russia, communists in those countries still come running to evil Western capitalists *to show them how to become capitalistic*. This one fact, which fills our newspapers each day, tells more about the merits of capitalism and the failure of communism than any book could ever explain.

Nor is this naiveté limited to the young. So-called liberal adults in this country talk of the "purity" in the cultures of places like Vietnam, China and Russia, failing to note that it is the communist countries who are so obsessed with industrial growth. China's recent decision to accomplish industrial growth at any cost is a perfect example of this. Industrialization has now been placed head and shoulders above its communist ideology, and for good reason: the ideology does not work in the real world!

And what effect does this have on liberal American adults? At a White House dinner for Vice-Premier Teng, actress Shirley MacLaine was quoted as saying that she had "mixed feelings" about the "relaxation of standards" that was taking place in China. Ms. MacLaine, whose intentions and sincerity are no doubt beyond reproach, is one of a number of liberal Hollywood "activists." For many years it has been chic in the world of show business to praise collectivism and admire inhumane communist regimes throughout the world.

Many knowledgeable people tend to disregard Hollywood liberalism, dismissing the most vocal of their numbers as simply uninformed. I agree that it is mostly a case of lack of knowledge (coupled with self-imposed guilt), but I think it is a mistake to dismiss their statements. Whether one likes it or not, the fact is that show-business celebrities are able to reach millions of Americans through the media. While most of these celebrities, albeit poorly informed, no doubt have good intentions, they have the potential to do great damage to our country. The only way to reduce the damage which they unknowingly inflict is for people who do understand the concepts of human freedom to do a much better job of making the public aware of the real facts.

Amid all the hubbub of China's whirlwind initiation into the world of capitalism, amid all the hugging between President Carter and Vice-Premier Teng, amid all the celebrating and dancing, the most important point about China's overtures to the West was missed by most of the media. When China opened its doors to Western capitalists, the message was plain and simple: "We admit it; the revolution has failed. Communism does not work."

With a per capita annual income of $350, China's leaders decided, after thirty years of experimentation with a system wherein "goods are owned in common and are available to all as needed," that it was time to throw in the towel—just as Lenin had decided back in 1921.

It is no big mystery why communism does not work. It does not work, and cannot work, because it defies human nature. There is nothing in it for the individual. It was this same kind of restraint of human nature that was a key factor in keeping the slave-oriented economy of the Old South perpetually depressed. If men know that everyone will receive the same, regardless of how much each one produces, everyone has a tendency to become more "needy" and less productive. When motivation is eliminated, producers disappear. This is why, as Rose Wilder Lane noted, a communist economy is a static economy. No ideology can change the nature of man.

As a result, both China and Russia not only import Western technology but have had to resort to "creeping capitalism." In desperation, they have given peasants small incentives for increased production. The communism of Russia and China has lost its "purity."

One of the most glaring examples of capitalism versus communism is found in the comparison of Taiwan, a tiny nation of but 17 million inhabitants, with China, whose population is close to 1 billion. Taiwan, notwithstanding its size, is one of the top 20 trading nations in the world. Taiwan's foreign trade in 1977 was $17.9 billion, as compared to Communist China's $16.4 billion.

It is no coincidence that a country more than fifty times the size of Taiwan cannot equal it in production. Nor is it a coincidence that in countries like China, where free enterprise is outlawed, human freedom is most restricted. The connection between freedom and free enterprise remains: without property rights, no rights are possible!

Before leaving the subject of communism, I feel it is my duty, as a libertarian, to point out if people wish to enter into a communal existence *voluntarily*, and to form communistic societies without forcing others to join, that is certainly their right. The key word, as always, is *voluntarily.*

Few people, however, choose such a life voluntarily— *including* those in Western nations who are the most vociferous in singing its praises. I believe communism will always fail (to make people happy), because of the reality that people instinctively seek to improve their well-being. That is why all communist societies must be held together by firm dictatorships. Communism, as an ideology, is not a threat to freedom-loving people. The threat of communism stems from the fact that its dictators have been clever enough to assemble powerful armies and mighty arsenals of weapons.

THE ECONOMICS OF "NOTHINGISM"

I refer to socialism as "nothingism" for two reasons. First, theoretical socialism, by dictionary definition, is virtually the same as communism. Therefore, if one were to be concerned only with the theoretical aspects of socialism, there would be little reason to use the term at all; communism fills the bill quite well. The only significant difference between the definitions of socialism and communism is that socialism is referred to as "a transitional state of society between capitalism and communism."

In view of the rapidly accelerating trend toward collectivism in all Western nations, including the United States, this is a rather discomforting thought. Marx, in other words, foresaw the current trend toward collectivism. He saw "socialism" only as a temporary, intermediate step, with communism ultimately become firmly established. The only catch is that Marx did not live to see what communism, in real life, would be like. In *real* communism, the State does not "wither away" (as in the definition of communism). The State stays on to terrorize the people, and no one but the State has *any* rights.

The second reason for seeing socialism as a non-system is that *real* socialism is neither fish nor fowl. It is a contradiction. In all Western nations, both capitalism and communism exist, with the mixture referred to as socialism (although the governments of most countries, such as the U.S., conspicuously avoid using the term). In some countries the tilt is toward capitalism, while in others (Sweden, for example) the balance is shifted much closer to real communism. Socialism, in the real world, is nothing more than a mixture of impure capitalism and impure communism.

The reason that so many countries cling to the contradictory system of socialism, as opposed to communism, is that it provides the opportunity for politicians to meet the expedient demands of citizens by exploiting what *does* work—capitalism. Capitalism fuels the socialist economy, with much of the fruits of capitalism being confiscated to help expediency-minded politicians meet the expediency-minded demands of their constituents.

While the Expediency Factors of both citizens and politicians put constant pressure on governments to lean more and more toward socialism, there are two other factors which help to flame socialist fires. The first is fear. Governments have made intelligent use of fear, urging citizens to conform or run the risk of being left out in the cold, particularly in old age. It is this drive for conformity that leads frightened men down the collectivist path like sheep, a path at the end of which the god of socialism is presumed to be waiting, ready to wave his magic wand and instantly dissolve one of nature's strictest laws—the inequality of men.

The second factor that inspires socialism is envy, which is at the heart of the true socialist's attitude. The hardcore socialist is bothered by the fact that, in a free society, people can rise to the level of their ambitions, abilities and willingness to work. Through socialism, the envious socialist hopes not to make everyone well off, but to make everyone equally miserable. It is no wonder that the socialist admires societies like Russia and China, where most of the population live barely above the poverty level.

Socialism leads us to where government has evolved today, with its distorted concepts of what the functions of government should be. The U.S., one of the last bastions of substantial capitalistic activity, is rapidly accelerating down the socialist path. The realities of The Vote seem to have left its power-conscious officials no alternative if they wish to stay in power.

In vying for The Vote, one of the excuses politicians use for injecting greater dosages of socialism into society is the "mysterious-multiplier" concept. This is the curious notion that the laws of mathematics, economics and common sense somehow change when one goes from small to large transactions. While government successfully perpetrates the myth that, as society becomes larger and more complex, problems are too difficult for individuals to solve, the truth is quite the opposite. In reality, the more complex problems become, the better they can be solved by individuals. That is because an individual has his own well-being at stake.

An individual knows himself better than some bureaucrat in Washington who has never met him. An individual understands his own needs and desires, his own personality, his own special circumstances—none of which are exactly like those of his neighbors. The larger a society grows, the *less* capable government is of solving the problems of individuals.

In addition to the "mysterious-multiplier" concept, government works hard at trying to make voters believe that economic law can be ignored and that something can, in fact, be created from nothing. People are led to believe that when money is taken from one group and handed to another, something greater results. Again, the opposite is true, for two reasons:

First, on the way from one group to another, a substantial portion of the booty ends up in the hands of the government employees who administer such "transfer-payment" programs. Second, there is a loss, not a gain, when wealth is confiscated. What is lost is the new technology, products, services and jobs that could have been created with it.

What allows Uncle Sam to violate economic law so blatantly is his adeptness at using an old magician's ploy—the strategy of getting the audience to look at one hand, while doing the trick with the other hand. In the case of government functions, the politician always emphasizes the hand that holds the *short-term benefits* of his actions. This, he hopes, will translate into V-O-T-E-S. But the hand he hides behind his back holds the *long-term ramifications* of his expedient, vote-getting actions. And, as we are witnessing today, such long-term effects are almost always disastrous to everyone—*including the people who receive the short-term benefits of such actions.*

It is the continual use of this short-term-patching approach which, when combined with the normal bungling, inefficiency and corruption of government, is most responsible for our national insolvency. It simply does not work.

If I may borrow an example from *Looking Out for #1,* the use of short-term, politically expedient solutions to cure the "problems" of individuals is akin to trying to bail water out of a sinking ship by using a bucket riddled with holes. Government effectively succeeds in keeping the public's attention focused on all the water it throws out of the boat (the short-term benefits), but it succeeds even better in hiding the far more important fact that the ship is sinking a little more each day.

This short-term-patching approach was facilitated by the works of the late John Maynard Keynes, the British economist. Keynes believed in injecting varying dosages of communism into a capitalistic economy, which means he believed in a contradiction. So-called Keynesian economics is the belief that increased government spending stimulates the economy during periods of recession, thereby decreasing unemployment, while decreased government spending slows the economy during inflationary periods.

The 1970's, however, shattered Keynes' theories, because the U.S. experienced both unemployment *and* inflation, the worst of all possible worlds for the average worker.

What Keynes did not understand at all was The System and its dependence upon Expediency Factors. He was politically naive in that he believed that power-hungry politicians actually would cut back on government spending during inflationary times. But the realities of The Vote have made the politician's spending habits like the proverbial snowball accelerating downhill. He *can't* stop spending, because voters are hooked on it. People want *more* each year. Either you give it to them or you don't get reelected.

The fact is that when people blame capitalism for the mess in which the United States today finds itself, they are looking in the wrong direction. Unfortunately, we have never had the opportunity to try laissez-faire capitalism in this country, and though capitalism has done well even with one hand tied behind its back, ever-increasing government intervention has rendered it less and less effective. What has failed is our "mixed economy," i.e., a contradictory economy comprised of *some* free enterprise and ever-increasing governmental restrictions.

The result is that the U.S. productivity rate has fallen close to zero. Between 1966 and 1977, our cumulative productivity rate—about 24%—was, along with Great Britain's, the slowest of all industrialized nations. Japan's, by way of comparison, was 105% over the same period.

Clearly, these statistics are an indication of the obvious—that real socialism must fail in the long run. Socialism must fail because it is an irreconcilable contradiction. Freedom and restraint cannot coexist, particularly when the emphasis is on restraint.

The failure of our economy would make Karl Marx look like a very good prophet but for the fact that it is Marx's own socialism which has failed, not capitalism.

Also, it is not Marx's theoretical utopian communism toward which we are rushing. We are moving rapidly toward the same kind of totalitarian situation that exists today in other communist countries throughout the world.

Socialism eventually must evolve into extreme totalitarianism, because it kills off incentive. As we have been witnessing for the past several years, lack of incentive, in turn, causes a nation's gradual economic collapse. This collapse triggers anarchy and chaos, which forces government to resort to strong-armed totalitarian measures to restore order.

Sincere collectivists make the presumptuous mistake of believing that they are the only people who would like to see everyone in the world as well off as possible. But among freedom lovers and men of goodwill, such a desire is assumed without a second thought. The disagreement lies in the *proper means* of improving the welfare of the greatest number of people.

NIGHTMARE RESULTS OF SAMMY'S PROMISES

Now that we have concluded our "economic detour," we are in a good position to appreciate the ramifications of the functions modern government performs. These functions today are a direct result of the lethal combination of human Expediency Factors and The Vote. The necessity for Sammy's stealing can therefore be formulated as follows:

Expeciency Factors + The Vote = Government Functions

Because the realities of The Vote bring out the expedient worst in people, when Sammy attempts to make good on his campaign promises, the resulting "government functions" are a nightmare of violations of human freedom. It is precisely because of Sammy's expedient promises to deliver more of everything to everyone that the once-clear function of government has been transformed into the fulfillment of as many of those promises as possible, no matter how immoral in concept or how economically unfeasible they may be.

Obviously, these functions have little to do with the *proper* function of government. We already know that government's only legitimate function, assuming it is to be conceded any function at all, is to protect the individual from aggression. For most libertarians, this means, *at most:*

1) Providing physical protection for the lives and property of citizens.

2) Providing a system of arbitration for contractual disputes.

3) Providing for a so-called national defense.

Protecting a person from aggression, *with his explicit consent*, certainly is within the framework of Natural Law. But whenever government goes beyond this basic function and acts in violation of men's rights, *it* becomes the aggressor. Consequently, for some people to take it upon themselves to try to solve the "problems" of millions of other people, either against their will or at the expense of others, necessitates a *violation* of Natural Law. The American Revolutionists were well aware of this, which is why there were no provisions in the original Constitution providing for government to fulfill the needs and desires of individual citizens.

But the reality of The System is that it takes votes to get elected, it takes expedient promises to get votes, and it takes expedient actions to stay in office. What the politician's expedient actions translate into are a new set of functions for government, functions far removed from those originally outlined in the Constitution.

THROWING OUT THE CONSTITUTION

Though the erosion of the American Dream began over two hundred years ago, a tremendous acceleration in the rate of that erosion occurred in the 1930's under Franklin Roosevelt. Said FDR: "Government has the definite duty to use all its power and resources to meet new social problems with new social controls."

With those words, FDR took it upon himself, in effect, to throw out the Constitution of the United States and to redefine the function of government. His statement was, at best, unintelligible, and, at worst, immoral—a dangerous combination:

First, government has no "power" (i.e., legitimate power) except that granted to it by the *individuals* who explicitly consent to be represented by it.

Second, government has no "resources" except those it arbitrarily expropriates from citizens.

Third, there are no such things as "social problems"; only individuals have problems, and since each individual's circumstances are unique, so too are his problems.

Fourth, government has no "duty," either moral, divine or legal, to "meet" *anyone's* problems.

Finally, there are no such things as "social controls"; society is an abstract entity, and controls therefore can be imposed only on individuals (even businesses are comprised of individuals). Government has no right to control the lives of individuals in any way except to prevent them from forcibly interfering with others. All other government control is aggression and is therefore immoral and illegal.

Logic and morality notwithstanding, Franklin Roosevelt was determined to be a generous man—with other people's money. Among a seemingly endless list of short-term, expedient actions, he established the Social Security

Act, introduced farm subsidies, brought us minimum-wage laws, and created a multitude of government jobs programs.

Worst of all, he initiated the "soak-the-rich" policy of taxation which subjected persons with high incomes to *unequal* tax treatment, thereby initiating the economy-crippling trend toward lack of incentive. While the New Deal may have put a chicken in every pot, the long-term consequence, as is always the case with socialistic reforms, was a gradual erosion of personal freedom.

The New Deal was a classic example of political expediency—emphasizing the immediate benefits to certain voters, while ignoring the inevitable long-term devastation caused by such actions.

Roosevelt was, indeed, a generous man. And today, almost fifty years later, we are still paying for his generosity. Even FDR could not create wealth from nothing—although, to his credit as a politician, he was able to defer the payment for his actions far longer than were any of his successors. As a result, he did not live to have to face today's taxpayers.

It was the Great Depression of the 1930's that allowed Roosevelt to change the rules of the game dramatically. The Depression gave politicians a far greater range of issues to use in vying for The Vote. It allowed them to hold out more carrots to more people, because virtually everyone was in need. As a result, politicians offered redistribution-of-the-wealth programs to the "poor," business subsidies to favored businesses, and, eventually, special legislation to special-interest groups to "promote the general welfare."

Now, in our rapidly crumbling democracy, government's function has been tragically altered. Government today is in the business of "helping people to fulfill their desires." What this means is that government attempts to fulfill the needs and desires of people who cannot do so on their own in a free society, a society which gives them the opportunity to deal with other free men on a value-for-value basis. And when men no longer fulfill their needs and desires on a value-for-value basis, the code of ethics necessarily becomes "every man for himself" and "anything goes."

In the next three chapters we will be analyzing some of the most notable functions of modern government—functions fathered by the Expediency Factor and mothered by The Vote. Again, we should carefully consider both the moral validity and economic realities of these functions.

Morally, there is little to analyze. An action either complies with Natural Law or it does not. If a "function" violates the natural rights of *any* individual, it is immoral.

As I stated earlier, liberty must be given a higher value than all other objectives. Personal integrity demands that one's belief in Natural Law not be betrayed on an emotional whim. The "good" that a particular government function may purport to accomplish for some people is not a justifiable reason for committing aggression against other people; *no end* justifies the violation of *any* individual's right to his own life and property.

I again emphasize that men do not have the right to force other men to be concerned, sympathetic, helpful or charitable toward others. Men do not have the right to dispose of other men's lives or property, no matter what their personal rationalizations may be. If needs and desires were relevant, then any group of men would be justified in taking forcible control over other men's lives merely by claiming that such action is necessary in order to "fulfill their needs and desires."

It should also be mentioned that when people speak of "problems" or "injustices" that need to be corrected, they are merely voicing an opinion. When one talks in terms of the need for government to correct a "social problem," he is, in reality, stating his *opinion* that a problem does, in fact, exist; in addition, he is advocating the use of government force to fulfill *his* desire to change a circumstance that *he* defines as a problem.

As a result, when government intervenes to correct what certain voters deem to be an injustice, it virtually assures that a greater injustice will be committed. More often than not, the injustice originally alleged is merely a reflection of someone's moral beliefs—usually relating to personal needs and desires. And since government itself has no source of wealth, such needs and desires can be satisfied only by instituting *real* injustices against those who do produce wealth.

4

The Gourmet Banquet

Conservative economists used to refer to it as the "free lunch," while trying in vain to explain to the public that there was no such thing. But we've come a long way since FDR. What started out as a ham sandwich and a glass of milk has evolved into a gourmet banquet, with all 220 million of us pushing and shoving one another in an effort to stuff ourselves with as many of Sammy's "free" delicacies as possible.

This mania is a result of Government Function Number One: *Redistribution of the Wealth.*

Though it isn't worth much anymore, money still talks. Politicians are smart enough to know that top priority still goes to the dollar. So the expediency-minded politician, through The Vote, strikes up a bargain with the expediency-minded voter. After all, a potential candidate cannot just come right out and tell people he wants power over them. He must promise them something. Sy Leon, in *None of the Above*, describes the understanding this way:

"If (the politician) simply laid his cards on the table and said, 'I want to give you orders,' he would be ignored or despised. So he comes bearing gifts. 'I will give you education, or food, or housing,' he says, 'and all you have to do is give me some control over your life. Let me make the important decisions for you, and I will reward you.' "

In the final analysis, the main plank of *every* candidate's political platform promises redistribution of the wealth. The only differences lie in the degree and method each one advocates.

What does government's number one function mean to the American taxpayer? It means that there now are approximately 1,000 government programs which redistribute the wealth, as opposed to about 100 in 1960. It means that more than 60 million Americans now receive regular government checks of some kind. It means that, theoretically, a person in this country can qualify to receive money from 13 different government agencies *at the same time*.

Who is in charge of handing out these massive sums of money? Well, for one, Senator S. I. Hayakawa. But his appointment to the Budget Committee perplexed even him, since he admitted to having "the greatest difficulty balancing (his) own checkbook." Hayakawa himself considered his appointment "appallingly irresponsible on the part of the United States Senate."

If you are nervous about *who* is handling your money, listen to Senator Hayakawa's description of *how* it is handled:

A member of the committee will say, for instance, "Here's an appropriation for such-and-such. It was 1.7 for 1977. So for the 1978 budget we ought to make it 2.9." So all we do is add 1.2; that's not hard. The next item is 2.5. The members discuss it back and forth, and someone says, "Let's raise it to 3.7." They look around at each other. "Everybody in favor?" "Yes, sir. Okay." So in five minutes we have disposed of 2 *billion* bucks— 2 billion, not 2 million. I never realized it could be so easy. It's all simple addition. *You don't even have to know subtraction.*[11]

Like William Simon, Senator Hayakawa was the victim of culture shock when he made the transition from private to government life. Sounding almost like a naive child abruptly introduced to a new experience, he pointed out the obvious fact that the people of the United States never amended the Constitution to the effect that government's main function should be to redistribute income. He now concedes, however, that this is, indeed, the number one function of government. Franz Oppenheimer described this unapproved redirection of government purpose as "the institutionalization of the 'political means' of acquiring wealth."[12]

As we know from the last chapter (and, indeed, as I assume everyone already knew), wealth can be produced only through effort. Redistribution of the wealth as government's chief function consequently poses an uncomfortable multiple question: How much of whose wealth shall be given to which people? This in turn raises, once again, the inevitable question: *Who shall decide?*

If one believes in Natural Law, he knows there can be only one moral answer to the last question: *each individual must decide for himself.* The reality, however, is that politicians decide. And their decisions, of course, are tied directly to The Vote. What does this mean in numbers? Obviously, that politicians must take from the smallest number of people possible and give to the largest number possible if they hope to stay in office.

And who constitutes the small and large "numbers?" This is an interesting question, because the original "majority" (the "poor") no longer exists, and the new "majority" (the "middle class") has fuzzy demarcation lines. This is why politicians now run around like zombies out of control, picking *everyone's* pockets.

"RICH" VERSUS "POOR?"

Even though the original "majority" has disappeared, I think it is important, before analyzing today's "majority," to understand some realities concerning the original voting groups. George Orwell, in fact, places them in *three* categories:

> Throughout recorded time, and probably since the end of the Neolithic Age, there have been three kinds of people in the world; the High, the Middle, and the Low. . . . The aims of these three groups are entirely irreconcilable. The aim of the High is to remain where they are. The aim of the Middle is to change places with the High. The aim of the Low . . . is to abolish all distinctions and create a society in which all men shall be equal.

It is important to recognize that these groups are created by nature, and that to change them artificially means to ignore the natural instincts and abilities of men. This artificial change may be instituted by Majority Rule or by violent revolution, but in either case nature, in the end, will have its way. Events in modern-day Iran are a perfect example of Will and Ariel Durant's description of the inevitable:

". . . violent revolutions do not so much redistribute wealth as destroy it. There may be a redivision of the land, but the natural inequality of men soon re-creates an inequality of possessions and privileges, and raises to power a new minority with essentially the same instincts as in the old."[18]

THE PROMISE OF EQUALITY

Over the centuries, many people have tried to erase from the earth the natural presence of inequality. Virtually everything has been tried, but, in the end, nature always asserts itself. Marx's ideological dreams were grand, indeed, but inequality has not been erased in the Soviet Union. Russian shoemakers, carpenters and truck drivers still live like shoemakers, carpenters and truck drivers;

basketball, hockey and track stars live like a privileged elite; and politicians eat caviar.

Why is the fact of inequality so difficult to accept? I accepted it long ago. Millions of people on this earth are superior to me in endless ways. I am *not* equal to O. J. Simpson when it comes to running a football. So the free market pays him millions of dollars for his skill, which seems natural and right to me.

I cannot write lyrics like Alan Jay Lerner; I am not the least bit equal to him in that respect. I accept that fact as a reality of life.

I do not have Jonas Salk's ability to discover a cure for disease. I applaud him and accept my inequality without resentment. I am very happy that there are men and women whose "unequal" abilities make this a better world in which to live.

I believe that one of the things which has caused inequality to become an obscene word in today's world is confusion over the phrase in the Declaration of Independence which states that "all men are created equal." The document itself makes it very clear that the founders of our country had no illusions about transforming nature. It makes it very clear that *all men are created equal* was intended to mean that *all men have equal rights*.

Every libertarian, every freedom lover, every proponent of Natural Law and every man of goodwill certainly agrees that all men have equal rights. Everyone has an equal right to sole dominion over his own life; he has the right to do anything he wishes with his life, so long as he does not forcibly interfere with those same rights in others. Every man should have the right to pursue his life, his liberty and his happiness, without fear of aggression from his neighbors. These rights truly are inalienable. But other than in their rights, men most certainly are *not* born equal.

In our increasingly socialistic society, however, equal

rights has come to mean *unequal* rights for some. It has come to mean that those who produce the most wealth do not have the same rights as those who produce the least. It is interesting to note that in the old American phrase, "life, liberty and property," there is no mention of equality. This is because life is not equal; liberty and equality are conflicting objectives; and property rights and equality have no relation to one another.

If one believes in equal rights, one cannot simultaneously believe that some men should be allowed to *force* other men to share the fruits of their labor. This means, once and for all, facing up to the reality that if one man has $1 million and another man has only $1, no one has the right to force the first man to give any part of his $1 million to the second man. On the contrary, it means that the man with the $1 million has just as much right to his $1 million as the second man has to his $1.

Even many economists today are influenced by the question of inequality—both among individuals and nations. They cannot accept the fact that freedom and free enterprise only give everyone a better opportunity to improve his well-being, but do not make everyone equal. Egalitarianism is a philosophical issue, and, as previously discussed, philosophy has nothing to do with economics.

As we also have discussed, one of the chief causes of the eventual collapse of all democratic experiments throughout history has been the clash between equality and freedom. In their zealous efforts to achieve equality, utopian proponents have had a tendency to violate the rights of those whom they deem to be the "rich." And when the rights of *any* person are violated, cracks begin appearing in the basic structure of a democratic civilization.

NEEDS AND DESIRES VERSUS MORALITY

Assuming, for the moment, that there existed in America today those two mythical groups called the "rich" and the "poor," one would, in addressing the "problem," encounter the same difficult questions mentioned earlier: Who, exactly, are the "poor?" Who is "in need?" How much should be given to the "poor" and "needy?" Whose assets should be confiscated in order to give to them? At what point should a person no longer be considered poor? And, above all, who has the *moral right* to make these decisions?

Let us consider "need" first. How do we define it? Is a man in need if he earns only $5,000 a year? Or should the figure be $7,000? Or $10,000? What about the man who earns $20,000, but has five children and elderly parents to support, a wife who is dying of cancer, and a house that is badly in "need" of repairs? Or the man who has an income of $100,000 a year, but owes $300,000 in bills and is on the verge of bankruptcy?

I feel I have neither the divine right nor the wisdom to decide who is in need and who is not. One would have to be omniscient to know where to draw the lines.

Now let us look at "desire." How about the desire for a "decent living?" Is everyone entitled to one? Fine. What *is* a decent living? Is everyone entitled to a home? If so, at what price and in what neighborhood? Is everyone entitled to a car? A Chevy? Why not a Buick, if that is what a person desires? In fact, if desire is relevant, what about the poverty-stricken individual who desires a Rolls-Royce? Why should his desire be any less relevant than that of the man who is willing to settle for a compact car? This is not an attempt to be humorous. It is an attempt to demonstrate that desires are personal and arbitrary.

Clearly, if one insisted that needs and desires were relevant, then moral standards would be out the window. It would mean that one man's desire to steal would be on an equal moral footing with another man's desire to work. One man's desire to be free would not have greater moral validity than another man's desire to violate his freedom. A person who places needs and desires above liberty does not believe in *human* freedom. What he believes in is freedom for *some* humans. He believes it is moral to violate the rights of certain men in order to help certain other men whom he deems to be in need.

The relevant question is not whether someone desires something or believes that he needs it. If human rights are to be respected, the relevant question is whether he has the ability to pay for it and/or the willingness to work for it. Every man should get what he deserves. And what he deserves is exactly what the highest bidder will pay him in a free market, regardless of what he thinks he should get or what his desires are.

That some people are poorer than others is a reality. That these people desire a better way of life is perfectly natural and understandable. And for them to *pursue* a better way of life is their natural right. But that is where Natural Law draws the line. For anyone to force you to hand over to others an arbitrary percentage of the fruits of your labor is a violation of *your* natural rights.

You have a natural right to your life, liberty and property; someone else's *desire* for your life, liberty or property is inconsequential. Needs are subjective opinions and desires are personal wishes; one cannot sacrifice his standard of ethics to opinions or wishes. Your human rights are superior to any desire I might have to take your property.

Each of us has many personal needs and desires. These needs and desires not only are of a financial nature, but of an emotional nature as well. Are emotional desires also to be considered relevant? Should, for example, others be forced to give love to every person who needs or desires love?

Years ago, when I was flat broke—literally without $10 to my name, evicted from my home, my car repossessed—I had many needs and desires, to say the least. I experienced what it means to go hungry. But never did I run to Sammy and ask him to slip me some of his stolen loot. My needs were *my* responsibility. My desires were subjective, personal wishes, and certainly were not binding upon anyone else.

Even now I desire many things I cannot have. I also have subjective opinions about my needs, and I realize that some of them may never be fulfilled. It would be easy to have a bitter attitude and to insist irrationally that life has not been fair to me. But years ago my mind was set straight on the validity of needs and desires when someone very quizzically asked me, "Who ever said life was supposed to be fair?"

Since then I have come to realize that I have two morally valid options with regard to my needs and desires. I either can try to satisfy them through my own honest efforts or I can make the decision to leave them unfulfilled.

Government loves to cloud the issue of needs and desires versus morality with a strange adaptation of the same "mysterious-multiplier" concept it applies to economics. The idea is that needs and desires acquire moral validity if one thinks in terms of large numbers of people. It is this illogical notion that forms the shaky foundation for Majority Rule. If 3 million people vote to steal from 1 million people, proclaiming that the theft is justified because it is *their* opinion that they need the money for a worthy cause (say, to send a man to the moon), one is supposed to accept their action as moral.

To demonstrate the absurdity of such a position, eliminate six zeroes from each figure: If a group of *3* people gets together and decides to rob *1* person, insisting that they are a "society" and that what they are doing is in society's (their) best interest, virtually everyone would agree that their claim is ludicrous. How can the same action be declared morally right just by multiplying by millions? On the contrary, it would be that much more *immoral*, because the number of people whose rights would be violated would be substantially increased.

Men of goodwill, who respect the rights of their fellowmen, must reject the notion that an act of aggression can be justified by arbitrarily claiming that it is for a "worthy" cause. It says something about the moral decay of our society when a fictional character—Robin Hood—is seen as a "good guy" because he steals from those he deems to be "rich" and gives the stolen loot to those he deems to be "poor." The drift toward "justifiable" aggression in our society, as noted in "Fundamentals of Liberty," makes it easier to understand the corresponding drift toward increased criminal activity.

> If a man grows up believing that trespass is all right whenever he deems himself as having a 'just cause"; if a man is continually reminded that "property rights are not absolute"; and if a man witnesses governments interfering with the property rights of other men, all with the approval of business, professional, civic, religious, and labor organizations; if such is the background in which persons are raised, it is not too difficult to understand why criminal behavior is on the increase. If men who are respected in the community can sanction property trespass and violence, then why not the criminals?[14]

ECONOMIC REALITIES OF REDISTRIBUTION OF THE WEALTH

Again assuming that the mythical groups "rich" and "poor" still existed in America, let us go one step further. For purposes of this discussion, we will temporarily ignore the moral aspects of redistribution of the wealth and look only at the economics involved.

The "soak-the-rich" philosophy used to be very popular among politicians and economically ignorant liberals. But Henry Hazlitt did some calculating a few years back and came up with some interesting—and embarrassing— figures. Hazlitt noted that if the government had confiscated 100% of the income of every person in the country who earned over $50,000 in 1968, it would have netted an additional $24 billion in tax revenues. Had that additional booty been distributed equally among the approximately 200 million people then living in the United States (assuming no administrative costs whatsoever), each person would have received the grand sum of $120![15]

This, of course, does not even take into account an even more important economic fact: if Sammy did resort to such extreme theft, it would be the last time he could do it, because people simply would stop earning high incomes if they knew that all of their earnings would be confiscated.

To a lesser but increasing degree, this, in fact, is exactly the kind of reality that has been destroying the American Dream for years. Potentially super-productive individuals have curtailed their efforts; their incentives have been reduced by the economically destructive "soak-the-rich" philosophy. Those who still cling to this suicidal philosophy would do well to think about the old cliché of "killing the goose that lays the golden eggs."

The truth is that the welfare state, which politicians would have you believe was designed to aid the "poor," is, in reality, devastating to the "poor." Among other things, it kills incentive, which decreases productivity, which in turn increases unemployment. In addition, it is a major contributor to inflation, as we shall see in a later chapter, which is one of the worst enemies of the poorest people in our society.

Perhaps the aspect of redistribution of the wealth I most deplore is the politician's ploy of making it, like so many other actions, a black-versus-white issue. Unfortunately, uninformed liberals, as always, mistakenly support vote-conscious bureaucrats in this race-issue sham. In truth, it is a vicious, politically expedient scheme on the part of politicians.

I consider this ploy to be an insult to the millions of proud, self-respecting black individualists throughout the country. Such blacks are well aware that the road to security and economic success is paved with self-esteem, hard work, ambition, determination, and, above all, a respect for human rights. Politicians insult the intelligence of these people by believing that they buy the notion that the road to riches is littered with dollars which Sammy has pilfered from their neighbors.

The issue is *not* black versus white. The issue is *freedom* versus *coercion*. Human freedom relates to *all* men, black *and* white.

THE NEW MAJORITY

The politician does not like to be bothered with mundane topics like morality and ethics; his interests lie solely in numbers. He wants to know only one thing: what group or groups form the "majority?"

When the lines were more sharply defined by nature alone, his task was much simpler. He could easily see that The Vote could be won by offering the free lunch to those in the lower income brackets. Had nature made more people capable of becoming rich, the politician simply would have wooed the "rich" instead. Wherever the numbers lie, that is where he makes his pitch.

But government has done its job too well. After making such clever use of a rich-versus-poor issue for so many years, it now finds itself in a dilemma. The wealth has been so thoroughly redistributed that the "poor" have virtually disappeared (relative to yesterday's standards), and certainly there are very few super-rich (again, relative to yesterday's standards).

In losing the "poor," liberal politicians have lost their favorite pawns. Not that they are giving up without a fight. The government is perfectly willing to resort to fraud to avoid losing the rich-versus-poor issue. The U.S. Census Bureau reported that in 1976 there were still 25 million people living in poverty in this country. Between 1964—when the total was 36 million—and 1975, annual "transfer payments" (cash payments from the government) to these people increased from $27 billion to $156 billion.

Such figures might lead one to believe that these 25 million people not only are not poor, but, in fact, are very well off—assuming that all the money went directly into their hands, which it did not. But the least that can be said of them is that they now live far better than the great majority of people throughout the world.

So why are they still listed as poverty cases? Because, believe it or not, the Census Bureau does not count the money they receive from the government as income! Therefore, no matter how much money they receive, they always will be officially listed at below the poverty level.

This neat little trick is very convenient for politicians who want a poverty *issue* rather than a poverty *solution*.

But the new majority—the gigantic Middle Class—has learned well from the politician. It, too, thinks expediently. This huge majority no longer is interested in doctored-up poverty figures, as evidenced by the passage of California's Proposition 13 and other tax-cut measures. "The people" have turned on Sammy; he has made them too healthy, too wealthy and too wise.

Try as government does to pit one member of the Middle Class against another—through occupation, race, sex, nationality, and even religion—the fact remains that its members are aligned by a common bond: they have been weaned on the milk of false prosperity (receiving more than they produce), and they are not about to settle for less.

To maintain such an attitude means to embrace the irrational beliefs that economic law *can* be violated and that Natural Law *should* be violated. To refuse to believe that a free lunch is possible and that theft is moral, one would have to be prepared to give up the false prosperity he has come to cherish over the years.

What is government to do about this quandary? It now has virtually *everyone* hooked on getting more and more of the pie while doing less and less of the baking. Yet the same people who form the new Middle-Class majority have become—through government's redistribution-of-the-wealth policies—government's major source of funds.

If you ever wondered why government actions seem so confused and contradictory, sometimes bordering on the insane, it is in no small way due to this irreconcilable dilemma.

Now, virtually everyone in the new majority wants tax reform; everyone wants government spending lowered; everyone wants to see inflation brought under control; everyone believes that the other guy's benefits are an unnecessary government expense. But *no one* is willing to accept a reduction in *his* share of the plunder pie.

People, now hooked on the benefits of the gourmet banquet, no longer are capable of being objective. As a result, they give up a little more of their freedom each time they need a quick fix. And this is why the power-holders, notwithstanding the dilemma they have created, still hold the ace card. They know we all want more, so they continue to offer us more—in exchange for more power over our lives.

So long as most voters believe they are getting an increasing share of the national pie—regardless of where it comes from—government will be able to continue controlling their lives. The secret to maintaining this voluntary control, which is the backbone of The System, is contentment. "Without economic security," said Aldous Huxley, "the love of servitude cannot possibly come into existence."

THE DEATH OF PRODUCTIVITY

As we already know, there is only one way to create wealth—through productive effort. But there are two ways to *obtain* wealth. One is through productive effort; the other is through plunder. Workers and entrepreneurs obtain wealth by producing goods and services on a voluntary-exchange basis. Those who receive government checks obtain wealth by taking from those who produce it.

Eric Hoffer has referred to our era as the "Age of the Labor Faker." To an extent, it is hard to argue with his tag. But it implies a blanket indictment, so I think it should be examined more closely. There are varying degrees of "labor faking."

At one end of the scale are those who still retain pride in their work, insist on being individualistic, and want nothing from government. Such people can be found in all occupations and at all income levels. Whether a man is janitor or a business executive, he is an economic plus to the national economy if he *earns* his income and steadfastly adheres to the principle of nonaggression.

At the other extreme are those who produce virtually nothing and live off the efforts of producers. This group consists primarily of those who are capable of earning their own way and who would do so if they had no other means of obtaining food, clothing and shelter.

A smaller percentage of the nonproducing group is

made up of those unfortunate people who are physically or mentally disabled to the extent that they are not able to care for themselves. The regrettable circumstances of such people are a concern to every humane individual, and I will address myself to their plight toward the end of this chapter.

In between the maximum producers and the nonproducers are the millions of people who "labor fake" to varying degrees. Each, of course, rationalizes that *his* form of government dole is justified, that *he* is honest and hard working, and that it is *he* from whom the government is stealing. Few people are able to be objective about their own contributions to the free-lunch/loss-of-freedom evolution we have been experiencing for years.

In fairness, one should always keep in mind that government has been the precipitator of this evolution, encouraging nonproductivity by offering handouts in exchange for votes. While there is no question that every person must accept ultimate responsibility for his actions, government's role should not be ignored.

The result is that we have become a society which rewards people for doing less. And, in such an environment, that is exactly what people will do—*less*. This fact notwithstanding, Jimmy Carter, at the time of the writing of this book, was proposing a direct cash payment to families below certain income levels. Government always manages to outdo itself in coming up with creative labels for its ludicrous actions; the name given to this one is "negative income tax."

Any rational person could predict the unavoidable effect of such handouts. Quite simply, the more money people receive for not working, the less they work. And, in fact, that is exactly what a study recently conducted by the government itself has shown. Congress spent $112 million of taxpayers' money testing 8,500 low-income families, giving them various kinds of direct payments over a period of ten years. The government's own reports concluded that the more these families received, the less they worked.

Washington spent $112 million to find out something that any person with a layman's grasp of human nature already knew; then, after "studying" the results, Carter, in his infinite wisdom, concluded that more income and less production is a good thing. One could not ask for a more blatant example of a politician's totally ignoring the facts and basing a decision on political expediency.

So-called guaranteed incomes are death to productivity. The higher the guaranteed income, the greater the number of people at or even slightly above that line who will stop working and take the guaranteed income. And as more and more people take the route of the nonproducer, those left to produce will have to give up a greater and greater percentage of their paychecks to support the nonproducers.

All this certainly makes it no great mystery why our productivity rate is grinding to a halt. As human beings, we do not appreciate anything that can be obtained too easily. Things that are handed to us free, with no effort involved, are the least appreciated. In fact, our nature is such that we rebel. The more we get for free, the more we want. Indeed, we become belligerent; we *demand* more.

The inevitable catastrophic climax toward which we are rushing, as we jockey for positions at Sammy's gourmet-banquet table, was summed up by Roy Ash, former head of the Office of Management and Budget, when he admitted to Senator Hayakawa that "there will soon be more people benefiting from federal-government payments than taxpayers to carry the load."[16]

The producer segment of our population—particularly the most productive members of the massive Middle Class—is at the breaking point. It is on the verge of no longer being able to support both itself and the rest of the population. As William Simon said in an interview with *Reason* magazine, ". . . half the people in America work for a living and the other half vote for it."

Clearly, those who still believe in paying their way are becoming irritated. They began to show it through government's own system when they voted overwhelmingly for Proposition 13. The so-called tax revolt that Proposition 13 triggered was summed up by former Secretary of the Interior Walter Hickel. In a conversation with Paul Harvey, Hickel predicted that "the next revolution in this country will be when those who work refuse to support those who don't."[17]

In *The Discovery of Freedom,* Rose Wilder Lane reflected on our evolution into a society in which more and more people demand security without paying for it through their own risk and effort:

> . . . human beings are fighters by nature. Living is a tough job; only good fighters can do it. Like it or lump it, this planet is no safe place for any living creature. Living is fighting for life, and when anyone does not know this fact, someone else is doing his fighting for him.
>
> Anyone who says that economic security is a human right, has been too much babied. While he babbles, other men are risking and losing their lives to protect him. They are fighting the sea, fighting the land, fighting diseases and insects and weather and space and time, for him, while he chatters that all men have a right to security and that some pagan god—Society, The State, The Government, The Commune—must give it to them. Let the fighting men stop fighting this inhuman earth for one hour, and he will learn how much security there is.

Living in an age when Stoic virtues are thought to be passé, we cling to the belief that the world owes us a living. But the decaying of our democracy is a warning that neither nature nor the laws of economics have any intention of bending their ways to go along with our preposterous notion.

In the end, it is they, not we, who will have their way.

THE NATURE OF THE REDISTRIBUTION PROCESS

When one gets to the heart of most government "programs," he discovers that they are nothing more than varying schemes to redistribute income. Few people, however, recognize the more subtle means of accomplishing the redistribution processes. The schemes they do understand are those which involve taking dollars out of their pockets and handing them directly to others. This forcible transfer of people's assets has come to be known, in political jargon, as a "transfer payment."

FROM YOUR POCKET TO YOUR NEIGHBOR'S POCKET

It would be impossible to attempt to discuss here, in detail, even a small percentage of the transfer-payment programs that exist today. Unemployment compensation, Aid to Families with Dependent Children, food stamps, and Social Security are but a few examples. All of them, however, have one thing in common: they are government-perpetrated frauds. They encourage voters to pursue the harmful illusion of something for nothing.

Government would have us believe that it is a boost to the economy when transfer dollars are put into the hands of more consumers. But, in point of fact, the opposite is true. When money changes hands involuntarily, with no product or service being given in return, no additional purchasing power is created. In this type of "transaction," one person's gain is simply another person's loss. The productive person who relinquishes the money in taxes has lost the exact amount of purchasing power the recipient has gained; the economy is no better off.

But the economy *is* worse off. The more they have to cough up for transfer payments, the less incentive there is for workers and businesses to produce. And because they produce less and are taxed more, companies have to raise their prices. The result? *Everyone* is worse off than before the transfer took place. The people whose money is taken now have fewer dollars and are faced with higher prices to boot. (Sound familiar?) And the people on the receiving end can never seem to get enough to keep up with the steady increase in prices.

The Unemployment Myth

Unemployment compensation is an old transfer-payment favorite. Government causes unemployment (in myriad ways, including minimum-wage laws, taxation and unemployment compensation itself), then uses it as an excuse to increase its pilfering; after all, transfer payments must be made to the unemployed to keep them from starving to death. This all sounds very humanitarian until one examines some conveniently ignored facts.

Isn't it rather curious that, at a time when so many people are drawing unemployment compensation, the classified-ad sections of virtually every newspaper in the country are jammed with employment opportunities? Since want ads continue to fill page after page of newspapers, the law of supply and demand obviously is telling us something: The reason millions of jobs are going begging is that the *supply* of jobs is greater than the *demand* for jobs.

If all this seems rather confusing, I assure you it is not. As I said, government itself *causes* unemployment. The reason that the job supply is so high and demand so low is that people do not *have* to work if they don't want to.

The government will pay them for *not* working. Politicians love to talk about unemployment, but don't be fooled. It is one of their bread-and-butter "issues." Those unemployed people out there represent a lot of votes if office holders do right by them.

I happen to have a solution to the unemployment "problem" that really works. I offer it here as the *Quick-As-Hell Full-Employment Theory*: Simply remove all forms of welfare and unemployment compensation, and people who "can't find jobs" will find them *quick as hell*.

When a person says he cannot find a job, you can be sure he almost always is misstating his problem. Most likely, what he really means is that he cannot find the *exact kind of job* he wants, under the *exact working conditions* he wants, at the *exact wages* he wants. This is no such thing as unemployment for the man who is willing to work.

One of the things for which I most respect my father is that throughout the Great Depression he never failed to earn enough money to provide food, clothing and shelter for his family. Even though he had virtually no education, he was always employed, working 16- and 18-hour days if necessary. Whatever it took, he made sure he brought home the bacon—*his* bacon, not his neighbor's.

"Fundamentals of Liberty" states that "no involuntary unemployment can exist . . . in a market where the price of labor is free to fluctuate in response to demand for labor. The only men who would remain unemployed in a free market would be those who voluntarily chose not to work at a given wage."[18]

The always candid Senator Hayakawa has identified a sort of corollary to the belief that involuntary unemployment is theoretically impossible. One of the reasons unemployment statistics are so high, says the Senator, is that "there has been an enormous increase in voluntary unemployment."

Mr. Hayakawa notes that secondary wage-earners (i.e., wage-earners in addition to the primary wage-earners of households) and people who collect unemployment benefits are able to be choosy about taking jobs. Thus official government unemployment figures are greatly misleading. Unemployment in the face of eviction or starvation is one thing; unemployment in a case where the head of a household earns a decent living or a person collects unemployment compensation *instead* of working is quite another.

Our "illegal aliens," particularly those from Mexico, again are an embarrassment—this time to those who cling to the favorite unemployment myths. These aliens help to bear out the Quick-As-Hell Full-Employment Theory. Labor unions, of course, constantly complain about illegal aliens, claiming they take jobs away from U.S. citizens and "undercut" wages.

In reality, most of the jobs they "take away" are jobs which legal residents, secure on the government dole, are not willing to perform. And "undercutting" really means that, unlike the aliens, legal residents are not willing to sell their services at a price which the free market is willing to pay.

A good example of this occurred in Presidio, Texas in 1978. When farmers there advertised the need for 4,000 domestic agricultural workers at the then-minimum wage of $2.20 an hour, only 300 people replied. Finally, realizing that the farmers' problem could not be solved due to the comfortable welfare status available to U.S. workers, the government itself allowed the farmers to bring in illegal aliens from Ojinaga, Mexico—aliens who *were* willing to work at that wage. To the aliens, that "insulting" wage was symbolic of the American Dream.

It is pretty sad when government has to admit that the only way to get certain production accomplished in our country is to allow illegal aliens to come in and do it, while taxpayers simultaneously support millions of citizens who claim they "can't find a job" and thus need unemployment and other forms of compensation.

Ironically, the aliens, because of their nonresident status, are able to operate in somewhat of a free-market atmosphere. There is little or no government intervention between them and prospective employers. They are not restricted by minimum-wage laws and they must work in order to eat.

The final benefit from the aliens is that their employers are able to produce products at lower prices and/or achieve greater profits, both of which are good for everyone in the long run, as discussed in Chapter 3. Far from being inhumane, the abolition of welfare payments would be a long-term capitalistic boost to the "poor." By cutting down on the excessive expropriation of assets of producers, productivity would increase, prices would decrease, and employment and wages would rise.

Finally, of utmost importance, those now relying on handouts would regain their self-esteem. The worst part of being poor (and I speak from personal experience) is the degradation. Charity tends to make one feel inferior, though in some cases charity is unavoidable. *Forced* charity, however, is worse. Since the recipients know that the money has not been given willingly, there is a backlash of bitterness and resentment.

Government, aside from the direct handouts already discussed, also claims to help the unemployed by "creating jobs."

How is government's creation of jobs for the unemployed a form of redistribution of the wealth? Because the money used to pay for these jobs comes from producers. Worse, the jobs created are ones for which there is no demand in the free market. As a result of the taxes which fund these jobs, businesses have *less* money to employ people in private industry. Therefore, unemployment is not reduced; once again, government intervention merely causes one person to gain at the expense of someone else.

Perhaps this sounds like a zero exchange, but it is not. The job that is lost in the private sector is in a business that creates a product or service that is in demand. The government-created job provides a service which many or most taxpayers do not want; in some cases, a service virtually no one wants. In addition, because of the bureaucratic waste common to all government programs, it takes more dollars to pay the same employee to do an equivalent amount of work as in private industry.

Finally, the taxpayers who no longer have the money which was used to create the unneeded government job have less to spend on products and services that they desire, thus production is slowed and unemployment in private industry is actully *increased*. A typical government solution!

Dr. Milton Friedman, in exposing the old political trick of holding out the short-term benefits for all to see, while hiding the long-term results behind one's back, described "the visible vs. the invisible effects of government measures" as follows:

> People hired by government know who is their benefactor. People who lose their jobs or fail to get them because of the government program do not know that that is the source of their problem. The good effects are visible. The bad effects are invisible. The good effects generate votes. The bad effects generate discontent, which is as likely to be directed at private business as at the government.[19]

Government's whole approach to unemployment is upside down. To improve the well-being of people, the emphasis should be on full production, not full employment. You move toward full production as you produce more goods and services that people want. If full employment was the horse instead of the cart, government could just put unemployed people to work building pyramids in the Mojave Desert. After a few years, it could have them tear down the pyramids, then start all over again. Obviously, nothing would be accomplished, but you would have full employment.

The point is that merely creating jobs does not produce wealth. An economy will fail if people are employed in jobs which do not produce goods and services that the public wants to buy on a voluntary basis. Russia and China have full employment, but the people have no wealth. Worse, they have no freedom.

Is full employment in a free market possible? Theoretically, yes. But only if government stays *completely* out of the marketplace, which it never has done. While full employment may not be possible other than in theory, one thing is certain: the closer you get to full production, the closer you get to full employment.

In the end, however, I always feel most comfortable falling back on basic libertarian principles. The fact remains that, even if the economic realities of government's meddling in the unemployment issue were not harmful to the economy, no one has a "right" to a job. No one has a "right" to a "decent living." No one has a "right" to a home, a car or a TV set. On the other hand, everyone *does* have a right to *pursue* all of these things by dealing with others on a noncoercive basis.

Those who proclaim that someone has a right to a job really are saying that certain other people do *not* have human rights—that an unemployed person has a right to *force* others to satisfy his desires.

While it is true that government can, by the use of force, guarantee a man a job—and even a minimum wage—such a man is being led to the dangerous belief that his needs and desires are superior to the liberty of others. But there is a price tag for everything. When government removes the burden of his having to sell his services for what they are worth in the free market, the very least he can expect to pay in return is an equal loss of freedom.

Life on the Dole

The sad reality is that welfare has become a way of life in this country. Few people take seriously the notion that welfare is primarily for "those who cannot help themselves." Welfare stories make for entertaining chatter at cocktail parties—i.e., stories about those at the parties who are receiving it! It's the "in" thing for people to joke about their successes in grabbing some of government's redistribution dollars.

I was shocked by one such story not too long ago. An acquaintance of mine, a reasonably successful businessman, had just dissolved his partnership. His intention was to go into the same type of business as before, with a new partner, but he was marking time until the conclusion of a court dispute involving his ex-wife. He casually informed me that, while waiting for the case to be resolved, he was drawing unemployment compensation!

At first I thought he was joking. And he was; i.e., the story was true, but he thought of his accomplishment as something of a joke. If I had a strange expression on my face, it was because I was picturing him taking his "transfer payment" directly from me—at gunpoint. Because, in reality, that is exactly what he was doing. It was just that government was furnishing the gunpower for him.

If taking money from those who earn it has become something to laugh at, then Americans have slipped a long, long way down the moral ladder.

Where does it all end? More than 4 million people a month receive Social Security and welfare checks. Transfer payments now make up about 45% of the federal budget. This means that nearly one out of every two dollars taken from you is handed to someone else. Since 1960, total welfare expenditures have grown from $52 billion (federal, state and local) to close to $300 billion.

The Social-Security pyramiding scheme has become the biggest transfer-payment scandal of all, a fact of which virtually everyone is now aware. With the system on the verge of collapse, government desperately continues to increase Social-Security taxes in a vain effort to prop it up.

Most Americans now realize that there is no such thing as a Social-Security "fund." The truth is that politician-spenders have dissipated the fund's proceeds about as fast as they have been received from citizens. Social Security has finally been exposed for what it is: a glorified Ponzi Scheme.

Ponzi was a famous swindler, who, in 1920, raised enormous amounts of capital from unwary investors, promising to pay them huge returns. Which he did—for a while. The problem was that his ability to repay both principal and profit to old investors depended solely on his ability to raise money from new investors. After one investor became suspicious, panic spread, new investors were hard to come by, and it was only a matter of time until the whole Ponzi Scheme collapsed.

This practice, tried many times by both big- and small-time con artists over the years, is also commonly referred to as "pyramiding." So-called chain letters are an amateur's version of this con game.

The only way you or anyone else who has been paying Social-Security taxes over the years can ever hope to get anything back is totally dependent on Sammy's ability to confiscate ever-greater amounts from future generations. The notion of a "fund" is a myth. Dr. Milton Friedman disrobes Social Security quite candidly:

"Social Security is *not* a system under which 'nine out

of ten working people in the United States are now building protection for themselves and their families' (as HEW misleadingly describes it). Social Security *is* a system under which nine out of ten working people pay taxes to finance payments to persons not working."[20]

The problems inherent in any pyramiding scheme are now growing out of control with the Social-Security program. Increasing Social-Security taxes, coupled with astronomical increases in pension benefits for government employees, make a showdown between working people and retired people inevitable. By the year 2030 those who work will outnumber those who don't by a relatively small margin. The median age will be 50. and those over 50 almost certainly will use the power of Majority Rule by voting with those already retired, since they, too, will soon be retired.

The question is, how much longer will a smaller and smaller segment of the population be willing to support an ever-increasing percentage of the population that is retired? This is a particularly appropriate question when one considers that, contrary to popularly believed myths, older people, on the average, are better off financially than most other age groups. The highest per capita income is enjoyed by those between the ages of 55 and 64, with those over 65 not much worse off. In addition, people over 50 normally do not have the financial burdens that face younger people, such as home mortgages and the many expenses connected with the raising of children.

There is no question that Sammy is in big trouble with the new voting majority—the Middle Class—on the issue of transfer payments. This method of redistribution of the wealth is too easy for voters to see. which is causing them to become restless. The irony, however, is that those same Middle-Class voters, who are now making menacing gestures at politicians, were created by government's own politically expedient redistribution-of-the-wealth programs, about which they themselves are now up in arms.

THE SUBTLE APPROACH TO REDISTRIBUTION

Redistribution of the wealth goes far beyond the blatant transfer of cash from one citizen's pocket to his neighbor's. Government provides thousands of "services," on a federal, state and local level, which accomplish the same thing. For every government service that you either do not want or do not use, your dollars are being taken to supply other people with those services.

The gourmet banquet now includes about everything you can think of, from welfare items like housing assistance, day care, medicaid, and family planning, to seemingly essential public services like garbage collection, public utilities, fire protection and mail delivery. Local, state and federal governments provide legal services, student loans, book-making facilities, lotteries, and subsidies for art, publishing, opera, theater and museums, to name but a few.

Whether you want or need any of these services is beside the point. Indeed, you may not even qualify for many of them. But you pay for *all* of them—whether you like it or not!

This situation is not quite as galling to taxpayers as are transfer payments, because the redistribution of income is camouflaged by the providing of services. The economic problem, however, is that these services do not produce wealth. Therefore, the economy suffers to the extent that money is taken from taxpayers to support such services, because the money otherwise would be used to purchase goods and services in the marketplace or for investment in new plants and equipment.

The collectivist, of course, argues that the services government provides are necessary and valuable. But he conveniently overlooks three important realities:

First, that *any* service provided by government could be provided better, less expensively and more efficiently by private industry. Second, that only a small percentage of the population would be willing to purchase most government services if they were offered on a voluntary basis. Third, that many people who receive these services could not afford to pay for them in the free market; therefore, other people are *forced* to pay the cost of these services for them. We have already covered the issue of needs and desires versus morality, so I shall not embellish the latter point any further.

Then there is the last-ditch argument that some projects are too large to be undertaken without the aid of government. This is, of course, an absurdity on its face, since all projects already *are* provided with private capital. Those "too large" projects are paid for by funds taken from individuals and businesses.

It is preposterous to conclude that the term *general welfare*, as used in the Constitution, was intended to mean that government should have the right to take billions of dollars from workers and use the money to provide services for others. And it is even more preposterous that government forces millions of people to accept services they do not even want.

It should be noted, once again, that those who argue that government, overall, provides valuable and essential services are missing an important libertarian point: Many other people may *not* think the services are valuable or essential and may prefer to do without them, but they are forced to pay for them anyway! It always gets back to the same presumptuous belief that bureaucrats can, and have the right to, determine what is best for individuals. And that belief already has been rejected on both moral and practical grounds.

Certainly I am not going to attempt to dissect every government service to make my point. All of them, of course, are invalid from a moral standpoint if one believes in Natural Law. I will, however, touch on a small number of these services in order to expose, in addition, their false economic foundations. Also, I hope to bring to light the fact that many services which people assume can be provided only by government can, in fact, be provided better, less expensively and more efficiently by private industry.

Essential Services

People have become so accustomed to government monopolies or near-monopolies in such areas as police and fire protection, garbage collection, education, and operation of streets and highways, that it is hard for them to imagine these services being provided in the free market. Often when one suggests that such services could be provided much more efficiently by private industry, on a voluntary basis, the response is one of disbelief. People want to know in detail how such government services could possibly be handled by private companies. But the answer is quite simple: they would be handled just as everything else is handled in the free market.

Consider if government had for years been providing the public with refrigerators. Some people might get the impression that you were against refrigerators if you suggested that government turn the refrigerator business over to private enterprise. After all, how could people be certain that private companies could handle such a large project? How could they be sure enough refrigerators would be produced? Who would see to it that the quality would be satisfactory? What if the selling price were too high?

The answer to all these questions, of course, is the very reason that private enterprise *does* turn out more than enough high quality, low-priced refrigerators: profit motive—profit motive that is guided by trial and error, competition, and the law of supply and demand. Entrepreneurs will always find ways to create the most desired products and services at the most competitive prices.

The exact opposite is true of government services, where low quality, high prices and inefficiency are trademarks. The Postal Service is a prime example. Everyone has had the experience of standing interminably in line to buy postage stamps or waiting a week or more for a letter to arrive from a few hundred miles away. While service continues to deteriorate, the cost of postage continues to skyrocket.

Let it suffice to say that what United Parcel Service has accomplished in the package-delivery business—putting the U.S. Postal Service to shame in the process—other companies could accomplish in the delivery of mail.

To the embarrassment of the U.S. Postal Service, even a unit of the government itself—the U.S. Government Printing Office—recently began using United Parcel Service for all shipments to libraries east of the Mississippi. The Government Printing Office announced that it expects to save between a quarter-million and a half-million dollars during the first year alone as a result of the switch. A GPO official also admitted that "there are fewer damaged packages and we are enjoying fewer missing shipments, and when we report them they find the missing shipment immediately."

If mail service were a competitive industry, you and I would get the benefit of better service at lower prices. If not, we would take our business to a competitor, just as we do when contracting for pest control, a plumbing job or a haircut.

There are other scattered examples of private companies providing "government services," always on a more efficient basis than government. In garbage collection, for example, small pockets of private competition have appeared in some cities. A 1971 study by New York City's then-deputy city administrator concluded that it cost the city $49 per ton to collect garbage through its own garbage-collection service, but that private companies could perform the same job for $17.50 per ton.

A 1975 study showed that it cost the city's Sanitation Department $297 per year to provide garbabe-collection service twice a week to single-family homes in the Queens section of New York, but that a private firm was providing *three-times-a-week* service, just a few miles away, in a similar neighborhood in Nassau County, at a cost of only $72 a year. The government service was more than four times as costly as that provided by private industry!

Nor was New York a special case. Across the country, in San Francisco, two private companies were servicing the entire city at an average cost of $400 *per year*.[21]

Fire protection is another business where private industry, when allowed to compete with government, has provided far better service at less cost. In Scottsdale, Arizona, with a population of approximately 100,000, a fire-protection service is handled for the entire community by a private firm, Rural/Metro Fire Department, Inc. Rural/Metro provides exceptional quality service at an average cost of $6.67 per person per year (1974/75). For other cities in the same population range, the average fire-protection cost was $24.39 per person per year (1972/73 figures, when Scottsdale's cost was only $5.70).[22]

Here again, the cost of the government-provided service is more than four times that of comparable service provided by private industry. In fact, the service is not even comparable; it is superior. Scottsdale's per capita fire loss for years has been less than half that of the national average.

What these examples of private garbage-collection and

fire-protection services mean is that not only do taxpayers normally pay for government services used by others, but they pay much more than necessary because of government's insistence on trying to be an entrepreneur.

This is not blind stubbornness on the part of politicians, either. It is based on the fact that the people on the payrolls of those government-provided services represent a lot of votes. By keeping their pay exorbitantly high and their production pitifully low—*enough so that the cost to the public is as much as four times what it should be*—expediency-minded politicians hope to keep pulling in the votes of government employees.

In any discussion of so-called essential government services, it is necessary to confront the subject of public education. The idea of the government's not providing everyone with a free education is shocking to some people, but this usually is because they have never considered the moral implications. Like most other government-provided services, the reality is that public education is another method of redistributing the wealth.

Why should a childless couple be compelled to pay for the education of their neighbor's children? As with garbage collection and fire protection, the issue is clouded by the fact that government provides the service. But if all schools were privately owned, the only way government could force some people to pay for the education of other people's children would be through direct transfer payments, the type of redistribution discussed earlier in this chapter. Then the matter of mass, compulsory education could be more clearly seen for what it is—another redistribution-of-the-wealth program.

And, as is always the case, the quality of government service in this area is atrocious. In fact, the public-education system has become a national embarrassment. Students are being turned out who can barely read and write. That is not surprising when you consider a 1978 report which showed that more than half of the 585 new teachers in Dallas schools failed an IQ test for persons over 13![23] But don't be alarmed; it's okay, because all the teachers were "state certified."

The result of the public-education disaster is that people are rebelling. They are transfering their children to private schools, voting against bond issues for public schools, and demanding tax credits to offset some of the cost of private schooling. When people begin to realize that redistribution of the wealth is not in their best interest, they start to fight back.

There are many books available which deal exclusively with each presently provided government service, but the facts they present are always the same: 1) Government services are always of lower quality and higher cost than could be provided privately; 2) people who do not want the services are forced to pay for them anyway; 3) some people are forced to pay for the cost of these services for other people.

As Murray Rothbard has said, the true libertarian does not just want the separation of Church and State. He wants to separate *everything* from the State!* This would be a big step toward cutting government down to size and thus cutting back its politically expedient, but economically disastrous, habit of trying to redistribute the wealth.

THE GREAT REVELATION

The so-called tax rebellion in this country that was precipitated by California's passage of Proposition 13 has again forced politicians to change their strategy. In the

---

*If you are interested in further study of how everything from police protection to streets and highways could be more efficiently provided by private industry, I suggest you read Murray Rothbard's *For a New Liberty,* an excellent treatise on pure libertarianism.

old days, the numbers were easy to figure. It was simply "rich" against "poor," and politicians had no trouble calculating that the "poor" were in the majority. Hence, in order to win over this majority, vote seekers simply proclaimed their number one function to be redistribution of the wealth.

Thus government itself created today's voting dinosaur—the Middle Class—and continued to promise these millions of comfortable Americans still more of its magically created wealth. Everything seemed to be going along fine, until a large number of this huge voting bloc began to come to the realization that no matter how much they received from government, they still ended up with less. Thus came the great revelation about the gourmet banquet:

Sammy was now stealing from the Middle Class to give to the Middle Class!

All of a sudden, redistribution of the wealth no longer looked so attractive. The Proposition-13 message to government was clear: "You keep your services; we'll keep our money."

Most members of the Middle Class had been in favor of redistribution of the wealth only because they believed they were coming out on the plus side, particularly *prior* to their emergence to Middle-Class status. After their emergence, however, few had any concern about helping those less fortunate than themselves. A *Los Angeles Times* poll made that point clear. When it asked those who thought government provided too many services which services they would most like to see cut, 69% answered *welfare*.

The revelation could also be seen as the realization by many people, for the first time, that an old axiom was, indeed, true: *there really is no such thing as a free lunch.* Voting "yes" on Proposition 13 did not necessarily mean that a person was against all government services. What it did mean was that *he was not willing to pay for them*.

In conducting your personal financial affairs, you do not buy everything you want. In fact, you realize it would be impossible. Therefore, you consider how badly you want a product or service and how much money you have available, then you make your decisions accordingly. You are *selective*—or you are soon bankrupt.

Many stubborn politicians, blinded by political expediency, seemed unable to comprehend the revelation of the voters. Both before and after the election, they threatened the citizenry with the loss of "essential" services, from garbage collection and fire protection to educational facilities and lifeguard protection at the beaches. They could not comprehend that some voters were saying that, even though they wanted many of the services, they were *not* willing to pay for them. Wanting something and being willing to pay for it are two different matters.

The votes of still others represented a more libertarian statement: they were saying that they did not want *any* government services, regardless of cost.

All this poses a very interesting question. If what government has to offer is so helpful to people—if they really want government services—why does government have to *force* them to accept these services? Because, in point of fact, government services are unconscionably overpriced, low in quality, unwanted or unneeded by millions of people, and a violation of the natural rights of every individual who would choose not to pay for them if he were given a free choice.

THE SAMMY CORPS

One would think that government could easily solve its self-created dilemma by recognizing that The Vote is now in the hands of the tax-rebelling Middle Class. After all, helping the "poor" never was a serious moral objective of most politicians; it was simply a matter of numbers. It was the most politically expedient method of garnering votes.

But the new majority presents a more complicated problem. Along the way to creating the new Middle-Class majority, politicians also created a mini-monster—millions of government employees who were needed to carry out redistribution-of-the-wealth programs. Some are officially called "civil servants"; others are unofficially referred to as "bureaucrats"; and many are not referred to at all—they just receive healthy paychecks for very little work.

Government now is by far the largest employer in the country. Approximately one out of every six working Americans is employed by the federal government or its "subsidiaries"—local and state governments. The federal bureaucracy alone has grown approximately 500% since 1930. By 1976, the total yearly payroll of the more than 15 million federal, state and local government employees was more than $157 billion.* If you happen to be one of those individualists who wants little or nothing from government, $167 billion represents a lot of redistribution.

The problem? These millions of government employees now comprise a sizable percentage of the Middle-Class majority. And, unlike the 70 million or so eligible voters who refuse to play the voting game, you can be sure that government employees vote—and they never let politicians forget it. They have a good thing going and they have no intention of moving backward.

---

*If one takes into account the millions of people not "officially designated" as government employees—consultants, university researchers, attorneys in the Legal Services Corporation, and many others—but whose salaries are paid either directly or indirectly by government, the total number of government employees looms in the area of 22 million. It is interesting to conjecture why government finds it necessary to hide some 7 million of its employees from public view.

Yet I believe that if these government employees fully understood that they are a major factor in the destruction of the U.S. economy, that financial collapse—due in large part to their high-pay-low-output employment—is inevitable (just as it was in New York), that economic disaster always brings with it chaos, and that chaos virtually assures totalitarian rule and loss of freedom, they undoubtedly would feel that their temporary false prosperity is not worth the long-term price.

But, as I said at the outset of this book, the unfortunate reality is that most people do *not* understand the situation.

So the Sammy Corps presses relentlessly forward. Government employees do not want to hear about the desires of other voters to curtail government spending. A good example of this was seen when a representative of the Service Employees International Union stated, in reference to Los Angeles County's lack of funds after the passage of Proposition 13, "Where they get the money may turn out to be a problem, but it's their problem, essentially, not ours."

Few statements have ever depicted the Expediency Factor of human beings so clearly. Few statements have ever explained so clearly the long-term consequences of violating the laws of economics. And few statements have ever symbolized so clearly government's current dilemma.

The creation of full-time government jobs is itself another subtle method of redistribution of the wealth. We have already discussed the economic effects of all government-created employment (i.e., "jobs programs," etc.), but full-time government employees present uniquely disastrous problems. As we shall see, government employees breed more government employees, which gives the Sammy Corps increasing voting power, which in turn causes an increase in public-employee salaries and benefits and a corresponding decrease in work.

The growth of the Sammy Corps has resulted in government's becoming a gigantic, but incredibly inefficient, middleman. A staggering amount of the money which originally was supposed to go from the producers to the "poor" gets lost in the shuffle, and it is shuffled right into the pockets of the 15 + million members of the Sammy Corps.

The whole system breeds increases—in numbers of employees, in salaries and in dollars spent. Agencies feel compelled to spend whatever monies are allocated to them each year, knowing their budgets will be cut if they don't. In other words, government agencies work exactly the opposite of private businesses: employees are rewarded for being *inefficient*—for spending *more* money than necessary.

Those who work for welfare agencies, for example, do not want a solution to poverty. On the contrary, it is in their best interest to see the welfare system grow, rather than decrease, so that their jobs are safe. This is one of the reasons why poverty statistics do not reflect the billions of dollars received through transfer payments. It is imperative to the administrators of welfare programs that poverty remain a problem.

In reality, all programs designed to help the "poor" are programs to improve the well-being of those who administer them. The welfare state is most beneficial to those who run it. While Uncle Sam displays the "welfare" sign in the hand he holds before the public, the hand behind his back contains the real trick—the fact that millions of Middle-Class-elite government employees make off with most of the funds being redistributed.

As William Simon has pointed out, between 1965 and 1975, the cost of federal welfare programs increased by $209 billion—to a total of $286.5 billion a year. If each of the 25 million people who were listed as "poor" by the government in 1975 had been given just the $209 billion increase, without government as a middleman, it would have amounted to about $8,000 per person per year. That means that a "poor" family of six would have received a yearly income of $48,000!

While the poverty issue may be enormously distorted, even I concede that welfare recipients are not taking this much potentially productive wealth out of the economy. The bulk of the dollars obviously goes to government "administrators," "planners" and "counselors" of the "poor."

It is little wonder that Washington, D.C., has the highest average annual household income in the country—a whopping $23,602 (for 1977), far in excess of, for example, Los Angeles and New York. If we really had "government by the people," I hardly think that those who govern us would be far more privileged financially than the people they govern.

The attitude, "What the hell, it's only taxpayer money," is established at the top of the ladder. Congressmen recently raised their salaries to $57,500, and, of course, increased the salaries of their aides, too. Senator Alan Cranston of California, that great redistribution-of-the-wealth champion, makes sure that a nice chunk of the redistribution stops off at his office, where he has five aides earning in excess of $45,000 a year.

And in Chicago, shortly after voters, by an 82% margin, let government officials know that they wanted maximum *restrictions* put on government spending, some of the leaders of the local Sammy Corps answered the voters this way: Cook County Commissioners, by a vote of 14 to 1, voted big pay *increases* for county officials, including 30% increases for themselves, while aldermen of Chicago's City Council fought for 71% pay increases.

The civil-service level of the federal government, however, is where the plunder party has grown totally out of control. There are 18 civil-service "grades," each with 10 longevity levels. People get the longevity increases almost automatically, and, unlike in the real world, virtually no one ever gets fired and certainly no one ever takes a pay cut. The jobs are so attractive that there are thirty applicants for every person hired. As an example, there are 300,000 civil-service workers in "grades" 12 through 15, each with salaries of between $20,442 and $43,923.

The secret to this inflated pay scale is what has come to be known as the "inflated job description." The key to getting ahead faster in the civil service is to overstate your duties and responsibilities. The best way to accomplish this is to have a lot of civil-service employees working under you and also to overstate their duties (and salaries). Even government's own General Accounting Office has admitted that as many as 40% of civil-service jobs are overclassified, which probably means 100% is nearer the truth.

The bottom line is that everyone in civil service has a vested interest in seeing government get bigger and spend more each year. That puts still more pressure on Sammy to steal, because this vast civil-service segment of the Middle Class not only votes, but it justifies its own income by administering the very redistribution programs politicians use to win over other voters.

If all this makes you feel frustrated, you'll feel worse after reading the following statement by a civil-service worker, originally reported in *The Washington Monthly* in April 1977: "I have had no meaningful work to do since June 1965 and my present annual salary is $29,168. I share an office with another employee who is in the same salary and non-work category."

The politically expedient government-employee situation which bankrupted New York City (though officials still refuse to refer to it as bankruptcy) was, and is, a smaller model of a problem that is helping to destroy us on a national level. William Simon points out that there were 260,000 city employees in New York (prior to its financial collapse), and that, when you realize they had husbands, wives and other family members old enough to vote, their desires, no matter how unreasonable, were very important to local politicians. The New York City situation was a real-life example of the majority tyrannizing the minority—of the immorality of Majority Rule.

The most devastating aspect of redistributing wealth to the Sammy Corps, however, is hidden from the general public. As explained by Marjorie Boyd in a revealing *Washington Monthly* article, it is accomplished through the use of pensions; government pensions are far in excess of the average private pension plan. Politicians long ago discovered that they could partially appease Sammy-Corps voters and obscure the true cost of maintaining them simply by providing inordinate raises in their pensions.

As an example, military personnel can retire after twenty years, some as young as in their late thirties or early forties. Enlisted men receive 59% of their final pay, officers 62%. In addition, military retirees also receive Social Security and sometimes end up receiving a third pension check from private industry. Incredibly, they do not even have to contribute to their own pension fund during their years of service.

Military pensions now cost taxpayers $8.4 billion a year (1977), and are estimated to reach $34 billion a year by the year 2000. All of this represents wealth taken out of the economy and handed to nonproducers.

Congressmen and their aides do even better on pension pay, receiving 75% of their final salaries; federal judges top the list at 100% of final pay. By contrast, private pensions average only 40% of final salaries. And remember, congressmen and judges, too, can go into private industry after leaving government, earning considerable incomes while building yet another pension for themselves.

If none of the other economically disastrous actions of government existed, Sammy's politically expedient pension crisis would, by itself, probably be enough to guarantee the eventual financial collapse of this country. The total unfunded portions of government pensions (federal, state and local), combined with that of the Social-Security program, is in the area of *$5 trillion!**

This figure is so mind-boggling that the government avoids owning up to it publicly; officials refuse to mention it as part of the national debt, thus intentionally misleading those who will have to pay it: taxpayers. That is not surprising when you consider that it is at least *seven times greater* than the publicized "national debt!"

When one analyzes the awesome numbers involved in government-employee salaries, along with the nation's staggering pension obligations, it certainly is not hard to understand why our economy is falling apart. It is one thing for producers to be forced to support legitimately sick, elderly and disabled people. But to have healthy, financially secure people retiring at forty or fifty years of age puts an intolerable strain on the ever-smaller percentage of people still working for a living.

HAD THE SAMMY CORPS KNOWN ...

Contrary to what these statements may lead you to believe, I am not "against" government employees, nor do I believe that every government employee is lazy. I believe that government employees, like all of us, have been victims of the temptation of politicians' vote-oriented, free-lunch philosophy. Since the days of FDR, most of us have

*A recent article in *The Libertarian Review* reveals that the Department of the Treasury now officially lists the "Actuarial Liabilities of Annuity Programs" at nearly $12 trillion and the total liabilities of the United States Government at more than $15.6 trillion.

fallen into the trap of believing that wealth can be created without work; like the people of the 1920's, we have developed a feeling toward life exemplified by the spirit of "let the good times roll."

And it has a snowballing effect. Government employees, like everyone else, quite naturally have justified their actions with the attitude, "Why shouldn't we get everything we can from the redistribution process, too?" Most of these employees are innocent to the extent that they have little knowledge of the economic realities involved and certainly never have taken the trouble to think through the moral implications of living off money taken by force from others.

I have several relatives who either work for the government or are now retired from government service. Every one of them is honest and hard working. I feel certain that none of them has any idea that his or her income is derived through a violation of the rights of others. These are basically good people who have been misdirected by the realities of The System. Specifically, they have been misdirected into government jobs, jobs created by politicians' vote-oriented, redistribution process, and thus directed *away* from jobs in private industry. And the final effect of government jobs—*always*—is that they replace private jobs.

Had my own relatives, along with millions of other government employees, understood the realities of the situation, I believe they would have chosen to work in private industry instead. Perhaps they would have worked a little harder, but I don't think the extra effort would have bothered them. Perhaps they would have made a little less money, but that would have been misleading; for if it were not for the billions of dollars government takes out of the private sector to pay its employees for services that do not produce wealth, the dollars they would have earned would have been worth far more than their inflated government paychecks.

And perhaps their pensions would not have been as great, but at least they would have been secure. At the rate our economy is crumbling, those fat pension increases which government hands out so freely may not be there for millions of people when they reach retirement age.

However much less a government employee might have made in private industry and however much harder he might have worked, he at least could have felt confident that the future held freedom for him. What good are temporarily inflated incomes and benefits if they have to be repaid at a later date with a loss of liberty?

John Hospers chillingly describes the inevitable consequences of our redistribution-of-the-wealth philosophy:

> . . . when it is no longer worth the producers' while to produce, when they are taxed so highly to keep the politicians and their friends on the public payroll that they themselves no longer have a reasonable chance of success in any economic enterprise, then of course production grinds to a halt. . . . When this happens, when the producers can no longer sustain on their backs the increasing load of the parasites, then the activities of the parasites must stop also, but usually not before they have brought down the entire social structure which the producers' activities have created. *When the organism dies, the parasite necessarily dies too, but not until the organism has paid for the presence of the parasite with its life.* It is in just this way that the major civilizations of the world have collapsed. [*Italics added*.][25]

THE FATE OF THE "POOR" IN A FREE SOCIETY

What would happen to the "poor" and disabled in a truly free society, a society in which government did not use force to redistribute the wealth?

This question can best be answered by asking another question: What happens to the "poor" and disabled in societies that are *totally* controlled by their governments, governments whose purported purposes are to achieve equality for their people? In such countries throughout the world, *everyone* is poor and everyone *remains* poor; that is, if they are lucky enough not to be imprisoned or killed.

The question of the fate of the "poor" and disabled in a free society raises a number of other questions and points. First there is the same old problem of defining just who the "poor" and disabled are, which in turn gives rise to the same old question of who should have the power to make such arbitrary decisions.

Then there is the assumption that, in our redistribution-of-the-wealth society, government does, in fact, do a good job of aiding the "poor." Unfortunately, this is a false assumption. As we have already discussed, most of the money earmarked for the "needy" ends up in the hands of government employees who administer the aid programs.

But even if we ignore the problem of defining who the "poor" and disabled are and disregard government's waste in administering welfare programs, we still end up at the confrontation between needs and morality; i.e., while it may be true that many people are unable to care for themselves, that does not justify a violation of the rights of those who *can* care for themselves.

No matter what the circumstances, trying to solve the problems of some people by using force against others is *always* immoral. The moral objectives of any person or group can never transform theft into a moral action. You do not solve problems by creating bigger problems, which is precisely the mistake government has made with its redistribution-of-the-wealth philosophy. Applying force to a problem only produces resentment, backlash and chaos.

Helping the needy is a matter of personal morality, not

force. Rational men realize that there is no such thing as absolute morality. Each individual must decide for himself what is right and wrong, his only boundaries being the natural rights of others.

As Lysander Spooner rightly pointed out, even though a man may feel other men have a moral duty to feed the hungry, shelter the homeless, care for the sick, and enlighten the ignorant, these are *personal moral beliefs*. If people are to be free, then each person must make his own moral judgment as to how far, if at all, he wishes to go in providing these things.

Many people erroneously believe that to be in favor of personal freedom (i.e., sovereignty over one's own life and property) means that a person is heartless and is against helping those who are disabled. In point of fact, one has nothing to do with the other. Freedom is one subject, charity another.

I believe voluntary charity is admirable so long as the giver is fully aware of the final destination of his contribution. I am sympathetic toward people who are far less fortunate than I (although I do not presume to be in a position to arbitrarily label some individuals "poor" and others not), but I also believe in freedom. And because I place a higher value on liberty than on anything else, I do not believe that I or any other person has the right to *force* other men to be charitable. In other words, I am *not* against charity, but I *am* against the use of force.

What individual would not like to see every hungry child fed, every disease victim cured, every disabled person made comfortable? I assume that anyone who had the power to do so would make all misery in this world disappear instantly. The question is not whether people are for or against human suffering; all humane persons are concerned about human suffering. The question is whether some people should be forced to give money to programs which certain other people feel are helpful to those they deem to be in need.

CHARITY

Charity that involves the use of force is, in reality, the sacrifice of one human being to another. And sacrifice is not the mark of a civilized society.

Voluntary charity is not sacrifice, because a person is basing his actions on his own moral standards. Voluntary charity does not involve the resentment and bitterness associated with redistribution-of-the-wealth "charity."

What would happen to the "poor" if there were no redistribution-of-the-wealth programs? It seems to me there would be no problem. After all, in a truly free society each man would be free to give as much as he wished to charity; no one would stop him from giving. Therefore, if as many millions of people are as sincere as they claim to be about helping the "poor," such people could do two things, in particular, that would go a long way toward easing the misery of those whom they believed to be in need of help:

First, they could give self-determined percentages of their own incomes to whomever they pleased. Second, they could spend as much time as they wanted working for, and/or forming, voluntary charitable groups to raise money for *their* favorite causes. And because they undoubtedly would work on a gratis basis, the recipients of their charity would be far better off than now; the expensive government middleman would be eliminated.

In response to this point, people sometimes ask, "But what if people did not give enough voluntarily?" The answer is that it would mean they did not *want* to give in amounts that others may deem to be "enough." In the final analysis, all questions of this nature must be measured against the belief that human freedom is a higher moral objective than the arbitrary fulfillment of certain people's needs and desires.

Fortunately, however, the history of America is replete with hard evidence that the freer and more prosperous the society, the greater people's desire to give. And, although the creation and possession of great wealth does not need to be defended on the basis of the charitable acts of the wealthy, the fact is that it is the wealthiest families who have given the most to the "poor" and disabled. There are some 12,000 private foundations in existence that donate hundreds of millions of dollars yearly to causes they deem to be worthy. Among some of the more prominent ones are the Ford Foundation, Rockefeller Foundation, Carnegie Corp. of New York, and the Alfred P. Sloan Foundation.

Andrew Carnegie alone contributed some $350 million to various philanthropic causes, including more than 2,800 libraries in the U.S. and Canada. John D. Rockefeller, founder of the family fortune, gave away more than $530 million. His projects included the Rockefeller Institute for Medical Research, the General Education Board (which helped to establish schools for Negro teachers and children), and the Rockefeller Foundation ("to promote the well-being of mankind throughout the world"). All told, the Rockefeller family has donated well over $1 billion to various charities and charitable programs through the years.

Notwithstanding their charitable acts, however, the greatest contributions the super industrialists have made to the welfare of mankind have been through their use of the free-enterprise system.

My personal belief is that men basically are humane and that, given the opportunity to act *freely*, they would, as in the past, respond charitably to those whom they deem to be in need. But I also believe that men place an even higher value on their liberty, and that the less free they are to improve their own well-being, the less charitable they will be. As government has increased its attempts to redistribute the wealth, it simultaneously has decreased man's desire to be charitable.

Government also has succeeded in making the superrich virtually extinct, which in turn has made superphilanthropy virtually extinct. And the near extinction of the super-rich symbolizes the near extinction of the American Dream.

Charity is just another of the many services in which government should not be involved. People should be left alone to act voluntarily in a spirit of goodwill. A good example of private charity is seen in the Mormon church. Virtually no Mormons are on public welfare; instead, the church has its own welfare system.

Mormons provide millions of dollars in aid each year to needy members, and financial aid even goes to nonchurch members. For example, the Mormons gave assistance to Vietnamese refugees at Camp Pendleton in 1975 and to victims of the Teton Dam disaster in Idaho in 1976.

THE PRESENT FATE OF THE "POOR"

The cruel irony is that all of the so-called liberal acts of politicians to help the "poor" are really the worst enemies of those who are unable to care for themselves. Such acts are based on The Vote, and consequently they are structured to show immediate results; that translates into short-term solutions.

Long term, however, political do-gooders are setting up a disaster for those whom they purport to be helping. Bureaucratic waste is bankrupting our nation, which can only lead to less for everybody in the long run, including less freedom. If you consider yourself a humanitarian and you really do care about the "poor" and disabled, ask yourself this question: *How will "poor" and disabled people be better off if our economy experiences a total collapse?*

Clearly, it would be the worst thing that could happen to them. The best way to help the "poor" is not to interfere with the producers of the world. The results of a laissez-faire economy have already been detailed in Chapter 3. It is unfortunate that the "poor," as well as most people who purport to be concerned about them, do not understand the simple reality that you can only redistribute wealth if wealth exists. If you kill incentive, and production of wealth stops, there is nothing to redistribute.

It is time for us to stop killing the goose that lays the golden eggs. Let's restore the American Dream and allow the producers to produce so that *everyone* can be better off!

Murray Rothbard, in *For a New Liberty*, makes no bones about it: "What . . . *can* the government do to help the poor? The only correct answer is also the libertarian answer: Get out of the way."

THE GOURMET BANQUET IN ROME

Santayana warned of those who cannot remember the past, but my concern is more than with those who do not *know* the past and who do not understand it. If Americans are not aware that we are repeating errors of the past, then certainly there is a great danger that the results of the past will also be repeated.

The U.S. Government is not the first to offer the gourmet banquet. Over 2,000 years ago Romans enjoyed a glorious redistribution-of-the-wealth feast under Caesar Augustus. The government took care of every citizen from the cradle to the grave, providing schools, welfare, social security, hospitals, and much more.

In order to pay for all this, taxation reached the point

where producers lost the incentive to work. Society became a free-for-all, with lawyers devising ways to evade taxes and government creating new laws to prevent evasion. Everyone was so wrapped up in enjoying his false prosperity that the great productive ingenuity that had built Rome slowly disappeared.

As Rome decayed, the government took an increasingly firm hold over the lives of its citizens, until the original republic ultimately evolved into an extreme totalitarian state. The decay of productivity led to the decay of freedom, which inevitably led to the extinction of the Roman Empire.

Are we reliving the Roman past? If you were to substitute the United States for Rome and Franklin D. Roosevelt for Caesar Augustus in the little history lesson above, you would not have a very difficult job trying to pass it off as a history of this country since the 1930's. Only the final two steps remain on the horizon: the evolution into an extreme totalitarian state and extinction. And it is these last two steps that I am sure all of us—"rich" and "poor," laborers and businessmen, men and women— want to avoid. Hopefully, we are completely united on this one critical objective.

We are now at the stage of decay where productive ingenuity is disappearing at an increasing rate. There is no need for people to be productive if they believe they will have prosperity without working for it. Senator Hayakawa compares this situation to what was happening in the 1960's and early 1970's in colleges, when most students were given good grades regardless of the quality of their work.

The result was that *good* students stopped studying, and many even became dropouts. Today, says Hayakawa, laziness and ignorance are no longer penalized. And, he warns, "*When there is no such thing as failure, there is no such thing as success either.*"

Hayakawa goes on to conclude the college-grades analogy by saying that "if everybody is rewarded just for being alive, you get the same sort of effect as you do when you reward every student just for being enrolled. You destroy not only education, you destroy society by giving A's to everyone. This is a philosophical consideration that bothers me very much as I sit in the United States Senate and see its great budget allocations going through."[26]

The redistribution-of-the-wealth philosophy has led to a prevalent belief that people are not responsible for their own actions, that the burden for their success or failure belongs to "society." Worse, it has led to a decline in morality that accepts an implied "anything-goes" attitude as being perfectly ethical. Redistribution of the wealth has degenerated into a game of who can get the most benefits for the least amount of work.

"Getting a piece of the pie" has become a misnomer. In today's atmosphere, it would be more proper to describe it as "getting a piece of the plunder."

John Hospers, in an article in *Reason* magazine, notes that Albert Jay Nock foresaw this evolution some fifty years ago when he properly described the "exploited" as those who trade their goods and services on the free market and who are forced to turn over a portion of their earnings to government, and the "exploiters" as all those who receive government checks or subsidies of any kind, checks made possible by the work of the producing class.

Government has played a cruel hoax on *everyone* by making handouts so freely available. First of all, it has robbed people of pride and self-esteem—of the desire to make it on their own. Autonomy and self-responsibility create an environment which breeds goodwill and allows people to develop themselves to the best of *their* abilities. By today's perverted standards, this is considered evil, unfair or a hardship.

Second, most of those on the receiving end do not understand that loss of incentive is a dire consequence of the free lunch. Not just loss of incentive on the part of those who benefit most from government's "generosity," but, worse, on the part of society's greatest producers and its most creative thinkers. An obvious but too little discussed fact of redistribution of the wealth is that people simply become less willing to risk their time, energy and money if they know that much of what they earn will be confiscated.

The money for "people programs" does indeed come from people. Government is now at the crossroads. Politically expedient promises have exceeded all possible resources. The super-rich are virtually extinct; the bloated Middle Class is taxed to the point of revolt, well aware that it now pays out much more than it receives in benefits; the productivity rate of the United States is grinding to a slow halt.

Redistribution of the wealth *does not work* and has *never* worked. Will Durant, the eminent historian who probably has studied every redistribution-of-the-wealth experiment in recorded history, assures us that, in the end, nature will have its way on the subject of inequality:

> . . . periodically wealth is redistributed, whether by the violent confiscation of property, or by confiscatory taxation of incomes. . . . Then the race for wealth, goods and power begins again, and the pyramid of ability takes form once more; under whatever laws may be enacted the abler man manages somehow to get the richer soil, the better place, the lion's share; soon he is strong enough to dominate the state and rewrite or interpret the laws; and in time the inequality is as great as before.[27]

What is interesting about Durant's message is to reflect on what has happened most recently in countries where there were revolutions to "redistribute the wealth." As we noted in Chapter 3, the inequality in Russia, China, Cuba and other communist countries, where "people's revolutions" have occurred, is now greater than ever. After those revolutions, the "race for power" began and the "abler men" were those who were "strong enough to dominate the state and rewrite or interpret the laws." In these countries, the "abler men" are the Brezhnevs, Tengs, Castros and others who had the superior ability to muscle their way to the top. As a result, they control *all* wealth in their countries.

But what made the American Revolution so unique was that the Revolutionists made no pretense of a desire to redistribute wealth. Their only objective was to throw out the government; they wanted to be *free*. They wanted every inhabitant to have the equal *right* to life, liberty and the pursuit of happiness. *This* was the birth of the American Dream.

But from the day the Constitution became law, politicians began implementing the anti-nature, economically impossible philosophy of "wealth without work." And since this philosophy gained a full head of steam under FDR, the U.S. more and more has come to resemble Rome under Caesar Augustus.

Should we collapse economically, you can be sure that the "abler men" will take firm hold of the political reins in a totalitarian manner. That is when we will be presented with the bill for our false prosperity. "In nature," said Emerson, "nothing can be given, all things are sold." If it is not soon brought under control, the ultimate price tag for the gourmet banquet—and remember this well—will be loss of freedom.

Though the popular question during the Lyndon Johnson years was whether the United States could afford both guns and butter, I never for a moment thought that to be the relevant issue. I believed then, and believe more so today, that the important question is whether we can afford both freedom and equality.

And both nature and history have repeatedly given us the answer to this question: *No.*

I urge every American to heed the advice of William Simon.

> *Stop asking the government for "free" goods and services, however desirable and necessary they may seem to be. They are not free. They are simply extracted from the hide of your neighbors—and can be extracted only by force. If you would not confront your neighbor and demand his money at the point of a gun to solve every new problem that may appear in your life, you should not allow the government to do it for you. . . . This one insight understood, this one discipline acted upon and taught by millions of Americans to others could do more to further freedom in American life than any other.*

5

Taking the "Free" Out of Free Enterprise

Technically, all government functions redistribute wealth to the extent that they are paid for involuntarily by working people who may not want government to perform such functions. The redistribution-of-the-wealth function discussed in the last chapter, however, is more easily discernible because it involves actions which take money from some people to provide money and services for others.

As a result of The Vote, however, modern government performs other functions, all of which share the objective of appeasing various voter groups. Government Function Number Two—so-called business regulation—like most other government functions, is an area in which there are a multitude of differing personal opinions; as a result, government intervention is, as usual, confusing, contradictory and wasteful. To satisfy thousands of differing expedient demands is, of course, impossible; so, naturally, the politician attempts to do it. Heaven forbid he should miss out on even one prospective voter, no matter how ludicrous that voter's demands may be.

Business regulation is just another form of personal regulation in that every action government takes to interfere with the marketplace directly affects individuals. As we shall see, government interference in the world of business causes increases in, among other things, the cost of living, taxes and unemployment. It also causes shortages in, if not complete elimination of, goods and services desired by individuals.

If the average person truly understood not only how the free-enterprise system operates, but the extent to which government regulation of business damages his well-being, there would be as great a revolt against business regulation as there now is against excessive taxation. Taxes, after all, are just one of the many devastating effects of business regulation in that it takes tax dollars to support the regulatory bureaucracy.

Today there are over 100 agencies on the federal level alone that regulate business, ranging from "worker safety" and "environmental protection" to "antitrust" enforcement and "consumer protection." The Federal Register, which lists these regulations, contained 3,450 pages of new regulations when it was first printed in 1937; today the number is more than 60,000.

THE PRICE TAG

Like money for "people programs," money for business-regulation programs also comes from people. The one absolute certainty of all government intervention in the marketplace is that the consumer ultimately bears the cost. Unfortunately, the vast majority of Americans do not realize that they are paying for these regulations, not only through the higher taxes necessary to support the bureaucratic agencies that implement them, but also through higher prices for goods and services. These higher prices are in great part the result of the billions of dollars industry must spend to comply with agency dictums.

What, exactly, is the cost? There is no accurate measuring stick; it can only be estimated. There are enormous indirect costs that are impossible to calculate. The waste of human life, time and energy, for example, is staggering. In dollars and cents, I have heard various estimates: Chase Manhattan Bank put the figure for complying with government regulations at $100 billion a year; former Federal Reserve Board Chairman Arthur Burns was a little kinder to government, putting his estimate at "only" $70 billion a year; Secretary of the Treasury Michael Blumenthal broke the figure down to $25 to $30 billion a year for the cost to business of filling out federal reports, while estimating the capital lost to the economy at $60 billion to more than $100 billion.

Another waste/cost perspective is man-hours invested. Estimates furnished by the government itself (which means, once again, that we may assume they are very much on the low side) revealed that 210 million man-hours were expended by business just to complete federal forms in the year 1977. To translate this into language that means something to you and me, 210 million man-hours is the equivalent of the total labor force used in the production of all of the Chevrolets that are manufactured each year—2.1 million cars.[28]

That means, theoretically, that if we lived in a laissez-faire society, the equivalent of over 2 million automobiles could be produced each year at no additional expense. And in turn that would either mean that automobile prices would drastically decline or employment and wages would increase, or all three.

Some miscellaneous details of the regulatory nightmare: the General Accounting Office has estimated that passengers could have saved $1.4 to $1.8 billion *per year* between 1969 and 1974 in the absence of CAB regulation; compliance with pollution regulations was estimated at $32 billion for 1977; auto-safety and pollution equipment costs for 1977 were pegged at $7.5 billion, which increased new car prices an average of $666, the steel industry has to comply with 5,600 regulations administered by 26 agencies, which makes it understandable why steel companies are in financial trouble.

More: the ICC has over 400,000 tariff schedules and 84 *trillion* rates;[29] the American Petroleum Institute reported that one oil company alone employed 115 technical people to work full time preparing reports to comply with government regulations, while another company had to prepare one special report that was *475,000 pages* in length; and perhaps the zaniest of all reporting requirements are those of the FCC, for which the estimated man-hours per year for compliance is six times greater than for any other agency and the average "program report" that must be filed with that agency takes 5,772 man-hours.

And to think socialists smugly argue that our economic difficulties prove that "free enterprise" has failed! *What has failed is government regulation.*

Of course, the simplest argument for the liberal "humanitarian" to make is that business simply should be restricted from passing the increased cost of government regulation on to the consumer. That sounds wonderful so long as you disregard the fact that a company that cannot raise prices to cover the higher costs of doing business goes *out* of business; the results of such a "solution," therefore, would be decreased productivity, unemployment, higher prices and scarcity of product. As it is, business profits in this country have been cut in half over the past decade—from about 10% of sales to 5%. That does not leave much room: As you near zero percent, you near economic collapse and dictatorial rule.

Too many companies, as it is, have already collapsed under the strain of government regulation. It is bad enough that excessive regulation often makes it nearly impossible to do business, but the time and money consumed either in conforming to regulations or in trying to fight them is enough to break even giant corporations, let alone small and medium-sized businesses. The use of potentially productive time and energy to fill out tax forms, safety forms, sanitation forms, equal-opportunity forms, and environmental-protection forms, to name but a few, has become a way of life for the businessman, a curious substitute for the American Dream this way of life has been helping to destroy.

Milton Friedman brings business regulation down to a personal level by maintaining that it is the greatest example of violation of human freedom one can think of. Among others, he mentions having to obtain a government license to engage in an occupation, being prevented from selling a product at a price one wishes to charge, and not being allowed to grow the amount of crops one wants to grow. These are called "economic restrictions," which is a nice phrase, but the fact remains that they are restrictions of *freedom*. Try as collectivists may, they can never separate freedom and free enterprise.

Business regulation really is just part of the larger "wealth-is-evil" philosophy. Over the centuries, ignorant and envious zealots have convinced great numbers of people that profit is sinful and that large concentrations of wealth ("bigness") are dangerous. This is the irrational attitude that has prompted overtaxation and overregulation of business in avalanche proportions. This in turn has helped to destroy the lifeblood of the American Dream—free enterprise—-the dream that inspired the technological progress which brought Americans health, comfort and material well-being unimagined in past centuries.

Those who favor such destruction display the same short-sightedness as those who revere redistribution-of-the-wealth legislation. Whenever some absolute moralist (someone who believes that his standards of morality should be binding upon everyone) is of the opinion that a problem exists, his solution is to appeal to government to pass new laws and create a new agency to enforce them. This means violating still more rights of more people, which once again is the mistake of trying to solve what certain people believe to be a problem by creating bigger problems.

THE RULERS WHO DON'T ANSWER TO THE VOTE

A truly terrifying aspect of the rapidly growing regulatory monster is that it is the most visible sign of creeping totalitarianism in our country. Most regulatory agencies operate outside the law, with nonelected bureaucrats in control, and act as judge, jury, prosecutor and executioner. They virtually can make or break a company or individual businessman at will. The whole concept of regulatory agencies is in direct contrast to everything America originally stood for; a company or businessman is deemed to be guilty until proven innocent.

What kinds of "experts" are these nonelected rulers? Just as Senator Hayakawa was shocked when he was named to the Senate Budget Committee, so too was William Simon when Richard Nixon appointed him chairman of the Oil Policy Committee (which made him, said Simon, a virtual "dictator" over the energy resources of the United States). The problem? Simon himself told Nixon that he knew nothing about oil!

Another case of government-culture shock was experienced by William T. Bagley, an attorney who left private practice to chair the Commodity Futures Trading Commission. He was amazed when the head of one of his departments boasted that he had never seen a commodity-exchange trading floor, had no plans to see one, and had no interest in talking to anyone in the commodities business. After a rather brief and disenchanted life in the government bureaucracy, Bagley concluded that "all they (civil servants) want is to write rules. They are not conscious of the real world."[30]

Like civil servants who administer "welfare programs," government regulators spend most of their time maneuvering to protect their vested interests—which means trying to increase the size of their agencies. Since they have no way of proving tangible results, government regulators, like their counterparts in "people-program" agencies, must increase paperwork, which in turn increases staff size; an increase in staff regulators brings still more regulations, which continues the cycle by bringing still more regulators.

It is imperative that bureaucratic regulators find problems, even if they do not exist. As is true of "poverty programs," if problems were solved and new problems could not be found, they would be out of jobs. I have dubbed this parasitic dilemma for today's businessman the *Regulatory Mousetrap Theory*. Simply stated, the essence of governmental regulatory policy is: "You build a better mousetrap, and we'll build a bigger mouse."

This intentional destruction of our economy and freedom by nonelected bureaucratic dictators calls to mind an all-too-true statement by Ayn Rand many years ago: "The man who has no purpose, but has to act, acts to destroy others."

Attorney General Griffin B. Bell, another member of the government hierarchy who acknowledges the cataclysm toward which we are headed, put it on the line about as clearly as anyone. Bell called the monstrous government bureaucracy "a prescription for societal suicide," saying it made him "fearful of what lies ahead for the nation. . . . If the republic is to remain viable," says Bell, "we must find ways to curb and then to reduce this government by bureaucracy. . . . More staff invariably means more time in which to evolve more ideas about how to increase government control over the lives of the American people."[31]

The reality that the American Dream is on the verge of extinction and that total loss of freedom is just over the horizon apparently is motivating more and more "insiders" to join William Simon in laying the cards on the table.

HOW THE DESTRUCTION GAME IS PLAYED

Business regulation, on the surface, appears to be an enigma. While unelected bureaucrats implement the regulations and have dictatorial powers, the agencies themselves are set up by politicians who pay homage to The Vote. Therefore, though business regulation for many people is an extension of their "wealth-is-evil" attitude, others want business regulated for different reasons. In fact, virtually *everyone* wants business regulated, including businessmen!

The enigma arises from the contrasting *types* of business regulation desired by various groups and individuals. Since virtually all business regulation grows out of subjective opinions and moral desires, and since no two people share the exact same opinions and moral desires, how can the government even begin to please everyone?

The answer is that it can't; but, thanks to The Vote, it tries anyway. Which is why business regulation sometimes takes the form of "consumerism," at other times burdens industry with totally unreasonable environmental or safety restrictions, and at still other times doles out special favors, on a selective basis, to companies and businessmen.

THE PERSUADERS

All this manifests itself in a phenomenon called "lobbying." Government regulation of business has evolved into a game of lobbying, and the playing field on a federal level is Washington, D.C. What politicians realize is that all lobbying groups represent votes, and, in the case of business lobbying in particular, there also are ancillary benefits to be had, such as campaign contributions and other forms of help from powerful businessmen. It is no coincidence that the lobbying game gets bigger as the American Dream diminishes. Lobbying has become such a major business in Washington that the city is overrun by lawyers; the number of attorneys in major firms in the nation's capital doubled between 1970 and 1978.

Moral desires show up in the lobbying game through small groups of politically active people. The objective of these people is to persuade government to force business to abide by their opinions regarding protection of the environment, safety of workers, the size of companies—virtually an infinite number of moral beliefs with which they feel others should be compelled to go along.

Notwithstanding the destruction such people have wrought upon millions of individuals and upon the economy as a whole, I can, after listening to their "arguments" for years, forgive most of them as well-intentioned individuals who not only are uninformed, but whose vision is limited to single issues which create a distorted view of specific situations. I believe that if these people were the only regulatory problem, producers might eventually be able to cope with them.

I am sorry to say, however, that they are not the only problem. A problem that is just as bad, and perhaps worse, is that cry-baby businessmen run to government to seek an edge over their competitors. As with labor fakers, virtually all businessmen are guilty to one degree or another. The result is the philosophical dilemma many businessmen have been trying to resolve for years: how to have their free enterprise cake and eat it too; i.e., how to bring about government intervention in the marketplace which favors their specific companies or industries, while holding down regulation that is detrimental to their interests.

When I sing the praises of capitalism, therefore, one should not take this to mean that I am praising businessmen. There are moral businessmen and immoral businessmen. There are businessmen whose operations are virtually dependent upon obtaining special favors from government; there are businessmen who reluctantly ask for government help only because "everyone else is doing it"; and there are businessmen who rarely seek government intervention and who, given a choice, would favor the advent of the world's first laissez-faire free-enterprise society.

Both small and big businesses are guilty of inviting government intervention in the free market. "Small businessmen" often decry the "unfair" advantages of "big business," but, to be sure, many small businessmen are just as guilty as giant corporations when it comes to government collusion. If you have ever read any literature put out by small-business associations, you know that they are not asking for an end to government regulations; they are asking for less regulation of small business and *more* regulation of big business. This short-term, expedient outlook has the same destructive effect on society as the expedient demands of welfare recipients, civil-service workers and the "unemployed."

Both large and small businesses are well known for their wide variety of appeals to government to step in and "protect" them. "Fair-pricing laws" are an old favorite; these laws artificially keep prices high and penalize efficient competitors.

Tariffs are another type of government protection which has been around for years, always helping inefficient domestic producers by forcing consumers to pay unnecessarily high prices for imported goods. While tariffs foster the impression that government is protecting workers in a particular industry, the long-term effect is not only an increase in prices, but a *decrease* in employment. Since tariffs force people to pay higher prices, people have less to spend on other goods and services, which results in less employment in the industries that produce such goods and services. The hidden reality is that the job protected by a government tariff is at the expense of a worker in another industry.

And then there are the companies that appeal to government to keep newcomers out of their fields, claiming their industries are "overcrowded." These claims are, of course, illogical, because if an industry is overcrowded, profits should be inordinately low; therefore, why would anyone want to invest capital in such an industry? The truth of the matter is that the entrenched businesses do not want the extra competition which would force them to become more efficient and produce better products and services at lower prices.

Subsidies and government loans to "businesses in need" are the same story. What really happens is that money is taken from efficient producers (and workers) to keep inefficient producers in business—all at the expense of consumers in the form of higher prices.

As Henry Hazlitt has noted, it is important that antiquated, inefficient companies die out so that new, efficient companies can grow faster; i.e., so capital and labor will find their way into more modern industries. Mr. Hazlitt uses the automobile industry as an example, pointing out that if government had tried to keep the horse-and-buggy trade alive through subsidies, the automobile industry would have suffered, which in turn would have meant a loss of great wealth and a subsequent loss of improved living standards for all.

In the case of farm subsidies, the government pays farmers *not* to grow crops. In 1978, the Department of

Agriculture paid farmers $620 million to cover the difference between the market prices of grain and the prices set by government.

When a businessman stops running to government for special favors, only then will he convince me that he really believes in capitalism. It is ironic that those businessmen who encourage government regulation *of any kind* use the very same tactics employed by antibusiness moralists who press for safety and environmental regulations— the same moralists whose actions businessmen so deplore. Businessmen who seek government favors are, in effect, admitting that they cannot compete on the basis of their own talents, and that they therefore wish to see the free-enterprise system eliminated.

ANTITRUST MYTHOLOGY

Many business regulations imposed by government are instituted under the guise of "protecting" the public from monopolies which otherwise, so the theory goes, would be able to charge virtually any prices they desired for their products. It seems rather strange, then, that it is often big companies that bring so-called antitrust or monopoly suits against competitors. Usually the objective is either to keep another company from entering its field or to get government to restrict a successful company in ways that would give the suing company advantages it has not been able to acquire on its own merits.

Antitrust legislation (including all antimonopoly laws) is just another fraud played upon the average American. The truth is that companies rarely are able to obtain a monopoly in an industry *without* the aid of government. It is interesting to note that the term *monopoly* originally meant: an exclusive grant or franchise from the king to operate in a given area, free from competition.[32]

Few people realize that the infamous "trusts" and cartels of the early American business giants failed. The main reason for their failure was that each company in a cartel was always trying to gain an edge over the very companies with whom it was allied, which was only natural.

As a result of this failure, some of the bigger corporations got the bright idea to use the coercive machinery of government to pass "antitrust" laws to knock out the competition that they themselves could not eliminate in the free market. Industry's antitrust alliance with government is probably the biggest mistake capitalists have made since prehistoric property owners agreed to let power seekers protect their lives and property.

Today government awards strict monopolies in most of the biggest industries in the country, and monopolies of one kind or another in literally thousands of other businesses. Service businesses such as gas, electricity, telephone, railroads, airlines and trucking are some of the more obvious examples. The absurd explanation given for such monopolies is insulting to one's intelligence. While claiming that its regulation of prices protects the public from "unfair" high prices, the truth is that government rate-setting protects the companies it "regulates" from having to charge *low* prices. Such companies are virtually guaranteed a fixed profit for their products and services.

This whole charade is exposed whenever some maverick comes along and tries to break into an established industry by offering better products or services and/or lower prices. In such cases, entrenched industry giants usually run to the government to protect them from the new price competition they claim will cause "chaos" (lower prices) in their industry.

Laker Airlines is a good example of this. It took Freddie Laker years to fight the airline-industry/government antitrust alliance. The fact that he finally succeeded in getting Laker Airlines off the ground, charging rates that were a fraction of those being charged by established airlines, was something of a miracle—and a tribute to his brilliance and determination to fight city hall. More important, his success meant that you and I now pay lower air fares on many routes than we did before he dared to fight the government-protected airline trusts.

A virtual admission by the government of its protection of monopolies was evident in a recent FCC ruling whereby the FCC decided, after all these years, to *allow* other companies to compete with Western Union for telegram service, money orders and mailgram business. If the objective of antimonopoly laws is to *stop* monopolies, why did other companies need government's permission to *compete*?

Incredibly, the FCC admitted that the only reason it was now going to allow others to compete with Western Union in these specified areas of its business was that these services no longer comprised a significant portion of its operations. Since the services now account for only about 10% of Western Union's total revenues, the loss of its monopoly was no longer considered important to its overall success.

In truth, licensing laws of *all* kinds are monopolistic, because they mean, plain and simple, that people are not free to compete with established businesses or individuals without government consent. No matter how much one may be used to thinking to the contrary, the same principles hold true even for such businesses as law, medicine, dentistry and pharmacy.

As in the area of public education, I appreciate that it is difficult for most people to accept this seemingly extreme point of view, having been accustomed all their lives to believing that government licensing is practically divine and that government possesses omnipotent powers to protect the public from incompetent and unscrupulous operators.

Unfortunately, however, even *with* government-monopoly licensing laws for most professions, the country is filled with incompetent and unscrupulous operators in all areas of occupation. And the fact always remains that elimination of competition through licensing, regardless of the nature of the service, lessens the motivation for efficiency, raises prices, and lowers quality, again at the expense of the consumer.

Now government antitrust coercion is being used by medium-sized and smaller companies in all fields in an effort to stop efficient competition either from becoming bigger or from entering their industries at all. "Bigness is badness" is just another way of expressing the ignorant notion that wealth is evil.

Edward Kennedy has been a leader in campaigning for new laws to stop companies from getting larger, even if they are not presently "violating" existing antitrust laws. At the time of the writing of this book, Justice Department officials had begun drafting legislation that would, in effect, stop the 200 largest manufacturing companies in this country from merging with *anybody*, regardless of how unrelated their business operations may be.

One of the more interesting results of the lobbying/antitrust game is that confused, contradictory antitrust legislation (and thinking) has now made it technically against the law just to be in business in this country. Consider:

1) If a company charges *higher prices* than its competitors, government reasoning is that it must have a monopoly in its field or else it would not be able to charge such high prices.

2) If a company charges *lower prices* than its competition, Uncle Sam assumes that it must be trying to acquire a monopoly by "undercutting" other companies in its field.

3) If a company charges the *same prices* as its com-

petitors (without government approval), then, of course, it is guilty of "price fixing."

What once was the American Dream has been replaced by the notion that virtually every businessman is breaking the law simply by being in business!

The truth about monopolies is that they seldom could occur in a free market, and even if they did occasionally exist, such companies could not charge any price they wanted. This is so because, in a *free* market, even if a company held a monopoly, it would have competition, as pointed out in "Fundamentals of Liberty." The three kinds of competition that always exist are:

1) *Parallel competition.* There are always alternatives to any product or service. If the price of anything—including seemingly essential products like gas and oil—become prohibitive, consumers will seek a substitute. They may not like the substitute as well, but at a certain point they become willing to sacrifice some degree of comfort and convenience for price.

2) *Dollar competition.* People only have so many dollars to spend, and, unlike government, they weigh their needs, desires and income against the cost of various products and services, then make decisions to purchase some and do without others. Again, they may not like doing without some items, but if the prices of those items are too high, that is precisely the decision they will make.

3) *Invisible competition.* No matter how entrenched a company may be, if it raises prices to levels considered exorbitant by consumers, it is practically inviting new companies to enter its field to compete with it at lower prices. *Potential* competition is always out there, in the form of ambitious entrepreneurs looking for ways to increase their wealth by offering better products and services at lower prices.

The greatest regulator is competition, and there is *al-*

ways competition in the absence of government intervention.

Above all, the fact that every consumer is interested in buying the best products and services at the lowest prices *guarantees* competition in a free market. This is precisely what makes black markets flourish. A black market is nothing more than a free market asserting itself in spite of government regulation. Only government intervention in the market—usually through "antitrust" legislation—can interfere with the natural forces of competition in laissez-faire capitalism.

The example of Alcoa Aluminum is cited in "Fundamentals of Liberty" to reinforce the point that a monopoly earned in the free market does not necessarily translate into higher prices for buyers. Notwithstanding the fact that for years Alcoa had a monopoly on aluminum production in the United States, it *lowered* its price over the years, so much so that it was only charging 20¢ a pound in the 1930's as compared to $8 a pound in 1888. Alcoa recognized the power of invisible competition.

But in the end, government made sure that the consumer was forced to pay higher prices by bringing an antitrust suit against Alcoa. Bureaucrats, using their infinite powers of reason, determined that Alcoa's defense—that other companies did not enter its field because it operated too efficiently—was not valid. The government, in effect, decided that it was illegal for a company to be too efficient!

In the case of antitrust laws, not only do consumers pay for the millions of man-hours required to comply with federal regulations and to fight antitrust suits, but they pay what is probably the biggest cost of all: the monopolistic rates government sets for virtually all major industries.

Some brief comments on a small sampling of agencies that help to implement government-enforced monopolies:

—*CAB* (*Civil Aeronautics Board*). This agency assures high fares, inflight meals that are often inedible, uncomfortable seating arrangements, and passenger inconvenience with regard to airline scheduling and routes. It accomplishes all this simply by keeping out competitors. If any company were allowed to go into the airline business at any time it desired, fly whatever routes it chose to fly, and charge any price it deemed to be feasible, it is you and I who would reap the benefits of such unrelenting competition.

As everyone knows by now, when the government finally announced that it was going to "deregulate" the airline industry, it was the airlines themselves who vehemently fought it. They insisted that deregulation somehow would be bad for passengers (though I never heard one of them offer an intelligible reason why).

The current deregulation is, of course, a mere token of free enterprise in the airline industry. The fact remains that you are not free to go into the airline business tomorrow, without government permission—permission that is virtually impossible to obtain—let alone to fly any routes you choose and to charge any prices you desire.

Do not be misled into mistaking government's version of deregulation for laissez-faire capitalism.

—*ICC* (*Interstate Commerce Commission*). As this book was being written, government also was threatening to "deregulate" the trucking industry. Most established truckers, of course, were adamantly in favor of keeping regulation the way it was, so much so that American Trucking Associations, Inc. ran a full-page ad in *The Wall Street Journal* in an attempt to convince readers of the evils that free competition in the trucking industry would bring. Apparently, these great giants of capitalism consider competition to be evil.

A humorous twist to the ICC is that its original purported purpose was to protect the public from railroad monopolies (which really meant to protect railroad monopolies from competition). It eventually evolved into an agency to protect the railroads from trucking competition, and finally evolved into a bureaucracy that protects trucking companies from new trucking competition.

The bottom line is the same: Trucking is just another government-protected business that you or I could not enter if we wanted to, let alone charge any rates we liked or cover any routes we deemed to be desirable.

—*FTC (Federal Trade Commission)*. This is one of those anything-goes agencies that plays ball all over the lot, sticking its nose into a wide variety of aspects of virtually every industry. Among other things, it can practically force a company to surrender, to competitors, patents that took millions of dollars and many years to obtain, arbitrarily decide what prices are "fair" on which items, and block acquisitions and mergers.

Robert Rowan, president of Fruehauf Corp., commenting on the fact that his company had been spending $1 million a year on legal fees fighting an FTC ruling against one of its acquisitions, summed up the FTC this way: "(FTC personnel) feel all business is bad. . . . I have never seen a group of people so antibusiness. . . . You walk into the room and there's a young guy (who) graduated from some Ivy League college and never worked a day for a living."[33]

Of course, it is business itself that helps the FTC to be antibusiness, as companies scurry around trying to convince that agency's bureaucrats that they should stop mergers they fear will improve their competitors' positions.

—*FCC (Federal Communications Commission)*. First and foremost, of course, the FCC guarantees the continuance of existing monopolies by established radio and TV stations. But it also crosses over into that vague, anti-freedom area of "protecting the public morals." Prodded on by expedient voters who want to impose their moral standards on others, the FCC excels at using curious terms like "public-interest programming."

Television stations, so the interventionist rhetoric goes, have a responsibility to the public to provide "quality programs." It is but another attempt to legislate personal moral judgments. Everyone's idea of what constitutes a quality program differs to one extent or another; a quality program is a program that *you* think is good. No one has a right to ask the government to force stations to offer programs that are to *his* liking.

I also reject the notion of the airways belonging to the "public." Radio and TV stations are privately owned enterprises, in business to make profits, particularly where shareholders are concerned.

I happen to be a virtual non-watcher of television, simply because there are very few programs that I consider to be of good quality. But that is only *my* personal judgment; I do not go running to the government in an effort to make others abide by my standards. Since God has not christened me His official guardian to watch over the quality of TV programming, I cannot see where it is my duty to decide what others should watch.

TV stations, even though they are government-backed monopolies, lose to "dollar competition" in my case. While there are many types of programs I would like to see produced for television, I accept the fact that apparently not enough people agree with my tastes to make it profitable for stations to create such programs. I therefore exercise my right to choose alternative forms of entertainment. And that's that. Simple; no problems; no interference with my neighbors; no government involvement.

WORKER- AND CONSUMER-PROTECTION MYTHOLOGY

All government regulatory agencies play the dual role of being both antibusiness and pro-monopoly to one extent or another. Some agencies, however, lean more toward imposing the opinions of various "consumer" and labor groups on the business world. These agencies make it possible for virtually anyone who is willing to spend his time crusading for an issue to disrupt the free market. Whether the issue is consumer safety, worker safety or environmental protection, the actions of such agencies always involve forcing business to abide by the opinions of lobbying groups concerning what is unsafe or unfair.

What complicates the problem is that not only do these groups make their demands known to vote-conscious politicians—politicians who create agencies and jobs for the non-elected bureaucrats who carry out the interference—but, more often than not, the nonelected bureaucrats themselves get carried away and impose *their own* moral standards on business. Under their "leadership," "consumerism" has evolved into a sort of social fascism.

Some brief comments on a small sampling of agencies that forcibly interfere with the free market under the guise of consumer, safety or environmental protection:

—*SEC (Securities and Exchange Commission)*. It would be more appropriate to refer to this agency as the Swift Execution Commission. It is easily the most gestapolike of all governmental regulatory agencies, continually expanding its powers into areas far removed from its original purported purpose of "protecting investors." It arbitrarily makes the law, then passes judgment on whether or not a person or company has violated it.

Like all government agencies, the SEC's efforts not only violate human rights, but result in the opposite of its stated purpose. For example, over the years it has forced public companies to increase the detail of their annual reports and prospectuses to the point that it is now virtually impossible for the average person to understand them. It takes a very sophisticated investor to be able to make sense out of the endless financial figures, facts and footnotes which are now mandatory in corporate public reports.

Incredibly, when the SEC accuses a company or individual of "wrongdoing," it does not have to prove guilt beyond a reasonable doubt, but is only required to show a "preponderance of evidence." Furthermore, defendants, in effect, are forced to provide SEC investigators with evidence *against* themselves.

Customarily, an SEC "investigation" results in individuals or companies signing a "consent decree," a nasty little document that states that they "consent to an injunction, without admitting or denying the allegations." The result of this is that the SEC achieves its desired objective of damaging the target company or individuals without having to prove violations of the law.

The damage comes from the bad publicity that accompanies such investigations, which, unfortunately, leads many investors, company suppliers, potential merger candidates and others to assume that "where there's smoke, there's fire." And that assumption usually leads to a drastic drop in the price of a company's stock—which in turn hurts the very investors whom the SEC claims to be protecting.

—*FDA (Food and Drug Administration)*. This is a virtual life-threatening agency in that, among other things, it takes it upon itself to outlaw various "drugs" and medicines that may improve the health of seriously ill people or, in some cases, even save lives. People die every year in this country who conceivably could be saved by drugs outlawed by the FDA.

A former college football player, Kent Waldrip, had to

go to Russia to obtain treatment for paralysis because the FDA refused to approve an enzyme injection that had been shown to be helpful in cases similar to his. Previously, a Florida man who was paralyzed from the neck down had gone to Russia for the same treatment, which, he claimed, led to his being able to walk across a room.

In another case, Mr. and Mrs. Gerald Green had to flee the United States to Mexico to obtain laetrile treatments for their leukemia-stricken three-year-old son. Incredibly, the assistant state attorney of Massachusetts then applied for a federal kidnapping warrant against the parents.

The question here is not whether certain drugs in certain cases help or harm individuals. The crux of the issue is libertarian in nature: government simply has no business deciding what medications companies should or should not be allowed to sell, and certainly has no right to make it a criminal offense for people to take whatever medications they desire. In addition, there prevails, once again, the general false assumption that government has some omniscient power to make such decisions, decisions which can be better made by individuals—both consumers and businessmen.

—OSHA (Occupational Safety and Health Administration). This agency, purportedly formed to protect workers, has, through its ludicrous, counterproductive and conflicting regulations, become a source of amusement to most observers, including the workers whom it is supposed to protect. In fact, it has become commonplace for workers to "cheat" to avoid the "protection" forced upon them by OSHA.

OSHA's absurdity recently hit home when I received in the mail, unsolicited, two rather lengthy booklets from that agency. To properly appreciate the waste of your tax dollars, I first must tell you that I employ a total of three people in a modern office building in a highly desirable area of the city. The nearest thing we have to a pollution problem are staples scattered carelessly around a desk now and then.

Nevertheless, as I write this very sentence, I am looking at the two booklets mailed to me by OSHA, the covers of which show a man wearing some sort of respirator/gas mask. The titles of the booklets are *Respiratory Protection . . . An Employer's Manual* and *Respiratory Protection . . . A Guide for the Employee.* Needless to say, these booklets have become the objects of numerous little jokes around our office.

But, in reality, it isn't funny. What I keep wondering is how many thousands, or perhaps millions, of other copies of these booklets were sent to people who do not need them or want them—all at the expense of the taxpayers.

—EPA (Environmental Protection Agency). A latecomer on the regulatory scene, the EPA has been making up for lost time. Presently, it is probably doing more to cripple the U.S. economy and endanger lives than any other agency.

Ironically, it is those who ramble on about the evils of capitalism and the need to curb technology to protect the environment who apparently place very little value on human life. Such people are afflicted with tunnel vision, being totally obsessed with "cleaning up the environment" at any cost. By stifling technology, they stifle the very thing that has ended misery for the masses, prolonged people's lives, and made life more comfortable for virtually everyone.

It is curious that people have grown up to relate capitalism with environmental problems; as pointed out earlier, even communist countries use the division-of-labor industrial system—though less successfully, because of lack of incentive on the part of workers. There is just as much pollution in Russia, if not more, as in the United States.

As with all regulation, the price tag for environmental

controls is hidden from taxpayers. All of us want clean air and water, but not at *any* cost; certainly not at the cost of losing our freedom. There is nothing wrong with being concerned about the environment, but it is impractical and tyrannical to allow it to dominate virtually every decision regarding technological advancement and business planning.

Energy is one of the most critical areas being endangered by the fanatical and dictatorial environmental attitudes of small numbers of bureaucrats and politically active groups. Our legal system—appropriately referred to by one source as "trial by endurance"—makes it possible for small groups to block, for interminable periods of time, what could be life-saving energy projects.

As I was putting the final touches on this book, the now famous Three-Mile-Island nuclear incident occurred. As usual, this immediately brought to the fore such professional agitators as Jane Fonda, Tom Hayden and Ralph Nader, not to mention Jerry Brown, who has become embarrassingly well known for his talent at preaching for or against any issue, depending upon popular sentiment at the time.

Publicity hounds such as these, if taken seriously by enough people, could eventually succeed in dooming mankind to a return to pretechnological times. More often than not, their efforts are a threat to the comfort, safety, health and freedom of future generations. Notwithstanding ego and power motives, it can be assumed that these "crises crusaders" are not consciously attempting to cause millions of people unneeded suffering. Therefore, if one is to give them the benefit of the doubt, one must also assume that their actions are simply based on a lack of knowledge.

In the case of Three Mile Island, for example, these crusader types were protesting for all the wrong reasons. In effect, they were protesting against free enterprise and advocating *more* government intervention. If they felt an irresistible urge to protest, what they should have been protesting was the fact that it was government intervention which created the Three-Mile-Island problems in the first place. The heavy hand of government, in fact, virtually created the entire nuclear industry.

A calm, rational, well-informed person might be more inclined to analyze a situation such as that of Three Mile Island in the following manner:

1) After all the hysterical talk is set aside, the reality is that not one person died in the incident (though one should not assume that future deaths may not occur as a result of Three Mile Island).

2) No one, to my knowledge, has *ever* died as a result of the negligent operation of a nuclear-power plant (though the same qualification as above applies).

3) If a fatality ever should occur as a result of a nuclear-power plant accident—or even if many fatalities should occur—the solution would not be to outlaw nuclear-power plants. The solution would be to allow free men to correct the problems which caused such deaths.

4) Government does not have unique powers to solve nuclear-plant problems, just as it does not have unique powers to solve *any* problem. Individuals, motivated by the desire to improve their well-being, solve problems; government bureaucrats, motivated by The Vote, only succeed in impeding progress.

5) Again, the automobile-accident analogy: Some 50,000 people a year die in automobile accidents, yet rational people do not advocate the outlawing of cars. Because one is in favor of the free use of automobiles and is against government regulation of the auto industry, however, does not mean that he is indifferent to the 50,000 deaths a year caused by automobile accidents.

6) While bleeding-heart liberals love to paint businessmen as evil capitalists who will do anything for profit,

common sense tells one that men who operate nuclear-power plants have no desire to fill the air with nuclear radiation. Remember, these men know that they too have to breathe the air on this planet.

7) Should someone eventually suffer physical damage as a result of the negligent operation of a nuclear plant, then such a person (or his heirs, in the case of death) certainly should have the right to institute civil and/or criminal proceedings against the nuclear-plant owners, just as a person is able to sue an automobile manufacturer if the manufacturer's negligence results in damage to him. Along with rational thinking and humaneness, this is precisely what prevents businessmen in *every* industry from endangering the lives of other people just for the sake of profit.

If government intervenes on *behalf* of an industry, however, as it did in the late 1950's and 1960's when the Atomic Energy Commission, through the Price-Anderson Act, limited the liability of nuclear-power-plant developers and utilities, it practically invites the companies in that industry to be negligent and thus negates this free-market principle. Government intervention, then, is the *real* libertarian issue involved in the nuclear-energy question—whether such intervention is helpful or detrimental to energy companies.

At the same time that "environmentalists" are stifling the production of energy in this country, we read about reports like that of Professor Petr Beckmann, of the University of Colorado, who has estimated that the "waste" now in storage, combined with available unmined uranium reserves, could produce another *1,750 years* of energy at present U.S. consumption rates.[34] A U.S. Geological Survey reported that we have 50 to 127 billion barrels of untapped oil, plus *proven* resources of 40.6 billion barrels, but "environmentalists" have fought tooth and nail to prevent oil drilling. There are enough coal reserves in this country alone to last another 800 years (at 1973 consumption levels), but the Coal Mining Health and Safety Act and the Clean Air Act of 1969 and 1970 have actually caused coal production to *decline*.

In *A Time for Truth*, William Simon relates how Gerald Ford caved in to political expediency and signed a "compromise" form of the disastrous Energy Policy and Conservation Act of 1975 in the hopes of winning votes in the New Hampshire primary. The act imposes so many regulations on the energy industry that it virtually puts government in complete control of the nation's energy resources. It is just one more example of a seemingly well-meaning politician giving into his Expediency Factor for the sake of The Vote, despite the devastating long-term consequences of his decision.

It seems that some people will never understand that the solution to every problem—particularly environmental problems—is not to outlaw the cause of the problem and set up a policing agency to enforce the law. Isaac Asimov made this point brilliantly and simply in a recent lecture by reflecting on prehistoric times, when men first discovered fire and learned that it provided a source of warmth for cold nights and winters. When these men brought the fire inside, however, they found that it filled their caves with smoke. But since there was no agency around to outlaw the use of fire in caves, man instead resorted to his greatest asset—creative ingenuity, inspired by a desire to improve his well-being. As a result, he invented, instead of a new regulatory agency, the chimney.

Narrow-minded environmentalists who want to eliminate all risks for mankind are forcing us to take the biggest risk of all: destruction. A risk-free society is a dead society! The people of this country must recover the willingness to take risks, for it was the risk-taking, spirited quest of a better life that made America the healthiest, wealthiest and strongest country in the history of the world.

The Hopeless Cause

Depending on popular voter notions that may be circulating at any given time, government intervention in business may also take the form of "wage-and-price controls" (as opposed to "fair pricing," mentioned earlier, which keeps prices artificially *high* for the benefit of certain companies). The implication is that Uncle Sam can use force to negate the law of supply and demand. Short term, this sometimes looks good to voters; long term, it never works; and, more often than not, it does not even work on a short-term basis.

What is amazing about wage-and-price controls is that they have been tried for centuries by governments throughout the world and, though they have *never* worked, governments refuse to toss them in the junk pile of old political schemes that have outlived their usefulness. On second thought, it probably is not so amazing, because, judging from newspaper and magazine articles, enough people still misunderstand the real consequences of wage-and-price controls to support politicians who espouse their nonexistent merits.

The most basic reason (although there are many others) that wage-and-price controls do not work is that it is impossible, without the aid of an extreme totalitarian regime, to put price ceilings on every product and service that exists. (New housing is just one good example of a product for which it would be impossible to limit price, simply because there are too many variables.) The result is that producers will produce fewer of those products on which prices are restricted, thus people will have more money available for other products (such as new houses), which in turn will cause the price of the nonrestricted products to rise *faster* than normal.

—*Rent control is one of the most popular forms of political price control.* When "crises crusaders" Ms. Fonda and Mr. Hayden were last seen, they were celebrating a rent control "victory" in Santa Monica, California—a "victory" which virtually assures renters in that area that not only will rents of the future be beyond the reach of all but a small percentage of the people, but that new apartment construction will be a rare occurrence and a great many existing apartment buildings will be allowed to slowly deteriorate.

Renters foolishly believe that government is doing them a favor by using force to hold down rents. But the result is always the same: Regulation of rents makes apartment construction an unappealing investment, which means there will be fewer apartments built, which in turn results in a shortage of rental units, which, ultimately, results in *higher* rents. Isn't it amazing how government regulations consistently achieve the exact opposite of their stated objectives?

Rent controls bring to mind my *Illusory Deregulation Theory:* Every time government blesses us with a "deregulation" of some kind, the long-term net effect seems to be a substantial *increase* in regulations. When the people of California finally stood up to the government and voted overwhelmingly to have property taxes lowered, via Proposition 13, the result was a broad assortment of proposed *new* regulations to make up for it. The most widely publicized of these was the instituting of rent controls in some areas, which drastically reduced apartment-construction activity.

—*Again, the energy industry must be mentioned, particularly the oil business.* Government intellectuals continue to ignore official data and insist that there is an oil shortage. But the only shortage is the one artificially created by government intervention. Not only do environmental regulations make it almost impossible to drill for oil profitably, but, by artificially restraining prices, government kills off the incentive to engage in risky and costly oil exploration.

The economics of oil drilling works just the same as in apartment construction. Higher oil prices mean higher profits, which allows for more exploration and, hopefully, more oil. More oil, in a *free* market, means lower prices—*naturally* lower prices. The profit motive will find us all the oil we need if government will just get out of the way and let oil companies go at it. It is a cruel irony that U.S. Government price restrictions on domestic oil in effect subsidize oil imports and keep us dependent upon other oil-producing nations.

—Government is even less effective at holding down wages, and all of the same free-market and Natural-Law principles apply to wage restrictions that apply to price restrictions. Government has no more right to hold down either prices or wages than it has to use taxpayer money to subsidize a company that happens to have a good lobbying man in Washington.

Promoting Unemployment

On the other side of the wage-and-price-protection coin is the compilation of laws which force employers to pay artificially *high* wages or charge artificially *high* prices ("fair pricing"). Artificially high wage levels include both "minimum-wage laws" and laws which force employers to negotiate with unions, no matter how unreasonable their demands. The long-term result, of course, is detrimental to those who are supposed to be protected by laws.

There is a simple business axiom which says that if wages are forced up, business hires fewer people. In the case of skilled union-shop workers, what good does it do a man to be told by his union that his skills are worth $20 an hour if he is unemployed?

For unskilled people at the lowest end of the wage scale, the problem is much worse. By pricing these people out of the labor market, government all but forces them to accept welfare, which in turn causes a loss of pride and self-esteem. Yet the minimum wage—that great creator of unemployment—keeps rising in quantum leaps, most recently to $2.90 an hour.

Minimum-wage laws promote unemployment, because people who might otherwise be hired at a lower wage simply are not hired. This is especially oppressive to minority groups; it is a fact that every increase in the minimum-wage rate since 1948 has brought an increase in the black teenage unemployment rate relative to whites.[35] Government achieves an amazing feat for workers by substituting unemployment for low wages!

During a more laissez-faire period in our history, Henry Ford did not need government force to raise wages. He *doubled* the wages of his employees, voluntarily, because he was smart enough to figure out that such a move would increase production and profits. It was the "invisible hand" of free enterprise that raised the wages of his workers. At a very early stage of our industrial development, Henry Ford understood that increased productivity (i.e., increase in output per man-hours worked) makes it possible to increase wages—*without increasing prices*. In a free market, wages should, and will, rise according to increased productivity.

It goes without saying that minimum-wage laws and union-enforced minimum wages are paid for by consumers, in two ways: first, in the form of the welfare and unemployment-compensation payments they bring about; second, in the form of higher prices which result from higher wages. The latter also means that the increased wages are really an illusion to the worker who receives them, because everything costs him more.

DOES ANYONE BENEFIT?

While it is true that many companies benefit from special government licenses, government-granted monopolies, government subsidies and the like, I adamantly maintain my position that anyone who gains anything through government intervention will suffer right along with everyone else in the long term. The professional welfare recipient and the corporate executive who vies for special government favors both are contributing to the destruction of our economy and our freedom. I doubt that even the bureaucrats who administer the devastating regulatory programs would enjoy living under a totalitarian government.

The regulatory game is a game of destruction. Regulatory agencies help to cause high prices and unemployment, stifle technology and production, and grant monopolies and subsidies at the expense of the overall economy. All of these actions are destructive and can lead only to financial collapse for America and a loss of freedom for all of us.

As I stated at the outset of this chapter, business regulation is an offshoot of the wealth-is-evil philosophy, so politicians love to play up that angle. The regulation of nasty capitalists, we are led to believe, will somehow help the "poor." We already have been through all the reasons why that is not true, but government nevertheless clings to the political poetry of defending the "poor" against the evils of businessmen.

The fact is that business regulations are most stifling to the impoverished. A person from such a background rarely has the means to cope with oppressive government regulations, thus he is restricted from becoming a businessman himself. The American Dream, which certainly was symbolized in part by the freedom to start a small business on a shoestring, has become a myth to such a person. This is such an important, but virtually ignored, result of business regulation that I feel obliged to quote at length from John Hospers' marvelous book, *Libertarianism*, which so clearly spells out the predicament.

> Though the regulations and taxes are enough to discourage anyone to the point of giving up, the effects have been especially harmful to racial minorities, such as the Negroes. Many blacks have had to leave farms in the South because of government intervention: the government paid large subsidies to the *big* farmers, but the small ones were put out of business by the thousands. They left home in droves for the large industrial cities, only to find that they had been priced out of the labor market by minimum-wage laws and government-created unemployment. For some of them, there was still another possibility: start your own business. But the taxes and regulations described above were enough to prevent that possibility in most cases, or to bring them to financial ruin if they did start.
>
> The liberals pretend to be friends of the Negro; but they have been the advocates of the very restrictions and regulations which stopped the Negro at every turn—as farmer, as worker, as businessman. And so there was no way out but the government dole, year after year, and life in a ghetto which would have been no ghetto if enterprising building constructors had not been shackled by government regulations and taxes. The message to the black race should be clear: the government is not your friend! And those who are responsible for all the government regulations which stop you at every turn are not your friends either, though they may wring their hands for you in their newspaper columns; if they know what their "humanitarian" measures are doing to you and support them anyway, they are hypocritical; and if they do not know, they are hopelessly ignorant of the economic facts of life.

As incentive continues to be smothered, Atlas is beginning to shrug. Businessmen more and more knuckle under to oppressive demands by government. It is now common for companies, particularly small ones, to comply with regulations out of coercion, realizing that to try to fight the regulatory bureaucracy is suicide. The number of businessmen who are simply giving up continues to increase, as they come to the conclusion that it is no longer worth the battle to stay in business. When too many producers give up, the pie will stop growing. And when the pie stops growing, there won't be any pieces left for *anybody*.

These regulatory "protectors of the ecology" and enemies of "business greed" are, as William Simon puts it, not "protectors of life, (but) . . . heralds of slow death." What is humanitarian about destroying the wealth-producing machinery that has brought us technological advancement and scientific discoveries that have made us the most advanced nation on earth?

Anything that is done to discourage business investment is bad for *everyone*. On that basis, business regulatory agencies would have to be classified as disastrous for *all* people. Are vote-conscious politicians aware of this obvious fact? As Simon further states, "It takes an immense resistance to logic and fact not to know that one cannot simultaneously control prices, inflate costs, ban production, increase taxes, grant counterproductive subsidies—and expect healthy, vigorous production to result."

Many politicians may be economically illiterate, but most are just hopelessly hooked on The Vote. As a result, government refuses to do what it needs to do to save the economy: totally disengage itself from economic matters. The more government neglects business, the better off the economy will be.

Senator Hayakawa, expressing deep concern over our

inability to rid ourselves of government intervention in the market, warns that "Washington is full of power-hungry mandarins and bureaucrats who distrust abundance, which gives people freedom, and who love scarcity and 'zero growth,' which give them power to assign, allocate, and control. If they ever win out, heaven help us!"

Man can survive pollution; environmentalists can relax about that. The question is whether he can survive regulation!

6

"Promoting the General Welfare"

Government Function Number Three is a sort of catchall function. It attempts to cover most of the other expedient desires of people, i.e., desires not directly related to matters of wealth and business. There is, of course, an overlap into these areas, but for the most part the function of "promoting the general welfare" covers moral desires outside the "wealth-is-evil" philosophy. Politicians are aware that the votes of many people can be won by promising to fulfill their expedient desires to impose their moral standards on others.

Any such attempts to do so obviously are flagrant violations of Natural Law, and anyone directly or indirectly involved in helping to carry out such violations is guilty of committing aggression. Yet virtually all regulations concerned with promoting the general welfare are, in reality, attempts to impose the moral desires of certain individuals or groups on others. Personal morality is not a very good guide for lawmaking, because men's ideas of morality change from place to place and time to time, so much that, as Will Durant says in paraphrasing Anacharsis, "if one were to bring together all customs considered sacred by some group, and were then to take away all customs considered immoral by some group, nothing would remain."

We have already discussed needs and desires versus morality, so we need not belabor the obvious point that it is immoral to force some people to abide by the desires of others—particularly moral desires.

And it certainly would be presumptuous, irrational and dogmatic—as well as immoral—to force the teachings of any religion on millions of others as a moral guide. A rational person realizes that it is unreasonable to attempt to base the law on religious beliefs, if for no other reason than because the tenets of Christianity, Judaism, Hinduism, Islamism, and all other religions contradict one another. Therefore, for one religion to be completely right, all others would have to be wrong. To complicate matters, different sects within each religion sharply disagree on fundamental issues (e.g., Methodists, Baptists, Catholics and Mormons are all Christians, but many of their doctrines are quite different).

Unfortunately, the reality is that it is human beings who determine by which moral standards other human beings should live, though it is true that some of them go so far as to claim that they are acting on the word of God. Aldous Huxley was skeptical of such claims, to say the least: "The gods are just. No doubt. But their code of law is dictated, in the last resort, by the people who organize society; Providence takes its cue from men." Enter Government Function Number Three.

There is a grave danger in putting men in a position to decide what is right and wrong. Yet that is the power we hand to politicians via The Vote. Through the workings of The System, the definition of sin becomes, as Bertrand Russell put it, "what is disliked by those who control education."

The term *general welfare* is meaningless for the same reasons that the definition of *good* as "that which is best for the greatest number of people" is meaningless. As pointed out in Chapter 2, every individual is unique in all respects; therefore, his welfare is enhanced by actions different than those which may be in the best interest of his neighbor.

Promoting the general welfare, then, translates into violating the natural rights of some people to satisfy the desires of others. Because, in reality, there is no such thing as "general" welfare; there is only individual welfare. And every individual should, and certainly has the natural right to, accept responsibility for his own welfare.

The fact remains that people's moral beliefs concerning matters of conduct, even when such conduct does not infringe on the rights of others, have been used as political tools by government since time immemorial. While this gives politicians "issues" to bandy about at election time, it causes deep-seated friction and hostilities among basically well-meaning people. Since every individual uses his own special circumstances, his own standard of ethics, and his own reasoning power to decide what is and is not moral, forcing him to abide by someone else's ideas of morality can only lead to ugly problems.

Those who insist on linking morals to the law invite unnecessary trouble. The desire to "save" people from themselves or to prevent them from doing things that other people feel are immoral is not sufficient cause for aggression. John Stuart Mill explained this point most eloquently over one hundred years ago in his essay "On Liberty."

> The sole end for which mankind are warranted, individually or collectively, in interfering with a liberty of action of any of their number, is self-protection. The only purpose for which power can be rightfully exercised over any member of a civilized community, against his will, is to prevent harm to others. His own good, either physical or moral, is not a sufficient warrant. He cannot rightfully be compelled to do or forbear because it will be better for him to do so, because it will make him hap-

pier, because, in the opinions of others, to do so would be wise, or even right.

Remember, a free person is one who is "not under the control or power of another." Freedom, in other words, is self-control. To the degree that one is controlled by others, he is enslaved. People living in relatively free countries may find it offensive to be told that they are enslaved to some extent, but I believe it is just that sort of blind attitude toward reality that has allowed the American Dream slowly to disintegrate.

All laws, therefore, that do not involve protecting individuals from aggression are laws that give government unwarranted power and control over citizens. To the degree that a man is restricted by such laws, he is not a free man. A person in India, for example, is not as free as a person in the United States, but is more free than a person in Ethiopia. Each of the three, however, is enslaved, but each to a different degree. It would therefore be just as correct to say that the people of the United States are the least enslaved people on earth as it would be to say that they are the freest people on earth.

All laws which criminalize conduct that does not involve aggression may be viewed as "victimless-crime laws." If there is no victim, there can be no crime. People who oppose victimless-crime laws tend to think only of laws prohibiting such things as "pornography," certain types of "drugs," various forms of consensual adult behavior regarding sex, and other obvious areas.

But victimless-crime laws—i.e., laws governing actions that involve no victim—must, by definition, include not only laws which prohibit certain noncoercive acts by individuals, but also laws which force people to *take* action against their will. Any control over a person's desire to act or *not* to act, other than to prevent him from aggressing against others, is unwarranted, since such action or nonaction does not harm anyone else.

The notion that someone is committing a crime because he does something to himself that others may believe to be immoral, self-endangering, or in some way harmful to him is ignorant, irrational and insulting. What actually happens to the person who insists on doing things which the "law" says are harmful to him is that the government will make him a victim of *its* aggression. In other words, he has aggressed on no one, but government may choose to aggress on him.

But laws that force an individual to *take* action against his will are just as bad as those which *prevent* him from taking action. In fact, they are worse, because these laws, in reality, *make* victims of those they force to take such involuntary action.

In either of the above cases, *external control* is exercised, as opposed to *self-control*. And external control of human beings is slavery, no matter how one tries to dress it up with respectable-sounding words.

All "crimes" other than crimes of aggression (crimes of aggression being crimes such as rape, murder, theft and fraud) must be categorized as victimless crimes. Whether laws keep you from exercising your will to do things you desire to do or force you to enter into situations against your will, they have one thing in common: they imply that the government, rather than you, owns your life.

And because legal authorities throughout the country spend billions of dollars stalking, bringing to trial, convicting, jailing and/or fining persons "guilty" of "crimes" against no one, police are too busy to protect taxpayers from *real* criminals. It has been estimated that the chances that an adult burglar will go to prison for any single burglary are less than 1%.[36]

COMPULSORY VICTIMLESS-CRIME LAWS

"Compulsory" victimless-crime laws are laws that force you to do certain things against your will. Can a man be defined as free if others can force him to do things involuntarily? Those who believe in Natural Law and who respect human rights believe that such a contradiction is impossible.

Examples:

—*The Draft.* No matter what name one ascribes to it, when a person is compelled to spend part of his life training for the military or, worse, risking his life in combat, he is a victim of involuntary servitude. The Selective Service System is a travesty on human rights. One may preach endlessly about the "duty to defend one's country," but the fact remains that conscription is slavery.

While enslavement can be made to seem respectable by the use of terms like "military duty" and "serving in the armed forces," words do not affect Natural Law; no one has the right to take a peaceable citizen away from his family and put him into a kill-or-be-killed situation against his will. The *desires* of some people to fight wars, or the *opinions* of some people that the draft is necessary to protect the country, are not sufficient grounds for violating anyone's human rights. (If one were to adhere to Natural Law, the only way in which the people of a nation could rightfully provide for a so-called national defense would be through the voluntary financial support of an all-volunteer army.)

The bodies of millions of innocent men which lie in military graves throughout the world serve as a monument to the true meaning of "promoting the general welfare." If government must make laws, it should pass a law requiring all congressmen who are in favor of war to lead the charge on the front lines.

—*Compulsory Education.* When a New Hampshire woman, Betsy Tompkins, recently was denied permission to educate her child at home, she joined thousands of others who have failed to convince the government that it is their right to educate their own children, or not to educate them at all, if that is their desire. Though Ms. Tompkins, like millions of other Americans, believed that the school system was not doing a satisfactory job of educating her daughter, when it came to a showdown, the government again made it clear that it owns everyone's life—including the lives of children.

Fortunately, Ms. Tompkins did not make the mistake of John Singer, a Utah man who was determined to demonstrate that government cannot force you to relinquish your children to its authorities. After a long legal battle, the government eliminated any doubt about its willingness to use force, when necessary, to make it clear to everyone that the lives of all men belong to the State. On January 18, 1979, Mr. Singer was killed by government "lawmen" on his own property. At the time, Singer was armed in last-resort preparation to defend his natural rights.

All Mr. Singer wanted was to educate his children his own way, without interference from the State, contending that he had a "God-given right to bring up his family the way he wanted." He did not feel that his children were getting the kind of religious and practical education he desired for them.

In addition to the repugnant immorality of government's claiming to own your child, compulsory education has been a disaster from the standpoint of results. Many children who might be better suited to learning a trade are forced to attend public schools, which explains why an estimated 13% of all high-school graduates are functional illiterates.[37] When a person is compelled to learn something, his mind tends to block it out. You can use physical force on people, but, as slave owners in early America discovered, you cannot force them to absorb thoughts.

Finally, there is the false notion that formal schooling is necessary in order for a person to be educated. A child learns when he plays, when his parents and others talk to him, and from everything he does in life. As he gets older, he learns through reading, through his job, and through conversations with others. I personally consider my formal schooling to have amounted to only a small fraction of my education.

Obviously, one of the reasons government insists on educating your child is so he will grow up learning history, philosophy and government itself from government's point of view.

—*Affirmative Action*. I have yet to hear anyone categorize "violations" of so-called affirmative-action laws as victimless crimes, but they most definitely are. These laws are another case of government's applying force to a situation of personal choice.

Supposedly free individuals are told that if they do not hire people whom the government says they must hire, they will be punished. Quotas for "minorities" have been established both for businesses and universities. Not only does affirmative action infringe on the freedom of employers and college administrators, but it creates another victim—the person who loses out on a job or college admission as a result; again, the only victims in this type of victimless crime are those created by government force.

While many people, particularly in government, would like to make the affirmative-action issue one that pertains only to blacks, the fact is that it is a *people* issue. Racism is not discrimination against any specific minority; it is discrimination against *anyone*. And the quota system— which has come to be known as "reverse discrimination"—is one of the most frustrating forms of discrimination.

What is particularly irritating about government meddling in this area is that both blacks and whites have rejected the concept of affirmative action in poll after poll. A Gallup poll in 1977 revealed that 64% of nonwhites interviewed rejected the idea of "preferential treatment" over "ability as determined by test scores," with an overall rejection ratio that exceeded 8 to 1. This presents a rather interesting question: If both blacks and whites are opposed to affirmative action, who *is* for it?

Thomas Sowell, a highly respected economics professor at UCLA, and himself a black, gives part of the answer in an article in the June 1978 issue of *Commentary:*

> . . . supporters of numerical policies have the powerful drive of self-interest as well as self-righteousness. Bureaucratic empires have grown up to administer these programs. . . . The rulers and agents of this empire can order employers around, make college presidents bow and scrape, assign schoolteachers by race, or otherwise gain power, publicity, and career advancement—regardless of whether minorities are benefited or not.

In other words, blacks, once again, have been used as political pawns, this time in the affirmative-action issue. It is just another appeal to people's Expediency Factors. Anne Wortham, a brilliant libertarian writer, and also a black, makes no qualms about it: "It is plainly not in the interest of black leaders and the State that blacks become individualistic, no more than it was in the interest of slaveholders that slaves learn to read and write."[88] In other words, if politicians and other power-hungry leaders were to lose the "black-versus-white" issue, it would not be in *their* best interest!

Affirmative-action laws not only are victimless-crime laws, and therefore immoral, but, in addition, they do not achieve their purported objectives. They do, however, achieve two other results: they create resentment and negative feelings among blacks and whites and they discourage blacks from self-reliance. Touching on some of these realities in a February 1979 article in *Reason* magazine, Ms. Wortham, who grew up in a segregated social system in Tennessee, states:

> During the first 20 years of my life . . . the federal government made five major advances in behalf of the civil rights of blacks. . . . With the possible exception of the right to vote, not one of these policies or the programs derived from them had any effect on my everyday life in segregated Tennessee. . . . Had my personal liberation and individuation depended on the knowledge that the State was in the process of increasing my civil liberty, I would have embarked on the road to adult maturity with no self-identity, self-respect, self-interest, self-sufficiency or self-initiative. . . . I would not be the person I am; I would not be such a passionate defender of human individuality and the philosophy of individualism.

A Rand Institute study supported the conclusions of black individualists like Ms. Wortham and Professor Sowell, noting, among other things, that "our results suggest that the effects of government on the aggregate black-white wage ratio is quite small and that the popular notion that . . . recent changes are being driven by government pressure has little empirical support."

What, then, is it that has allowed blacks to make important civil rights advances? Primarily, it has been the admirable actions of blacks themselves, particularly black leaders who have encouraged self-reliance. In truth, government force regarding such things as affirmative action and busing has created resentment and backlash, actually retarding the cause of freedom-loving blacks.

One of the most shining examples of what can be accomplished through peaceful means was the movement led by Martin Luther King, Jr., in the 1960's. King not only gave millions of blacks a new feeling of self-esteem, but, just as important, was successful in raising the consciousness of millions of whites to the injustices that blacks had endured over the years. While King's movement, in some instances, may indirectly have led to unwarranted forcible interference on the part of government, the real gains for blacks, as pointed out by Ms. Wortham and Professor Sowell, came as a result of their new feeling of pride and the emotional commitment on the parts of millions of whites.

What is particularly insulting to blacks about the quota system is that it implies that most minority-group members lack talent, which obviously is an irrational blanket judgment. Minority-group members, like everyone else, want respect—particularly self-respect—which does not come to them from being given special treatment for jobs and college admissions by virtue of government force. Says Professor Sowell:

> The message that comes through loud and clear is that minorities are losers who will never have anything unless someone gives it to them. The destructiveness of this message—on society in general and minority youth in particular—outweighs any trivial gains that may occur here and there. . . . By and large, the numerical approach has achieved nothing, and has achieved it at great cost.

Many black leaders, undoubtedly sincere in their intentions, make a grave mistake by calling for laws to force people to act against their wills. Some of them thoughtlessly accuse people of being racists if they are not in favor of affirmative action. But in reality it is they who advocate racism by calling for a clear distinction among blacks, whites, Mexican-Americans, etc., and by favoring special treatment for some people at the expense of the human rights of others. The fact that their ancestors were victims of slavery (i.e., external control by others) makes it ironic that they should wish to see men forced to act against their wills.

Affirmative action is morally wrong on at least three counts:

1) *No employer should be forced to hire anyone who either is not qualified for a job or is not as qualified as another applicant.* Such force is to the detriment of the employer's business.

2) *Innocent people should not be made to pay for the wrongs of others.* The mainstay argument behind affirmative action is that, since blacks were treated unfairly in the past, society now must conpensate new generations of blacks for that treatment. But how can men living today arbitrarily be held liable for the wrongdoings of people in the past? By the same token, why should members of a minority group receive special treatment today because other people were victims of discrimination in the past? Notes Professor Sowell:

> The past is a great unchangeable fact. *Nothing* is going to undo its sufferings and injustices, whatever their magnitude. . . . Neither the sins nor the sufferings of those now dead are within our power to change. Being honest and honorable with the people living in our own time is more than enough moral challenge, without indulging in illusions about rewriting moral history with numbers and categories.

3) But the most important reason that affirmative action is immoral is that *it defies Natural Law.* The owner of a business, whether black or white, has the right to hire and fire whomever he pleases, without having to account for his actions to anyone, simply because it is *his business.* When a person is not free to do as he pleases with his own property, in this case his business, his liberty has

been violated. It would be an unavoidable contradiction to refer to such a person as a free man.

Milton Mueller, in an article in *The Libertarian Review,* put the affirmative-action issue in proper perspective, noting that "affirmative action is the last gasp of a crumbling economic system." Mueller went on to say that:

> . . . if special exceptions and special laws are necessary to bulldoze minorities into the system, then something is clearly wrong with the *system*. If the regulations that burden the economy are so intrinsically racist that quotas are the only way to get minorities in, then something is wrong with the regulations. . . . A government-controlled economy is a static economy—the people on the bottom stay there. If the energies of a free, unrestricted economy are released, if the roadblocks are blown away, then minorities—and the rest of society—can advance.

—*Busing:* It is bad enough that Big Brother forces all citizens to send their children to school, but to make integration a function of the school system is preposterous. Schools are supposed to educate, not integrate. Busing is just another political weapon, and a very dangerous one: It implies that government can force people to change their emotions. And laws that attempt to regulate emotions never work.

Someone cannot unilaterally decide what is morally right or wrong, then go around cramming his ideas down the throats of his neighbors. Here again, a majority of both blacks and whites have let it be known that they are opposed to the wrongfulness of having their children shipped daily, like cattle, to distant areas of the cities. Professor Sowell contends that:

> Underlying the attempt to move people around and treat them like chess pieces on a board is a profound contempt for other human beings. To ignore or resent peo-

ple's resistance—on behalf of their children or their livelihoods—is to deny our common humanity. . . . The false practicality of results-oriented people ignores the fact that the ultimate results are in the minds and hearts of human beings.

As with all victimless-crime laws, the only victims involved in busing are those created by government. When a "busing law" is violated, the person found guilty of the violation is, in reality, not the perpetrator of a crime, but its victim. On the other hand, when these laws are obeyed, the children and parents involved, both black and white, become victims.

The concept of busing is particularly insulting to black children, because it implies that they must be surrounded by white classmates in order to achieve. The combination of both the aggression and insult inherent in busing has been an unnecessary political keg of dynamite planted under the feet of Americans.

—*Eminent Domain:* Back to the question of property rights once again. Through a very impressive-sounding term—*eminent domain*—government attempts to give respectability to the act of forcing people to give up their homes for the "general welfare." If the government decides that it wants your property, all other considerations are irrelevant—including the number of years you have owned your home or land, the emotional value it may have to you, and even what you think it is worth.

The fact that the government pays you for your property (at a price which *it* deems to be "fair") does not change the more important fact that your rights have been violated. If someone comes up to you on the street and demands your watch, then pays you what he deems to be a fair price in return, such payment does not change the reality that a theft has occurred.

As with all other victimless-crime laws, however, you

will be arrested and punished if you refuse to do as you are told by authorities—in this case, "sell" them your property. And if you try to defend your property physically, you will either end up in a jail or lose your life in the process.

History is filled with cases like that of Stephen E. Anthony, who refused to give up his half of a house to the government. Local politicians wanted to make room for a Hollywood film museum on his property. Anthony, who protected his property at gunpoint, eventually was arrested and put in jail for six months. A few months after his house was razed, the museum project was abandoned. The site of his former home is now a parking lot. Here again, the only victim in this "victimless" crime was the person victimized by the government itself—for refusing to give up what was rightfully his.

—*Seat Belts, Helmets and Other Protective Devices*. Millions of people do not use seat belts and therefore do not want to pay for them when purchasing a new car. Government, however, does not give the public an option on this extra. Everyone must pay for this protection even if the seat belts are never used and if they accomplish nothing more than flopping around on seats and causing discomfort to passengers.

Nevertheless, individuals who group themselves together under the banner of "consumer safety" still are not satisfied. They continue to campaign for the passage of a law which would force people to use the seat belts they already are compelled to buy.

Helmets and all other mandatory safety devices involve the same type of control over people. They force individuals to do what *others* believe to be in their best interests, even if they do not agree. Many motorcycle riders, for example, feel that helmets *cause* accidents by obstructing peripheral vision. But the motorcyclist is no different than anyone else: the government owns his life.

Because of their desire to capture the votes of "consumer-safety" advocates, helmet manufacturers, or anyone else who may be in favor of the compulsory use of "safety devices," politicians feel obliged to burden citizens with the cost and inconvenience of expensive equipment "for their own good."

PROHIBITIVE VICTIMLESS-CRIME LAWS

"Prohibitive" victimless-crime laws are laws which make it illegal for you to do certain things you may want to do. The same basic principle applies here as applies to compulsory victimless-crime laws; i.e., government prohibits your acting according to your will. Like compulsory victimless-crime laws, prohibitive victimless-crime laws involve external control and thus are forms of involuntary servitude.

Examples:

—*Gun Control.* Through the years there has been a great deal of heated debate over so-called gun-control legislation. Not only are all arguments that favor gun control invalid on the basic of logic, fact and morality, but even those who are *against* gun control usually miss the real issue. The issue is *freedom.*

A person has a right to own a gun for the same reason that he has a right to own *anything;* the corollary to this is that the government has no right to forbid anyone to own a gun, for the same reason that it has no right to forbid anyone to own *any* item. Gun control, therefore, is a misnomer. When politicians talk about gun control, they really are talking about people control.

Those who insisted on the Second Amendment to the Constitution—"the right of the people to keep and bear arms"—had important reasons for wanting this protection. Having been tyrannized by the government of Great Britain, they saw the right to bear arms not only as a means of protecting one's life and property from other citizens, but as a last resort of defense against an oppressive government. That is precisely why it is in the best interest of today's government to disarm the population. It has cleverly masked this violation of a Constitutional and natural right by appealing to the emotions of a frightened populace.

Owning guns has nothing to do with crime; if anything, it has to do with preventing crime. Notwithstanding their continual efforts to build a case against gun ownership, government legislators have failed in their attempts to show that gun control lowers crime rates; in almost all cases, in fact, the results of tests and studies have shown quite the opposite to be true.

The old slogan which maintains that "if guns are outlawed, only outlaws will have them," is a reality. Today, for example, it is illegal for most private citizens to carry concealed weapons. Law-abiding people, therefore, do not carry them. But you can be sure that *criminals* in every city in America are walking the streets carrying concealed weapons. Gun-control laws have the very real effect of giving criminals an advantage over noncriminals!

The view of government toward a citizen is that of a parent toward a child: "You mustn't carry guns, because you might accidentally hurt yourself or others." The assumption is that just because something *can* be used to harm someone, it *will* be used for that purpose.

Authorities estimated that approximately 9,000 people in the United States would be killed by handguns in 1979, which is an unfortunate fact of life. Nevertheless, this is only a small percentage of the number of people killed each year by automobiles. But the large number of automobile deaths is not sufficient cause to deny sensible, responsible individuals the use of automobiles. The exact same logic applies to guns; just because some people use guns negligently or for criminal purposes is no reason to deny prudent, honest people the right to own them.

Guns are a form of self-defense, and by removing a tool of self-defense from a man, government not only violates his rights, but endangers his very life. A gun is an individual's ultimate means of preserving his freedom; it may well be that there is a definite connection between government's stepped-up efforts toward gun control at a time when government itself is increasingly guilty of violating individual rights.

As Morgan Norval put it in an article in *Reason* magazine: " 'Order' may be the excuse; 'law' may be the argument; 'keeping someone else in his place' may be the emotional rationale; 'supporting the police' may be the civic slogan; 'ending violence' may be the dream—but the nightmare of reality is total tyranny of the state."

The right to bear arms should be defended to the bitter end. Because in the bitter end, as the American Revolutionists discovered, it may very well get down to a matter of whether or not you *do* have arms.

—*Zoning*. Remember, one of the true tests of ownership is whether or not you can do anything you want with your property. If you have to get government's permission to build the house of your choice, or even to do remodeling or put up a fence, how can you be called the owner of your property in the true sense of the word?

Aside from the moral implication of others telling you what you can and cannot do with something you own, the whole concept of zoning is based on the mythical vision of a vicious entrepreneur building a slaughterhouse adjacent to someone's $100,000 home.

For obvious economic reasons, this would never occur: Why would someone want to pay an enormous price for land on which to build a plant, when he could choose an industrial location at a fraction of the cost? Land prices negate the practical need for zoning laws. The beautiful city of Houston, with virtually no zoning laws, is living proof of why such laws are an unnecessary intrusion of privacy.

—*Usury.* The major effect of usury laws is somewhat analogous to the effect of minimum-wage laws. Minimum-wage laws force people to be unemployed; usury laws force people out of business. Because some voters think that "usury" (i.e., interest rates *they* deem to be too high) is immoral, politicians have burdened the public with yet another nuisance. They must protect the "innocent" citizen from being victimized by unscrupulous lenders.

No thanks. When I was down and out, I needed to borrow money badly, and I was a poor risk. When I did find people who were willing to lend me money at interest rates commensurate with the risk they were taking on me, we had to spend many days working out the legal details necessary to get around the law that "protected" me. Such time-wasting maneuvering goes on every day, particularly in the business world, between borrowers and lenders who must create legal facades to protect the lender from government usury laws.

Of course, banks and other lending companies with special government "licenses" are allowed to charge more than the official usury-law rate in most states; if government does not give them an outright exemption from usury laws, this is accomplished through special fees, "compensating balances" and a variety of other means.

—*Gambling.* Various voters conceive of gambling as "sinful," which gives politicians yet another opportunity to preach about "public morals." Gambling, of course, puts government in a slightly hypocritical position, since it does allow selected "licensees"—who give government a cut of the take—to conduct gambling operations.

Horse racing is licensed in most states, but only to privileged operators; this licensing arrangement contributes enormous revenues to state-government coffers. In Nevada, virtually all types of gambling are legal, and recently gambling was "legalized" in Atlantic City. Other states go further by operating the gambling apparatuses themselves, such as New York State's bookmaking facilities and the lotteries run by many state governments.

The rather strange implication is that gambling is immoral unless government is involved. Since every person who gambles loses money in the long run, I guess the reasoning is that citizens are protected so long as the government is the one who ends up with their money.

—*"Pornography."* "Pornography" is so subjective that it is an absolute absurdity for government to involve itself in this area. Obscenity, like everything else, is in the eyes of the beholder. The libertarian approach here, the same as to all victimless crimes, is best expressed by Murray Rothbard:

"The good, bad, or indifferent consequences of pornography, while perhaps an interesting problem in its own right, is completely irrelevant to the question of whether or not it should be outlawed. . . . It is not the business of the law . . . to make anyone good or reverent or moral or clean or upright."[40]

—*Sexual Behavior.* Government interference in the sexual behavior of consenting adults is one of the most flagrant violations of individual liberty. The idea that government has a right to say what goes on in your bedroom should make even the most unconcerned person think twice before laughing at the suggestion that we are beset with "creeping totalitarianism."

It is irritating even to have to argue for the rights of people to engage voluntarily in sexual acts of their choosing, because it dignifies the incredible gall of absolute moralists who believe they should have a say-so in the most private affairs of others. If you believe in the right of individuals to control their own lives, then you know that the sexual conduct of consenting adults is not the government's business and should not carry legal consequences. Big Brother has no place in the regulation of private conduct—period.

—*"Drugs."* Probably no other promoting-the-general-welfare function of government causes so many innocent people (including non-users of drugs) so many problems. As happens with virtually all outlawed products and services, government, by prohibiting the use of certain drugs, creates a black market for them.

As soon as something is outlawed, criminal elements will gladly jump in and provide the illegal product or service at substantially increased prices. The higher prices are due not only to the scarcity of the product or service, but also to the seller's need to be compensated for the government-created risks involved. These high prices motivate some consumers of such products and services, particularly "drugs," to commit crimes against innocent people in order to raise the money needed to obtain them.

Aside from the basic point that it is not government's business to run around protecting people from hurting themselves, "harmful drugs," like "pornography," cannot even be defined. Marijuana is outlawed in most states, though many experts believe it to be relatively harmless; yet people can consume all the caffeine they want, even though this "drug" is considered extremely harmful by many doctors.

Alcohol is another substance that is much more harmful than many others that have been outlawed, and indeed government once spent billions of dollars of taxpayers' money in a vain effort to stop people from drinking it. The result, of course, was that people drank *more* during Prohibition than at any other time in U.S. history.

Now people are free to put as much alcohol as they want into their bodies, and some may even consume so much that they virtually kill themselves in the process. But the reality is that people also kill themselves by consuming too much cholesterol. Does this mean that government should outlaw foods containing cholesterol? Where does it end?

I have no personal axe to grind regarding any of these substances, because I rarely indulge even in a social drink and have never taken so much as a puff of marijuana. These are products which just happen not to be of interest to me. But, just as I do not go running to the government over the quality of television programming, neither do I insist that government stop others from "harming" themselves by the use of certain "drugs." I figure I have a full-time job keeping *myself* in line.

Being against restrictions on the use of drugs does not mean that one approves of the use of cocaine, heroin, laetrile or any other substance. On the contrary, I consider it very unwise and unhealthy to use such substances indiscriminately. But the fact is that their use is not a political matter; it is a *private* matter.

Who would protect children from the harmful use of drugs in a free society? The same people who are supposed to protect them from touching a hot stove, getting run over by cars, or committing crimes against others: *parents*.

One thing certain is that government certainly does a poor job of it. The fact is that the finest work done in the area of drug rehabilitation has been accomplished, as one would expect, by *private* charitable organizations. Individuals can solve problems just fine—even "community problems"—if left alone to do so on a noncoercive basis.

It is time for Big Brother to get out of our private lives and off our backs and let us fend for ourselves. Self-responsibility was a major ingredient in the American Dream.

—*Smoking*. Most of the same points made in regard to

anti-drug laws are equally valid for anti-smoking ordinances. There is, however, one additional twist to anti-smoking laws: Some nonsmokers claim that they do not care if others smoke, so long as they do not do it in a "public place."

The problem here is the curious latitude people use in defining the term *public place*. A restaurant is one outrageous and commonly used example, yet a restaurant is a *privately* owned establishment. As such, its owner has the sole right to decide whether or not to allow people to smoke on his premises. If he chooses to allow it and a nonsmoker (like me) is bothered by the smoking, the nonsmoker can take immediate noncoercive steps to do something about it—on his own—simply by not frequenting that restaurant in the future.

On the other hand, if the owner does not allow smoking, a smoker either can refrain or he can take his business elsewhere; there is no need for the heavy hand of the law. Free men can settle differences by respecting each other's rights, especially property rights.

The "U.S. Surgeon General" may believe that smoking is dangerous to your health, and government can even force tobacco manufacturers to print such a statement on cigarette packs, but apparently millions of people still prefer to make their own decisions regarding their well-being. The continued increase in cigarette sales, in spite of government anti-smoking efforts, makes this point quite clear.

Should anti-smoking crusaders ever succeed in having smoking outlawed, look for organized crime to set up an elaborate black market in cigarettes that will make the days of Prohibition look like a nursery-school game by comparison. Smokers will continue to smoke; you can be sure of that. The question is whether smoking will be controlled by private industry or organized crime.

—*Suicide.* There is virtually nothing to say on this subject, except to point out the ridiculous fact that suicide is actually against the law in some states. The right to take your own life is perhaps the ultimate test of whether or not you own it. In outlawing suicide, government makes it absolutely clear that your life belongs to the State and that therefore only the State has the right to decide what will be done with it.

PRIVACY: LOST FOREVER?

As is true of the first two government functions, the aggression that is couched under the benevolent guise of "promoting the general welfare" continues to grow each year. People are becoming more and more complacent, accepting Big Government interference in their lives as normal. Consider:

—The Bank Secrecy Act (a deliberate reverse description of its effects) requires that you file detailed reports with the government any time you take more than $5,000 cash out of or into the country.

—You not only need a passport to travel, but must fill out detailed reports naming your destinations, your original point of embarkation, the nature of your business, how long you will be away, and many other personal details of your trip.

—A federal appeals court in St. Louis ruled that the government has the right to break into an unoccupied office to install electronic devices if a judge deems that to be the only "reasonable way" to obtain evidence and issue warrants.

—Pacific Telephone & Telegraph Co. admitted that it routinely releases unlisted telephone numbers of private citizens to the CIA, the military, the governor's office, and other governmental agencies and branches.

—The CIA and FBI have virtually unrestricted access to all of your tax information.

——The government has an incredible average of 18 files on each man, woman and child in the United States![41]

Was all this what our founding fathers had in mind when they threw out those oppressive rascals from England? I think not. Certainly not in the history I have read. I believe, in fact, that they had just the opposite of Government Function Number Three in mind when they signed the Declaration of Independence.

Can these violations of freedom be stopped? Not unless an awful lot of people get educated to the facts very quickly and get very mad about the situation. So long as millions of citizens play right into the government's hands and demand that their expedient moral desires be met, the number of victimless-crime laws—under the guise of "promoting the general welfare"—will continue to increase, along with invasion of privacy, which means a *decrease* in freedom.

Far from stemming the tide of this coercive government function, it appears that things are speeding up considerably in the direction of *more* government control over the lives of individual citizens.

7

How the Bill Is Paid

Alas it comes time to pay the bill. The government functions created by the calamitous combination of Expediency Factors and The Vote now represent an annual cost that is astronomical. For the sake of brevity, there are countless areas I have not gone into, such as the billions of dollars government spends on armaments, foreign aid, and grants for various absurd and wasteful projects. Nor have I mentioned the billions lost through outright fraud in government agencies and programs.

What is the tab? It depends upon when you happen to be reading this book. At last count, it was running in the neighborhood of $500 billion a year; that's nearing the level of $1.5 billion a day; which is roughly $60 million every hour, $1 million per minute, or more than $16,000 per second!

If you like growth, you should love the federal budget. It has grown 15,000%—that's *15,000%*—in the past fifty years.[42] But don't be misled into thinking that such growth has been steady or normal; the acceleration of the growth has been phenomenal. Since the mid-1960's alone, federal expenditures have nearly tripled.

It turns out, then, that government's overall objective to "help people fulfill their desires" is just a bit on the expensive side—and getting more so each year. Since governments have no way of producing wealth, such generosity must be paid for with wealth produced by others. Governments, as previously noted, exist off the surplus wealth of citizens, which means violating the rights of those who do produce wealth. This comes about through a well-structured process of expropriation of assets.

This process, referred to for thousands of years under a name—"taxation"—that avoids its true description, presents a philosophical dilemma for millions of well-meaning, honest citizens. It is instructive to note that, among the many dictionary definitions, a "tax" is described as: "a heavy demand"; "a burden"; "a *compulsory* payment of a percentage of income . . . for the support of a government." [*Italics added*.] All of these sound rather unpleasant, but the real heart of the matter, and what causes the philosophical dilemma, is the word *compulsory*.

If something is compulsory, it means you are *forced* to do it. And the use of force is a violation of Natural Law; it is the act of aggressing on a person's rights. While the sound of the word may make some people wince, the hard reality is that taxation is *theft*. While one may believe, however irrationally, that the end (that for which "taxes" are used) justifies the means ("taxation"), this still does not change the fact that taxation is the act of stealing. Until a person is prepared to face up to this, he is refusing to acknowledge reality.

Assuming one is honest enough with himself to acknowledge this reality, the philosophical question becomes one of morality. And that takes us back to the early part of this book and to Natural Law: personal integrity demands that one's belief in Natural Law not be betrayed on an emotional whim. Just as all government functions we have discussed violate human rights, so too does the means of paying for these functions. No matter how much good certain people may believe is accomplished with "tax" money, the good can never negate the immorality of theft. You cannot change the nature of stealing by calling it taxation and by explaining that it is a patriotic means of "raising revenue."

To argue that government gives people services in return for the money it expropriates from them is, of course, irrelevant for the same type of reason explained in connection with "eminent domain" in the last chapter. If someone takes your money at gunpoint in an alley, but gives you something in return that you either do not want or did not bargain for, it does not make him any less a robber.

Of course, street robbers never give you back anything in return, which is somewhat of an advantage over government. When a thief puts a gun to your head in an alley and says, "Your money or your life," he does not pretend, like the government, to be doing anything but robbing you. He does not claim to be your "protector" or offer you services that you did not ask for and do not want.

Best of all, after he robs you, the ordinary thief goes away and leaves you alone. He does not insist on "protecting" you or demand that you be loyal to him. He does not try to impose his moral standards on you or forbid you to do anything. If you do not obey him, he does not call you unpatriotic or apathetic. With government, you have all the disadvantages of being robbed, but none of the advantages of being robbed by a professional thief.

One of the emotional arguments of the "patriot" who cannot bear to hear his benevolent Uncle referred to as a thief is to insist that, unlike a common robber, the government does not go around sticking guns in the ribs of taxpayers. And he is right. That is because most people either have been conditioned to accept "taxation" as a way of life or because they realize it is futile to resist; therefore, there is no need for the use of guns.

If, however, you suffer from the delusion that Uncle Sam will not use guns to force you to hand over what he deems to be your share of the bill, try defending your assets to the absolute end. By "absolute end," I mean literal self-defense, involving whatever is necessary to protect your assets.

If you refuse to pay, you will receive notices at first, which will get progressively more threatening. Assuming you do not have property on which the IRS can file a lien (which is, in itself, an act of aggression), it ultimately will pay you a visit. If you refuse to talk to the IRS agents when they appear at your door, they will obtain a court order for your arrest. And that in turn will bring gentlemen with guns to your front door. If you try to use physical force to defend yourself against this aggression, these men will—if necessary—kill you, just as they killed Mr. Singer, who tried to defend his right to educate his own children.

Never deceive yourself about the gunpower that stands behind taxation. Were it not there, governments would be powerless to continue stealing. Because the physical force behind taxation was established long ago, it rarely needs to be used—or even discussed. Instead, politicians can concentrate on dressing up taxation's image by inundating citizens with slogans like "pay your fair share."

The man who thinks it unpatriotic to call taxation theft either has forgotten the American Dream or is too young to have experienced it. The American Dream was not about government's taking huge sums of money from citizens by force. The American Dream was not about government's "using all its power and resources to meet new social problems with new social controls."

The American Dream was about *people*, not government. It was about people who, for the first time in history, declared that they were *above* government. It was about individualism and the *opportunity* to achieve success without interference from others. Most of all, the American Dream was about *freedom*.

On the contrary, the last thing in the world that the American Dream was about was taxation.

WHO PAYS HOW MUCH?

When the Sixteenth Amendment to the Constitution became law in 1913, an important step was taken in laying the groundwork for the destruction of the spirit that had made America the freest, strongest and most prosperous country in history. We need not go into the technicalities here except to point out that the powerholders of that day arbitrarily decided (as they do through all Amendments) to take away a right guaranteed by the Constitution.

The key element in the Sixteenth Amendment was that it gave government the power, for the first time, to levy taxes against incomes. Just as important, it left the interpretation of the word *income* up to the courts, which meant that from that point on the rules could be changed at the discretion of the government.

As taxes mounted and the something-for-nothing attitude of the 1920's began to destroy productivity, the Great Depression befell America. That in turn brought us Franklin D. Roosevelt, who took the next giant step in helping to destroy the American Dream. This was accomplished through implementation of his politically expedient "soak-the-rich" policy of taxation. The result of this policy was the birth of the anything-goes attitude that is so prevalent in our society today, as well as the economically destructive idea of cradle-to-grave security.

Lyndon Johnson put the final cornerstone of the new philosophy in place, assuring us that we could have guns, butter, and anything else we desired—without even having to work for them. How could we resist? At last, the American Dream had been replaced by the "Great Society!"

Like Roosevelt, Johnson did not live to have to face today's taxpayers. And very few Americans understood that *they,* not Roosevelt or Johnson, were going to have to pay the bill some day. In fact, only a handful of the most economically sophisticated individuals realized that a bill was even accumulating. No one had bothered to tell them. Now, as the Expediency Factors of irate voters motivate them to scramble for a bigger share of the stolen loot in order to keep up with the game, government expenditures at the federal, state and local level continue to rise even higher, notwithstanding the threat of economic collapse.

As pointed out in Chapter 4, soaking the rich does not work anymore, and really never did (for reasons previously discussed). Today, though politicians still love to preach about the "injustices" of our tax system, the fact is that 75% of the total federal income-tax take is paid by 25% of the taxpayers; the other 75% of the people carry only 25% of the load.[48] And the biggest share of all is paid by the huge, artificially created Middle Class; there is no one else to turn to.

Income taxes, of course, are only a part of the story. The wild scramble among politicians and voters to increase government functions would be impossible to sustain through income taxes alone—particularly because the payment would be too visible to voters. So, along the way, government has thought up a few other methods by which to tax people, many of them very subtle and thus not so apparent to voters. Some of these "other ways" include excise taxes, sales taxes, amusement taxes, gasoline taxes, liquor taxes, cigarette taxes, real-estate taxes, Social-Security taxes, inventory taxes, capital-gains taxes, inheritance taxes, corporate-income taxes, excess-profits taxes, gift taxes, and estate taxes.

Then there are the *very* subtle taxes. A "tariff" is one example. When you buy an imported product, you indirectly reimburse the exporter of the product for the tariff (tax) he was forced to pay on it.

An even more subtle tax is the free labor contributed by every taxpayer in complying with government tax forms and, in the case of employers, extracting taxes from employees on behalf of the government. If this innocuous-sounding little gesture does not seem like a big thing to you, it should interest you to know that the U.S. Controller's office itself estimates that it takes about 613 million man-hours a year to comply with its requirements for reporting and recording tax information.

If you add to this the man-hours necessary to comply with business regulations, as discussed in Chapter 5, the total equals more man-hours than it takes to produce all of the cars and trucks put out by General Motors each year. In other words, hidden slave-labor taxes alone, in the form of man-hours, would be more than enough to operate the largest company in the country!

In discussing who pays Uncle Sam's annual bill, it is important to point out one other reality: Business taxes (including the cost of complying with tax forms and recording) are, for the most part, paid for by consumers. The fact that the consumer always pays increased business costs may be starting to sound monotonous, but, unfortunately, it is true.

Businesses merely pass along tax increases to consumers in the form of higher prices—and for good reason: If they did not, they would soon go broke. Business taxes are a great scheme for politicians, however, because they are hidden taxes to consumers; as a result, the average person blames greedy businessmen for high prices, not realizing that he really is being taxed (indirectly) by government.

All of these subtle and hidden taxes are impossible to calculate, so no one can be sure just how much anyone is paying to support government functions. But there is enough data available to give you at least a rough idea of where you stand. The average American worker pays about 45% of his income in *direct* taxes of various kinds.[44] The average taxpayer now works until well into May each year for the government, or approximately one-third of his life (about one-half of his working life) without compensation.[45]

No matter what one's opinions regarding the necessity of government functions, how can twenty years of labor without pay be called anything but slavery?

PROTECTING YOUR ASSETS

Is there any way to stop this theft? The outlook for putting an end to taxation on a nationwide scale is not bright. While it is true that you have a moral right to protect the fruits of your labor from *any* robber, whether it calls itself a street gang or a government, hard reality dictates that "tax evasion" is an unwise move. The question here is not one of morality, but of practicality. The IRS does not hesitate to check private records (such as bank accounts), search offices, use blackmail (as do all government enforcement agencies), threaten, and, ultimately, institute physical force if necessary.

Though the entire system of taxation is a shameful transgression of human rights, I would strongly advise anyone against resorting to so-called tax evasion (i.e., trying to protect your assets by not volunteering their existence to the entity that wants to take them from you). Tax evasion is particularly dangerous for high-income earners, whom the government monitors closely.

It goes without saying, however, that one is morally obligated to himself and his family to use every available "legal" method to avoid paying taxes. Certainly you should not be intimidated into going out of your way to help Uncle Sam take your money by responding to government-manufactured slogans or "shame" words. You are not a "crook" for finding every "legal" way possible to avoid paying taxes. You are not "unpatriotic" for keeping government theft to a minimum by taking every authorized deduction you can find.

In our upside-down society, where theft has come to be accepted as moral, a person is chastised for having used a "loophole" or having "received" a "windfall" when he protects his assets by playing by the very rules set up by the robber. In reality, a "tax evader" who goes to prison is a poor soul who is being punished for having tried to protect his assets.

In view of the risks involved, it is astonishing that various sources have estimated the number of people refusing to file tax returns at between 4 million and 15 million.[46] Since government relies heavily on the cooperation of a trusting public to calculate and submit a specified portion of its income in the form of taxes, it is no wonder that such a statistic concerns the IRS. Said the director of the agency's criminal division, Thomas J. Clancy, "If the public sees a small group getting away with not paying, very soon others would lose faith in the system, and voluntary compliance goes to hell—people quit paying."[47]

Had the average American taxpayer read the works of Lysander Spooner, perhaps he might have thought twice before being so trusting. Said Spooner, "Whoever desires liberty should understand . . . that every man who puts money into the hands of a 'government' (so called), puts into its hands a sword which will be used against himself, to extort more money from him."

Today the most publicized way of trying to cut back on oppressive taxation is the Proposition 13-type tax revolt. In passing Proposition 13, the voters of California deserve to be commended for a valiant attempt at the seemingly impossible task of stemming Big-Government spending. Understanding the realities, however, I felt almost a sense of dejection as I listened to well-meaning, enthusiastic "tax revolters" celebrate the passage of Proposition 13 and refer to it as only the "first step." I would like to believe they are right, but . . .

Observing the effects of "tax cuts" over the years has led me to coin a hypothesis I refer to as the *Tax-Cut Illusion Theory*. While hardly rating in complexity with Einstein's Theory of Relativity, it is just as dependable. Very simply, it states: All tax cuts are illusions! There is no such thing as a tax cut; there is only a change in the manner in which the money is extracted from taxpayers.

Were this not true, all of us would be paying less in taxes than we were ten or twenty years ago. Think of all the "tax cuts" we have been blessed with during that time. In 1979, for example, there was an $18.7 billion federal-income-tax cut. But most taxpayers will pay *more* taxes in 1979, because Social-Security taxes were simultaneously increased (not to mention that falsely inflated wages may have pushed earners into higher tax brackets).

The fact that all tax cuts have to be an illusion is based on the realities of The System, as discussed in Chapter 2: Sammy *has to steal*—not less, but more each year in order to keep up with his expedient promises to give more of everything to everybody without their having to work for it.

I should also mention here a type of tax rebellion that is the most commonly practiced, though most of those who engage in it are not consciously aware of it. It is also the method most destructive to our economy. I refer to it as the loss-of-incentive tax revolt.

As taxes become an increasing burden on producers, they lose incentive; such people opt to produce less and enjoy life more. When a person lowers his ambitions, he lowers his income. This is the taxpayer's last-resort method of keeping Sammy's confiscation to a minimum; short of the institution of a police state, government has no way of making people work harder or longer hours.

This increasing phenomenon in the United States can

be viewed in its more advanced stage in ultra-socialist Sweden. Swedes commonly refuse promotions, but take more and more vacation time. A Swedish citizen's income theoretically can be taxed up to 103%, but taking vacations and enjoying life are not taxable.

The Swedish government has figured out that if a married man with four children has earnings of $4,600, he will end up with $14,117 of net income (after subtracting taxes and adding in government transfer payments); if the same man earns *five times as much,* or about $23,000, his after-tax net income would still be about $14,000.[48] Would *you* work much harder and longer to earn five times as much if you knew your net income would remain the same?

The reason this latter type of tax revolt is so devastating to the economy is not just that an increasing number of people produce less, but, in addition, that it "forces" government to increase taxes on those who do continue to produce. Back to the blackboard: higher taxes mean lower profits and/or higher prices, which decreases demand, which decreases production, which decreases employment, etc., etc., etc. The laws of economics never change.

I will sum up taxation by saying that I agree (although for different reasons) with Jimmy Carter's observation, made during his 1976 campaign for the presidency, that our tax structure is "a disgrace to the human race." *All* taxation is a disgrace—a violation of property rights, which means a violation of human rights. Politicians love to talk about "tax abuses" and the fact that they must be stopped. Again I agree: *all* taxes are an abuse and *all* taxes should be stopped.

THE RED-INK SEA

Believe it or not, if the taxation just described were our only problem, we might make it. We would still be victims of theft, and certainly not totally free men and women, but we probably could continue stumbling along with remnants of the American Dream to sustain us. Unfortunately, however, taxation is not the only problem when it comes to paying the bill; it is not even the worst problem.

A bigger problem (or at least the thing that causes the biggest problem) is that government, in the words of John Hospers, has been "for more than four decades (on) a drunken orgy of spending," so much so that not even the incentive-draining confiscation of all tax measures combined can keep up with it. Taxes can no longer be increased rapidly enough to meet the costs of the gourmet banquet and all of government's other "functions" and "services."

The result is a massive sea of what accountants refer to as "red ink"; i.e., *deficits*. A deficit, plain and simple, means that a person's income is less than his expenses. If such a person continues to run up expenses in excess of his income, he is guilty of a practice known as "deficit spending." I tried it a few times when I was younger and bolder, and I went out of business; everyone I know who has tried it has gone out of business. But does this deter government? No. Why? Because deficit spending is a way for politicians to vote for programs that are popular with voters—without raising taxes.

Now let us examine where that puts the U.S. Government (as well as you and me) at this time: The "official" federal deficit is approaching $1 *trillion,* but that does not include the billions of dollars owed by such agencies as the TVA, the Export-Import Bank, and the Federal Home Loan Board. More important, it does not include the combined $5 + trillion (no one knows the exact total) Social Security and government-pension obligations, not to mention the official total liabilities of the government—$15.6 trillion (which includes future liabilities computed on an actuarial basis)—as listed by the Department of the Treasury. The interest alone on the acknowledged national debt (total deficit) now runs in the area of $50 to $60 billion a year, or about $1 billion a week!

This mean, theoretically, that you and every other taxpayer in this country owes anywhere from $100,000 to $200.000 (depending on whose figures you use), an amount for which you probably were not aware you were obligated.

Deficit spending has always been used by politicians, but usually with some degree of discretion (perhaps sanity would be a more appropriate word). As previously noted, however, Lyndon Johnson, afflicted with a severe case of kingitis, was carried away by delusions of a "Great Society"—a society so great that it could spend $200 billion on a no-win war in Vietnam, feed the "poor" at home, and satisfy the expedient desires of virtually everyone in America, all without producing anywhere near an equivalent amount of wealth. Johnson started the momentum of a new era of pre-election deficit spending that no president since has had the courage to stop.

I use the term *"pre-election" deficit spending,* because initially it was a scheme designed to ensure reelection for an incumbent president. Deficit spending has the short-term effect of stimulating the economy, which makes the reigning administration look good. But it is an illusion; what people actually experience from deficit spending is false prosperity. They do not understand that the goodies they receive have not been paid for; i.e., that they have unknowingly accepted goods and services on credit.

As Morgan Maxfield relates in *1929 Revisited,*

Johnson started the ball rolling with an unprecedented pre-election 1967–68 deficit of $34 billion. After a $.4 billion surplus in 1969–70 (*post*-election years), Richard Nixon went all out in the pre-election years 1971–72 with a $46 billion deficit. But by now people were getting hooked on false prosperity; they did not want to hear about economic realities.

As a result, even in the post-election years 1973–74, the deficit was $17.8 billion. But expediency-minded voters screamed bloody murder at the new president, Gerald Ford. How dare he cut back on handouts. So Ford, the theretofore fiscally conservative politician, let loose with a pre-election spending barrage in 1975–76 that just about sealed our fate: an incredible $110 billion!

With this record-breaking injection of false prosperity, deficit spending had developed into a virtually incurable disease. What started out as a pre-election-year scheme had become a year-in-year-out political necessity. Americans were addicted; they needed their "fixes" on a continual basis. As a result, Carter came right out of the starting gate in 1977–78, topping even Ford's pre-election effort by running up another record high deficit of $118 billion. It now appears as though no politician has the courage (or good sense) to perform the necessary surgery to put the disease in a state of remission.

Obviously, no entity can continue in business indefinitely without paying its debts. So how does government cover these massive deficits? They cannot be paid through direct taxation, because voters already are rebelling against onerous taxes. Thus government is left with only two ways to cover deficit expenditures.

PONZI SCHEME II

Earlier I pointed out that the Social-Security system was but a sophisticated version of the so-called Ponzi

Scheme. But in addition to Social Security, government implements the Ponzi Scheme to cover its deficit spending. The U.S. Treasury sells securities (usually in the form of bonds) to the private market to raise as much capital as possible to offset each year's deficits. There is no plan whatsoever to pay off these securities, other than through the sale of new securities. In the meantime, the interest obligations keep rising, and, as previously noted, are now running at the rate of about $1 billion a week. It does not take a degree in advanced mathematics to figure out that at some point in time the interest payments alone will exceed the total wealth-producing capacity of all U.S. citizens combined.

On top of all this, there is a side effect to Ponzi Scheme II that hastens the Economic Day of Judgment. When the government sells bonds to the public, it drains funds from the capital markets of the country. Much of this is money that would have been used to finance new plants, equipment, and research and development. The effect of government borrowing on the economy, then, is that it removes the lifeblood (capital) that is essential for production and employment.

The figures here, too, are astounding. Between 1946 and 1966, the government was borrowing an average of a little over one-half of 1% of the funds available in the capital market, or about $500 million a year. By 1975–76, the government was draining about *150 times* as much from the capital markets—38% or about $74 *billion* per year. As the U.S. deficit continues to climb, it eventually will become impossible to sell enough new bonds to pay off old ones, not to mention paving the annual interest obligations on the total national debt.

But, even worse, increasing government bond sales will render the economy increasingly unable to earn the wealth necessary to avoid a total financial collapse. This is one of the main reasons that the U.S. productivity-growth rate has dropped to virtually zero, and why we are now last in productivity-growth rates among all Western nations.

I hope all this has not upset you to the point where you can't take any more bad news. Because, hard as it may be for you to believe, the worst is yet to come. The government, "unfortunately," is not able to sell all the bonds it would like to sell in the open market, so it still comes up short. Even after exhausting the capital markets, Uncle Sam does not raise enough dollars to cover his massive deficit spending.

Of course, he could choose to end the policy of deficit spending (i.e., stop spending more than he can steal and borrow), but it's too late for that. The expedient desires of politicians to stay in office and the Expediency Factors of 220 million Americans have hooked up to form a self-destructing, economic nuclear bomb. The charade of false prosperity must go on.

After stealing and borrowing to the maximum of his capacities, there is only one place left for Uncle Sam to turn to cover the remainder of his unpaid bills: the printing presses!

THE INFLATION SWINDLE

The remaining portion of the federal deficit each year is paid for by a process that sounds like it is right out of Aesop's Fables: government merely prints up pieces of paper and uses them as money. But that's getting ahead of the story. In order to understand the mechanics of this sinister act, and to be fully aware of what this fairy-tale approach to fiscal matters really means, it is first necessary to explain some basics.

At the outset of this book I said that I could not resist the challenge to reduce the truths about Big Government to components so simple that they would be clear to virtually everyone. In that respect, this chapter is the highlight of the book for me. For inflation is the one government scheme above all others, that must be demystified if the American Dream is to be restored. I am convinced that only a very small percentage of the population has even the vaguest idea of what inflation really is and what causes it.

Among those who apparently do *not* understand inflation (and I make this assumption based on their own explanations) are a majority of economists, bankers, businessmen and politicians. (It is hard to be certain about politicians; some do speak out of genuine ignorance, while others intentionally try to mislead the public.)

I do not claim to be in an academic class with the likes of Henry Hazlitt or Murray Rothbard on the subject of inflation. I do, however, propose to impart to the reader in the simplest possible terms what I have learned from them and others on their academic level. For that reason, I have purposely avoided detail which I felt was not essential to a basic understanding of inflation. If you wish to pursue the subject further, however, I highly recommend many of their works, particularly Murray Rothbard's *What Has Government Done to Our Money?* and *The Case for a 100 Percent Gold Dollar,* and Henry Hazlitt's *The Inflation Crisis, And How to Resolve It* and *Economics in One Lesson.*

How important do I consider the challenge to explain inflation in easy-to-understand terms to be? It is my sincere belief that if a majority of the people in this country do not soon understand the true facts about inflation (which are virtually the *opposite* of what most people have been led to believe through government propaganda), our country will, in the near future, experience a total financial collapse, which in turn will result in the loss of most, if not all, of our remaining freedom.

I believe this collapse could occur as early as within the next five years (if, say, a Ted Kennedy gains the presidency) or as late as twenty-five to thirty years from now. The reason for the wide range of time is that government has the power, unlike a normal bankrupt business, to institute one illegal measure after another to postpone such a collapse. That is, in fact, exactly what it has been doing for many years via the printing of counterfeit money and by the arbitrary passage of laws which keep changing the rules of the game; these rule changes are specifically designed to shift the blame from the real culprit—government—to innocent parties.

"Inflation is the biggest killer of civilizations," says John Hospers, "even more than war itself." From the Sung dynasty in China a thousand years ago to the famous German runaway inflation of the early 1920's, the real executioner was inflation.

Again I say that it is not so much that people do not learn the lessons of history, as they do not *understand* those lessons. "Each generation and country," says Henry Hazlitt, "follows the same mirage. Each grasps for the same Dead Sea fruit that turns to dust and ashes in its mouth. For it is the nature of inflation to give birth to a thousand illusions."[49]

As a final preface to my explanation of this universally misunderstood subject, I reprint here, from an *Atlantic Monthly* article by Adam Smith (i.e., today's pen-named Adam Smith, George Jerome Goodman), a description by Pearl Buck of the devastation wrought upon the German people by the runaway inflation of 1923. (Buck's report was quoted in Fritz Ringer's *The German Inflation of 1923*.)

> The cities were still there, the houses not yet bombed and in ruins, but the victims were millions of people. They had lost their fortunes, their savings; they were dazed and inflation-shocked and did not understand how it had

happened to them and who the foe was who had defeated them. Yet they had lost their self-assurance, their feeling that they themselves could be the masters of their own lives if only they worked hard enough; and lost, too, were the old values of *morals,* of *ethics,* of decency. [*I have added the italics to emphasize the important nonfinancial results of inflation which are rarely discussed.*]

Like all other financial collapses brought about by inflation, the German hyperinflation brought with it a strong-willed savior who ended the resulting chaos by clamping down on freedom. His name: Adolf Hitler. Likewise, the French assignat inflation of the late 1700's helped bring to power another ironfisted dictator, Napoleon Bonaparte.

I have no desire to live under a totalitarian regime headed by a Hitler or a Napoleon. I have no desire to live under a totalitarian regime headed by *anyone*—not even an American politician. That is my inspiration for writing this book and my inspiration for writing this chapter.

Paul Johnson, in *A History of Christianity*, has formulated Goebbels' Law in a way that fits the inflation swindle perfectly: "The louder the abuse, the bigger the lie." The lies that government has spread about inflation are beyond belief. That is because inflation is the greatest abuse imaginable. The money/inflation scheme of government is so incredible that it defies imagination. Which is exactly why this gigantic swindle is the world's best-kept secret.

THE NECESSARY INGREDIENT

One cannot understand inflation without having an elementary understanding of money, for money is what makes inflation possible. Early men bartered with one another for goods and services—i.e., one man would give another his "product" in exchange for a product or service he desired as payment.

As we can imagine, this would be a rather cumbersome procedure. It was the advent of money that simplified this bartering process; the purpose of money was, and is, to facilitate exchange. Men could now exchange their goods and services for money, then use the money at a later date in exchange for other goods and services.

Since the beginning of civilization, almost everything one can think of has been used as money at one time or another. In earlier times, this included such items as ornaments, weapons, horses, hunting knives, and even wives. As civilization advanced, mining brought metals to the fore, with silver and gold eventually emerging as the most desirable forms of money.

What caused gold and silver (and especially gold) to emerge as the most acceptable forms of money were their features: they were durable, easily transportable, subject to precise division by weight, and scarce enough so that they could not be obtained in great quantities without considerable effort. Gold and silver, in other words, were not arbitrarily chosen commodities. They evolved as a result, and survived the test, of supply and demand over the centuries.

Money, then, is nothing more than a commodity. But it has one great distinguishing feature: It is highly acceptable to most people as a medium of exchange. In order for people to accept money in exchange for goods and services, they must have confidence that others will in turn accept it from them in exchange for things they subsequently will want to acquire.

Money, therefore, *is not wealth*. It is only a medium of exchange. Wealth is goods that you possess or desire. A refrigerator represents wealth. Money is a commodity that the owner of a refrigerator will accept as payment for the refrigerator, providing he believes he can use that money to buy other products and services he wants.

There are basically three kinds of money. One is "commodity money," which I have just described; i.e., money (such as gold coin) that is in demand because of its durability, transportability, etc., and which usually also has a utilitarian purpose (such as for manufacturing or ornamental use).

A second kind of money is "credit money." Essentially, this is when a person gives someone an IOU in exchange for something of value; i.e., he promises to pay for the item at a later date.

Finally, there is "fiat money." Fiat money is anything that a government, unilaterally and arbitrarily, decrees to be money. The normal way that fiat money comes into use is for a government simply to print pieces of paper and proclaim that they are "legal tender," with complete disregard to the factors that make money acceptable to people.

Now let us see what all this means in practice. To simplify what actually occurs, let us assume that a shoemaker has made one pair of shoes and a hatmaker has made one hat. The shoemaker needs a hat, but the hatmaker does not need a pair of shoes. Assuming there is no government fiat money involved, there are two ways these men can trade with one another.

The shoemaker can give the hatmaker an amount of gold or silver (or some other commodity acceptable to the hatmaker) that the hatmaker feels is adequate compensation for his investment of time, labor and materials. He must, however, feel confident that he can later use the commodity he receives to buy something which he believes to be of equal value.

The other possibility is for the shoemaker to give the hatmaker an IOU, promising to repay him a specified product, service or commodity at some specified later date. The hatmaker's willingness to accept the shoemaker's IOU will depend upon his faith in the shoemaker's ability to make good on his obligation.

We will leave the story of this hypothetical transaction for now, and return to it later in the chapter for reasons that will become obvious at that time.

UNCLE SAM GOES INTO BANKING

For many centuries, there existed well-established private coin minters and gold and silver warehouses. (For the sake of simplicity, we will restrict our discussion to gold from this point forward.) People would bring their gold to a private minter of high repute, who would form the gold into coins and stamp them with his official seal (which included a guaranteed designated weight for each coin). For this service, the minter would charge a fee, as would any other service business.

It is important to point out here that weights of gold were described by various terms in different countries. The word "dollar" came to be used as the *term* for 1/20th of an ounce of gold. The dollar itself *was not money*; it was simply the *name* given to a certain quantity of money. Therefore, not only was money not wealth, but a dollar was not even money! Similarly, other countries used words like franc and mark to describe various weights of gold.

Gold warehouses came into existence to accommodate people who did not want to be burdened with carrying gold around to make their purchases. Like a warehouse keeper of any other product, the operator of a gold-storage warehouse would agree to store someone's gold for a set fee and would give the owner of the gold a receipt for his stored merchandise. Whenever the owner desired to redeem his gold, he would simply bring in his receipt and the warehouse keeper would hand it over to him.

These early warehouses were the first "banks." Their deposits were gold, and the receipts they gave to its owners could be used as a substitute for money in most transactions. The receipts were acceptable to the sellers of goods and services to the degree that such sellers had faith in the integrity of the warehouse keeper; i.e., to the degree they had faith that the receipts could be converted into gold on demand.

But private minters and warehousers were a problem for governments. Throughout history, and particularly modern history, governments have realized that the most essential step in gaining control over people is to establish monopolistic control of the money system, for the monetary system is the jugular vein of the power game. Karl Marx, in *The Communist Manifesto,* made this very clear, stating that one of the most important aspects in achieving communist control was "centralization of credit in the hands of the state, by means of a national bank with state capital and an exclusive monopoly."[50]

Until a government can eliminate private minters and gold warehousers, it cannot use the money system to achieve the kind of control made possible through a monopoly. In this country, the history of achieving this monopoly followed the same "creeping-control" pattern government has used in all other areas of our lives.

The first step toward the ultimate goal of monopoly was Article I, Section VIII, Clause V of the Constitution, which gave Congress the power "to coin money, regulate the value thereof, and of foreign coin, and fix the standard of weights and measures." So as early as 1789, just thirteen years after the British had been overthrown and the American Dream of near-total freedom had been born, new power seekers were beginning to take control.

This was one of the earliest indications of how men of power would operate under the experimental democracy set up by our founding fathers; i.e., they would achieve control gradually, over long periods of time. The rugged colonial individualists were too independent to have tolerated abrupt tyranny. So Article I, Section VIII, Clause V was a subtle way of opening the door for the new government's entrance into the money business—a seemingly harmless act. This first step allowed government only to *compete* with other minters and warehousers.

It took government nearly seventy-five years to take the next significant step, the enactment of the National Bank Act of 1863, which, in effect, *outlawed* its competition. It is very interesting to note here how the passage of time can be used effectively to make people lose sight of what has taken place.

Few if any of the citizens who saw government pass an arbitrary law in 1789, allowing it merely to compete in the money business, were around to see it take monopolistic control of the entire system in the mid-1800's. Americans just after the American Revolution were distrustful of government, but, by the middle of the next century, government involvement in many areas, including the money system, had come to be accepted as "normal."

It is important to note that, even though government outlawed its competition and took full control of the money system, it did not try to change the system itself for more than another half century. The term *dollar* continued to mean 1/20th of an ounce of gold, and the United States remained on a fairly strict gold standard until 1914.

People had been taking their gold to government banks for years, either receiving minted gold coins or gold receipts in return. As time passed, however, it became less common to keep gold and more common to use gold "receipts" as money (actually the receipts were "money-substitutes"), simply because it was not practical to carry gold around. Again the passage of time worked wonders. People, influenced by government's encouragement to keep their gold safely on deposit with banks, erroneously began to refer to government receipts for gold as "dollars."

This clever transition in semantics became very important in later government monetary schemes. The receipts, of course, were *not* dollars; they were receipts for a specified weight of gold, that weight being defined as a dollar-weight (*1/20th of an ounce of gold*). The slowly evolving practice of referring to government gold receipts as "dollars" was a subtle but critical maneuver by government in carrying out its long-term inflation swindle.

December 23, 1913, was a day of infamy for our country. On that day, government passed the Federal Reserve Act, which provided for "the establishment of Federal Reserve Banks," gave government power to print "notes" (which it referred to as "currency"), established a system for "member banks" to exchange their gold deposits for government "currency," and a long list of other measures which pretty much gave government carte blanche to do as it pleased with the money system.

From that point on, banks encouraged people to take government "currency" when they wished to withdraw their money, assuring the public that its gold was safer in the hands of the government. Gold, after all, was "old-fashioned." Government paper currency became the "reserves" of member banks, while the Federal Reserve Bank retained everyone's gold as *its* reserves.

A nice little piece of maneuvering, I think you will agree!

Since then, of course, people have been fed a continual diet of government propaganda about the need for a Federal Reserve System. (I wonder how we got along so nicely—and *freely*—before 1913?) It is disheartening, yet almost humorous, that even in colleges many instructors teach students that the Federal Reserve System is necessary to prevent panic and disorder in banking. Few people stop to realize that the Federal Reserve was established 16 years *before* the great crash of 1929!

It is true that the Federal Reserve Act put government

in a position to prevent "runs" on banks. But such prevention is not protection—it is aggression! If people flock to banks to withdraw their money, it is because they have lost faith in those banks. It means that they want their property back. All the Federal Reserve Act and other related banking laws did was guarantee that government would use force to *stop* people from getting back their own money. Some protection!

(If private banks were allowed to exist, the reason they would rarely experience "runs" is that they would know that if one bank failed, it would be bad for the entire banking industry. Therefore, not only would they be forced, by the free market, to operate prudently in handling depositors' money, but they would be apt to bail each other out simply because it would be in their best interest to do so.)

Having taken firm control of the money reins, the government did not wait as long for its next major move. In 1917 it set the minimum reserves that a member bank needed to keep on deposit with the "central bank" at 10%. The 10% was retained by the Federal Reserve in gold, but the reserve ratio meant that banks could loan out *10 times as much* in paper money ("notes," "currency," etc.—take your pick) as they actually had on deposit with the Federal Reserve in gold. This meant that 90% of the receipts that banks could loan out were fraudulent! (Keep in mind that Federal Reserve notes, or "dollars," technically were only *receipts* for gold owned by others.)

The government arbitrarily printed these "receipts" and allowed member banks to lend them to unsuspecting individuals as though they were money. People, in effect, were paying interest on counterfeit receipts—receipts for gold that did not exist. The evolution toward paper money was well under way.

The next step? All too many people still living today remember it: government, in the early 1930's, "went off the gold standard." Gold receipts (which by this time were referred to by everyone as "dollars") could no longer be redeemed for gold. Not only were the gold receipts not redeemable, but the government stopped printing them altogether and replaced them with "Federal Reserve notes." Again government arbitrarily passed a law, this one forcing people to recognize Federal Reserve notes as "legal tender." People were forced to accept pieces of paper—fiat money—as the legal money to be used in all transactions.

The reason governments go off the gold standard is that it allows them to increase the supply of paper money more easily. People become confused, because there is no way to judge the value of the paper money. But experts are *not* confused. As soon as we went off the gold standard, the price of gold in the open market zoomed upward. This is because financial experts realized that gold was far more valuable than the paper money.

In less than 150 years, consider what had taken place: government entered the money business, in competition with other minters and warehousers; government then outlawed all competitors and claimed a monopoly on the money system; government established a so-called Federal Reserve System which, among other things, gave it the power to hold everyone's gold in its vaults and issue receipts far in excess of the gold it had on deposit; and, finally, government made it illegal for people to get their own gold back and declared paper money (as opposed to receipts for gold) to be the legally recognized money of our country.

It was the most protracted theft in history, but it certainly made a case for advocates of the slow, sure approach. It had taken *one hundred and fifty years* for government to complete the theft of the American people's gold.

But from that point on, the government was in a position to speed things up considerably. It now had all the gold; it could print paper money at will; it was in total control of the money system.

Almost immediately after going off the gold standard, government "devalued" the currency by about 40%. It is significant to point this out, because a devaluation is an admission of bankruptcy. What the U.S. Government was telling foreign countries (who, unlike American citizens, still had the right to redeem dollars for gold) was that each receipt they held was now worth only 60% of the amount of gold it originally had promised them. As with all shameful government actions, however, devaluations are always couched in terms designed to make people believe that some brilliantly conceived fiscal miracle has been achieved. What in fact has occurred when a government devalues its currency is that it has announced that it is reneging on its debts.

Nations, however, are a little more powerful than individuals, and they do not take kindly to the news that the pieces of paper they are holding are counterfeit. As a result, countries holding large quantities of U.S. dollars began increasingly to cash them in—a sort of international "run" on the central bank of the U.S.

Out of desperation, Richard Nixon, on August 15, 1971, threw in the towel and, in effect, admitted to nearly two hundred years of fraud: He shut the gold window to foreign governments. The game was over, from that point on, no one—not even foreign governments—could redeem U.S. currency for gold. We were now a 100% paper-money country.

Turn on the printing presses—full speed ahead!

To rub salt in the wounds of American citizens, the government now *sells* our gold from time to time in the open market. You've come a long way when you enter the game as just another competitor, force everyone else out of the business, steal billions of dollars in gold through outright fraud, then, finally, turn around and sell that same gold to the people from whom you stole it.

Harry D. Schultz, the renowned investment advisor, may be understating the case when he says: "(The sale of Treasury gold is) a crime against the people of the U.S. (It is) illegal, immoral and unconstitutional. The U.S. will grow weaker as the backing for its currency is sent overseas and other countries will grow stronger."[51]

THE WORLD'S BEST-KEPT SECRET

The fantastic gold theft just described is, unfortunately, only a small part of the overall inflation swindle. Everyone wants the president to fight inflation; everyone agrees it is a horrible problem; and everyone supports government officials who stride forward on their white chargers vowing to "fight" it.

There is only one problem with all this: the vast majority of people who pledge their support to inflation-fighting politicians and decry its ravaging effects have absolutely no idea what inflation is, let alone what causes it. Almost without exception, the politician who gains public support for his "inflation-fighting" measures usually proposes actions that will make inflation *worse.*

If this chapter is the highlight chapter of the book for me, then the upcoming paragraph must be considered the highlight *paragraph* of the book. If I were asked to name *one* thing, above all else, that I would want readers to understand and remember from this book, it would be the following:

Increased wages and prices do *not* cause inflation; in fact, they do not even contribute to it. Inflation is caused by only *one* thing: *an increase in the supply of money*. It is this increase in the money supply which *causes* wages and prices to increase; wage and price increases, in other words, are the *result* of inflation.*

This means that virtually everything politicians, government intellectuals, a majority of economists, and most members of the media tell Americans about inflation is not only false, but the *exact opposite* of the truth. Big business does not cause inflation; big labor does not cause inflation; it is *Big Brother* who causes inflation—and he is the *only* cause. He accomplishes this through big printing of paper money; he is the *only* one who has the power to increase the money supply.

I really should go one step further and correct my own explanation of inflation. I said it was *caused* by an increase in the supply of money. Technically speaking, inflation *is* an increase in the supply of money. (Even more technically, it is an increase in the supply of money-substitutes, i.e., receipts, over and above the supply of money—such as gold—itself.) When I refer to the inflation swindle as the world's best-kept secret, it is for good reason. Had every American in history simply taken the trouble to open a dictionary and read the definition of inflation, the government would have been caught redhanded.

Webster's New World Dictionary (1975 edition) defines inflation as "an increase in the currency in circulation or a marked expansion of credit, *resulting* in a fall in currency value and a sharp rise in prices." [*Italics added*].

Just as government cleverly succeeded in getting people to call gold receipts "dollars," which led to later generations thinking that the receipts themselves, rather than the gold they represented, were money, so too did government succeed in getting people to refer to an increase in

---

*Of course, in a free market prices may also rise if demand exceeds supply, but such rises are *natural;* market prices will always adjust to the ratio of supply and demand.

prices as "inflation," which took their attention off *real* inflation: government's printing of worthless paper money.

When most people talk about inflation, then, they use a misnomer. What they really are referring to are high prices. It also would be technically correct to refer to an increase in prices as "*price* inflation." When government puts out propaganda on the "inflation rate," it is really talking about the so-called consumer price index.

It also should be noted that the consumer price index is a very misleading indicator of "overall" prices, because it covers only a few hundred items out of thousands, and many of those thousands may play a bigger role in your life than in the lives of others. More important, however, is that the so-called inflation rate really does not tell you the rate of inflation at all. The rate of inflation, once again, is the rate at which government *increases the supply of money*. But, by referring to an increase in the consumer price index as the "inflation rate," government avoids discussing its irresponsible and fraudulent increase of the money supply.

Why is this little game of government-engineered semantics so important? Because it confuses virtually everyone, so much so that all but a small percentage of the population do not understand what causes prices to rise. And it is rising prices that people are concerned with; i.e., they are concerned with the *result* of inflation.

Inflation of the currency *falsely* increases prices. If most people understood this one simple fact, they undoubtedly would revolt against government's printing of money. That is why the semantics charade—and the resulting confusion—are so important to Uncle Sam. So long as people can be led to believe false explanations of what causes prices to rise, they can be made to believe in false solutions.

Mechanics of the Swindle

Why do prices rise when government prints too much money? Remember once again that money is *not* wealth; money is only a medium of exchange. Wealth is what you exchange the medium for (TV sets, automobiles, etc.). Wealth, in turn, can only be produced by labor. Today's money, on the other hand, is produced merely by printing pieces of paper.

The result is that when the Federal Reserve prints up money faster than people can produce wealth (i.e., products and services), the ratio between available money and available products and services increases. The supply of money, increasing faster than the production of goods and services, increases the demand for the available goods and services, which, as per the law of supply and demand, stimulates prices to rise.

Inflation, then, as Morgan Maxfield puts it, is "too much money chasing too few goods." Rising prices (what people think of as "inflation") are caused primarily by the money supply's increasing faster than the supply of goods and services.

Now it is time to get back to our shoemaker and hatmaker mentioned earlier in the chapter. If you recall, the shoemaker gave the hatmaker an IOU for the hat he purchased. The hatmaker accepted the IOU, because he believed the shoemaker to be creditworthy. He felt confident that he could use the shoemaker's IOU to purchase another product from someone else or, if he later decided he needed shoes, that he could "redeem" the IOU for a pair of shoes directly from the shoemaker.

In the meantime, however, two things have occurred, and the hatmaker is unaware of both of them. First, the shoemaker has stopped making shoes; i.e., he has ceased to produce wealth. Second, he has discovered that he can persuade other people to accept his IOU's, which has motivated him to go on a "drunken orgy of spending."

The shoemaker has passed out an additional 99 IOU's since he gave that first IOU to the hatmaker. None of the hundred people realizes, however, that the IOU he holds is not the only IOU that was given out by the shoemaker, hence each one believes that his IOU is "as good as gold" (i.e., as good as the pair of shoes behind it).

The problem arises when each of these hundred people goes out and tries to spend his IOU. Merchants, sensing the sudden increase in the demand for their goods, raise their prices. Due to the shoemaker's "printing" of excess IOU's, the hatmaker, who accepted the shoemaker's original IOU in good faith, theoretically (and, most likely, in reality) has had the value of his IOU reduced by 99%.

To compound the problem, sellers of goods, realizing that an excess of IOU's has been distributed by the shoemaker, become leery of the value of his IOU's. As a result, they raise their prices even higher to compensate for what they deem to be a bad risk in accepting the shoemaker's IOU's at all.

Of course, this situation would correct itself rather rapidly in a free market, with no government involvement. What would happen at a very early stage is that the community would realize what the shoemaker had been doing and not only would stop accepting his IOU's, but would demand that he make good on those that he had already distributed; this probably would result in his having to go to work in order to produce enough wealth to pay off his debts.

When government becomes involved, however, it destroys the smooth workings of the market. Government, in effect, legalizes the shoemaker's theft and, furthermore, allows the theft to go on indefinitely. It accomplishes this by forcing everyone to use *government* "IOU's" as money (technically they are warehouse receipts, payable on demand; as already explained, however, they can never be redeemed for anything). With government in the picture, the shoemaker would have given the hatmaker a government receipt (let us say for a dollar-weight of gold), instead of his own IOU, in exchange for the hat he purchased.

Now, with the government controlling the situation, what happens when the shoemaker stops working? The government *continues* to print up "receipts" (paper money) and gives the shoemaker a new supply of them each week, calling these handouts "welfare" or "unemployment compensation." In fact, government gives large quantities of this "money" to many other people in the community, for a variety of reasons, ranging from unemployment to grants for special projects. But what about the hatmaker who accepted the government receipt in good faith as payment for the hat he produced?

He has been the victim of inflation!

Every "dollar" the government printed up and arbitrarily passed out to the hatmaker's neighbors *decreased* the value of *his* "dollar." And all of those newly printed "dollars," with no wealth behind them, compete with the hatmaker's "dollar" for the available goods and services in the community. This, as already explained, raises prices considerably, which means the "dollar" the hatmaker was paid no longer has the purchasing power it had when he accepted it.

The problem is that he knows absolutely nothing about government's money-printing policies, so he hasn't the vaguest idea why prices are rising all around him while he still has only one "dollar."

Again government would like you to believe that its "mysterious-multiplier" concept applies here, and for good reason: the marketplace each day involves billions of individual transactions of every conceivable kind. If one can be led down a path toward this confusing maze of transactions, thereby directing his attention away from the *one, real,* and *only* cause of inflation, he can be made to believe that inflation is an impossibly complex problem which only politicians and government intellectuals can understand.

WHY GOVERNMENTS LOVE INFLATION

Now let us return to where we left off with government's deficit-spending dilemma; i.e., its problem of having spent more than it could raise through taxation and the sale of government securities to the public. A portion of government's deficit spending, you will recall, still was not covered, even after selling government securities to the public. Presto! Through Gutenberg's invention, all things are possible. Just turn on the printing presses and the money to cover the deficit can be created in no time.

Now you can see why it was crucial that government take monopolistic control of the money system and get off the gold standard as soon as possible. Once money was not tied to gold—once gold had become "old-fashioned"—government was free to print money in any quantity it desired.

This practice of indiscriminately increasing the supply of money—inflation—gives politicians the ability to have their cake and eat it too. They are cautious about raising taxes too fast, for fear of revolt (as we have seen in recent years); this revolt could result in their failure to be reelected or, if taxation became bad enough, they could be physically thrown out of office (à la the American Revolution). On the other hand, we know that the *surest* way to be voted out of office is to fail to respond to the Expediency Factors of voters, so vote-conscious politicians certainly cannot afford to cut back on government "functions."

Therefore, inflation provides politicians with a way out.

Inflation is a *hidden tax* (i.e., a hidden *form* of taxation). By printing up enough "money" to, in effect, cover the remainder of each year's deficit, Uncle Sam gets off the hook. Individuals see prices rising sky high as a result of this "solution," but they do not understand why. As a result, not only do they not revolt against government, but they take up government's battle cry to "fight inflation," following its lead in pointing a guilty finger at all the *wrong parties*. The whole ludicrous situation is tantamount to a bank robber shouting to a bunch of depositors, "The culprits went that way; let's get them."

Ponzi himself could not have done better. Not only have the victims been taxed without even realizing it, but they look to the tax collector to help them solve what only *appears* to be the problem—high prices.

RESULTS OF THE SWINDLE

The hidden tax of inflation allows government to continue its politically expedient, redistribution-of-the-wealth policies and other nonwealth-producing programs with virtually no restraints. In the earlier stages of a prolonged inflation, most people are fooled into thinking that government has "stimulated" the economy. Many economists, in fact, still believe in the Keynesian philosophy that inflation of the currency increases employment and production and improves the health of the economy. They not only totally ignore the long-term effects of inflation, as well as the moral implications (fraud and theft), but they are naive enough to believe that politicians will stop increasing the money supply once the economy is again "healthy."

There are many fallacies in such thinking, but I shall only point out a couple of the more obvious ones. First, the inflation "spiral" causes voters to continue to clamor for higher wages and more handouts in order to "keep up." Second, that old reality, The Vote, motivates politicians to satisfy voter demands, which means *more* inflation of the currency, which, in turn, leads to still higher prices. Third, since the economy is to a great degree artificial (in that it is "supported" by deficit spending and valueless paper dollars), it is only a matter of time until the laws of economics set in: higher prices and lower purchasing power leading to less production; less production leading to still higher prices and less employment; and so on.

The nice thing about inflation from a politician's standpoint, however, is that deficit spending (which necessitates an increase in the money supply) creates short-term, artificial prosperity, designed to win votes. It can take a year or two for prices to rise enough to make voters mad, but by that time the election, hopefully, has been won. When deficit spending was merely a pre-election scheme, the new administration would then cut back on spending once the election was over; as noted, however, this is no longer possible, because voters are hooked on government benefits and they do not want to hear about cutbacks.

In the meantime, the purchasing power of the dollar continues to erode. Just since 1967 the value of the dollar has decreased by 50%. This means that if you are not making at least twice as much as you were ten years ago, you are not living as well now as you were then.

One of the things that commonly confuses people who try to understand what inflation is all about is that, theoretically, it is true that the quantity of money in "circulation" makes no difference. In other words, if government handed everyone double the amount of money he now has, prices and wages roughly would double in a short period of time and no one would be any worse off. Likewise, if government took 50% of the currency *out* of circulation, prices and wages generally would fall by 50% and no one would be hurt.

But that is not what happens with inflation. Everyone does *not* get a proportionate percentage of the new money; nor do people even get equal quantities of the new money. In addition, it is those who receive the newly printed paper dollars earliest who gain the most from them. People who receive them the latest are the losers; i.e., they are *taxed*. This is so because by the time the new money circulates to them, prices have already risen considerably, thus they are victims of the inflationary spiral; i.e., they are at the bottom of the spiral.

The fellow who gets caught at the bottom of the spiral then, quite naturally, demands higher wages in order to "keep up." His increased wages in turn help to increase prices, thus the upward spiral continues. But his increased wages did not *cause* the increase in prices. The real cause was the increase in the money supply, which decreased his purchasing power; i.e., he was taxed so high that he needed higher wages just to keep up with rising prices.

The cause of the increase in the money supply, as explained, was an increase in government spending. And when government spends, most people lose in the long term. That is because government takes money from them to support its politically expedient functions.

Therefore, the higher wages most people continue to receive are just an illusion. From 1973 to May 1978, for example, gross income of full-time workers rose 43%, but consumer prices increased 47% during the same period. The 4% difference represents the "inflation tax" that these millions of people paid, though few of them realized that they had been taxed.

To get a bigger picture of this tax, consider that the growth of the economy (Gross National Product) was about 90% between 1960 and 1978, while the money supply increased close to 380% during the same period. In other words, today there is about four times as much money chasing goods, on a comparative basis, as in the year 1960.

Plain and simple, then, inflation is just another redistribution-of-the-wealth scheme. When someone else receives dollars without producing wealth, his dollars compete with yours for available goods and services. The result is that you see prices rising in relation to your income, which is a manifestation of government's increasing your taxes without telling you.

Inflation, in fact, can really cause you to be taxed in three ways. First is the hidden inflation tax itself. Second, if your wages are increased as a result of overall wageand-price increases, you will pay higher income taxes on your increased income. Third, your wages may increase enough to push you into a higher tax *bracket*, which means, in addition, that government taxes you at a higher *rate*.

These latter two items help to support the Tax-Cut Illusion Theory mentioned earlier. In addition to the increase in Social-Security taxes, these two items were expected to *increase* 1979 taxes by about $51 billion. So much, once again, for the $19 billion tax cut.

Inflation, then, encourages the free-for-all spirit among individuals and special-interest groups of trying to get more from the government than their neighbors. Henry Hazlitt noted that inflation fosters "the illusion in the great majority of voters that they will somehow get the better of the swindle, and profit at the expense of a few unidentified victims."[52]

Long-term, however, everyone loses unless inflation is brought under control. This is so because the continued onslaught of valueless money disrupts the market and causes confusion, apprehension and, eventually, panic. People are afraid to enter into long-term agreements, because they have no idea what money will be worth in the future. Businessmen decrease investments in new plants and equipment, because they do not know if their *real* profits will be worth the risk. The latter causes shortages, which leads to even higher prices.

Perhaps worst of all, everyone puts the blame on everyone else. Business blames labor; labor blames business; everyone points a finger at the other guy, yet the truth is that none of those accused are responsible for the higher prices.

If inflation is not eventually curtailed, a final collapse of the economy begins when people start to *guess* at what future prices will be. This sets off a chain reaction by which sellers increase prices even faster than the increase in the supply of money; i.e., panic eventually pushes prices up faster than government's inflation of the currency.

At that point, government faces its last chance to avoid a total collapse of the economy. As Henry Hazlitt puts it, "every inflation must eventually be ended by government or it must 'self-destruct.'"

And this self-destruction is exactly what has happened to nation after nation throughout history. The one we are most familiar with, due to its close proximity in time, is the German runaway inflation of 1923. If you doubt the ultimate results of a policy of continued inflation of the currency, consider these figures: between 1914 and 1923, the German government issued an additional 92.8 *quintillion* (92,800,000,000,000,000,000) paper marks, a 245 *billionfold* increase in the money supply; prices, in turn, rose 1.38 *trillionfold*. Interest rates rose as high as 10,000% per annum on some debt instruments.[53]

As you would guess, people eventually refused to accept paper money in exchange for goods and services. The economy collapsed; chaos and crime ensued; and waiting in the wings, preparing hysterical answers for hysterical people, was a man—Adolf Hitler—who understood all too well that only an authoritarian police-state regime could restore order.

CAN IT BE STOPPED?

The question of whether inflation *can* be stopped avoids the *real* question. Of course inflation *can* be stopped—simply by shutting off the printing presses. The question is whether those in power *will* stop it or whether enough people will ever sufficiently understand it to get mad enough to *force* those in power to stop it.

Realistically, for reasons that have been repeated throughout this book, it is wishful thinking to believe that politicians will ever stop it voluntarily. So long as their livelihoods and power depend upon The Vote, I cannot envision their turning off the power switch in the printing plants.

Therefore, the only hope that remains is that a great majority of Americans will come to understand the colossal inflation swindle for what it is and insist upon reform. To say the least, I rate that a long shot. But at least it's a shot. The probability of politicians' putting an end to vote-expedient spending on their own, and thus to inflation of the currency, is practically zero.

Education of the public is an uphill battle. Politicians and government intellectuals have virtually unlimited access to the media on a daily basis. That means that the public is fed a continual diet of false remedies for inflation, based on a continual flow of false ideas about what inflation really is.

Even many respected conservative economists have capitulated to government's twisting of logic and now accept "some" inflation of the money supply as "normal." Instead of talking about *stopping* inflation, such economists now argue the academic advantages of varying degrees of inflation; i.e., should the annual increase in the money supply be 2%, 5%, 7%, or some other figure?

But, as Henry Hazlitt pointed out many years ago, inflation either is good or it is bad. If it is good, why not inflate the currency 100% a year instead of just 5% or 10%? If it is good, we may as well have lots of it. But if inflation is bad, we should get rid of it altogether, so that everyone (except politicians) can be better off.

Five percent a year, for example, may sound like a "realistic" target, but even that seemingly harmless rate of inflation reduces the value of your dollars by 50% every 15 years—without giving any consideration to inevitable panic and subsequent runaway inflation.

People must start to ignore government ploys of treating the symptoms instead of the disease. When politicians vow to fight inflation, they lie. They are not talking about putting an end to the printing of money. Usually they are talking about intimidating "business" into not raising prices.

And intimidate is the right word: When it was announced that 1978 fourth-quarter corporate profits were up 26% (which many economists figured really amounted to only 8% after adjusting for "inflation" and taxes), "chief inflation fighter" Alfred E. Kahn called it a "catastrophe," saying that it "puts business on trial in the eyes of the American people."

This was the ultimate in logic twisting. Profits, the thing that makes the whole American way of life possible—*including* "free" handouts through government functions—were being termed a "catastrophe." Perhaps Mr. Kahn will be happy when Atlas finally shrugs and says, "You're right, profits are evil. I'm not going to waste my time earning them anymore. I quit."

Then where does government turn to raise money for its vote-oriented functions? At that point, the ball game is over.

All of this finger-pointing at the key source of the country's wealth—business—is nothing but an excuse to institute action intended to lead the public still further away from the real cause of higher prices. That action is known as "wage-and-price controls," which were discussed in Chapter 5. This is but another scheme to shift the blame erroneously to business and labor unions.

Wage-and-price controls have never worked and never will work. The most obvious reason why they do not work is because, as previously discussed, short of an outright dictatorship it is impossible to control the price of everything (land, housing, hospital care, interest rates, and imported oil are just a few examples). The result is that people will spend their excess money (such excess having been brought about by controls on the prices of certain items they want) on those goods and services that are not controlled, which will disproportionately raise the prices of the latter. Furthermore, as history repeatedly has demonstrated, when controls eventually are lifted, prices shoot through the roof on the controlled goods and services to compensate for their previous artificially low levels.

Finally, there is the old standby: The Dumb Act. It is imperative that every president foster the impression that, above all, inflation is a complex natural catastrophe, much like earthquakes and tornadoes, which man has not yet conquered. The result has been a procession of presidential faces on our TV screens, each one espousing "inflation-fighting" methods that would make witch doctors envious.

Gerald Ford's solution to this occult force was to print up "W.I.N." buttons. Though few people understood inflation, that one was a bit much. People may not know what inflation is, but they do know that wearing badges does not make *anything* go away.

Jimmy Carter should have won an Oscar for his "inflation-fighting" speech of October 1978. With a straight face, he appealed to his victims to "cooperate." Cooperate *how*? By not objecting to the government's printing up more money? He talked about business cooperation; he talked about labor cooperation; he talked about everything *except* the massive deficit spending incurred during his first two years in office and the resulting massive increases in the money supply. (At a later date, he outdid his October statement by saying that "a preoccupation with private pursuits and private gain at the expense of public purpose" was "a troubling challenge to efforts to control inflation.")

Carter never cracked a smile, acting as though he were trying to convince the American public (apparently with a great deal of success) that inflation was a mysterious force from outer space that was menacing planet Earth and that no one was sure how to combat this extraterrestrial plague.

And, as expected, "patriotic" intellectuals rushed to the fore, pleading with citizens to give President Carter's "program" a chance. *What* program? Had Carter appealed to Americans to give him a chance to stop printing worthless money, you can be sure that I would have been front and center in urging the public to give his program a chance. But, like all political "inflation fighters," Carter merely swayed back and forth between irrelevant issues and The Dumb Act.

THE REAL SOLUTION

The long-term solution to inflation is, I am afraid, an unrealistic one given today's climate: get government completely out of the money business and repeal the legal-tender laws. If the money business were returned to private minters and warehousers (banks not in any way connected to government), printing of false warehouse receipts (money-substitutes) would be controlled by the same forces that control all free-market activities. Banks that were guilty of irresponsibly inflating their warehouse receipts would soon lose their customers when word of their issuing of fraudulent paper became common knowledge. Originally, this is what inflation entailed—printing of excess gold receipts over and above the amount of gold being stored in private warehouses.

The powerholders in Washington, however, are not likely to give up their most effective tool for controlling people's lives, especially when one realizes that it took them some two hundred years to gain monopolistic control of the money system, to steal people's gold, to go completely off the gold standard, and, finally, to get into a position to inflate the currency at will for political purposes.

Back to reality: It is safe to assume that government, at least in the foreseeable future, is going to hang onto its most effective method of control. That means that the only way inflation can be stopped is to find a way to motivate politicians to stop it, since it is they who control government spending and the money supply. (As noted, government could stop inflation literally in one day simply by shutting down the printing presses.) And the only thing politicians respond to is The Vote.

With that in mind, let's start with the *result*—high prices (which is *not* inflation)—and see if we can work backwards to a solution:

1) Higher prices are the *result* of inflation.

2) Inflation (*an increase in the money supply*) is the *result* of deficit spending.

3) Deficit spending is the *result* of too much government spending in general (specifically, it is that portion of government spending not covered by taxes).

4) Government spending is the *result* of politically ex-

pedient actions—the desire of politicians to capture The Vote.

5) Politically expedient actions are the *result* of the Expediency Factors of voters.

So the story has a Hitchcock ending: It is the *voters* (albeit they are victims of misleading propaganda) who are responsible for inflation! The focus of most voters' Expediency Factors is on short-term well-being, which manifests itself in an attitude of wanting to get all they can right now.

Everybody wants something done about high prices, but nobody wants to be the one to get stuck at the bottom of the "spiral." Who will take the first step to stop this financial suicide?

We have two choices: We can all take our lumps together, let the "crash" come and take its toll (which is another way of saying that we will pay our overdue bills), let wages and prices settle to their normal market levels, and get back to living the American Dream that gave us our freedom and prosperity in the first place.

Or, by continuing to grab for all the short-term benefits we can get, we can keep fueling the political fires that in turn fuel inflation, which ultimately must lead to a total collapse of the economy and bring to power a dictatorship.

The mere mention of a dictatorship suddenly makes the first option sound much less terrible. Everything is relative. We've been so busy grabbing for "free" material benefits that we have forgotten that all the material wealth in the world is useless if one has no freedom. Wealth can be produced if men are free. If men are not free, then slaves produce wealth for those in power.

THE BOTTOM LINE

The bottom line is that the bill for government functions is paid, in one way or another, by the only source of wealth that exists: those who produce. The producers pay the bill for government spending either through "regular" taxation or through inflation taxes. Those who *produce* more than they receive from Uncle Sam are *net-tax producers;* in effect, it is they who pay all of the bill. Those who *receive* more from Uncle Sam than they produce are *net-tax consumers;* it is they (including all those who work for government) who benefit most from government's redistribution-of-the-wealth actions.

Because politicians and government intellectuals have done such a marvelous job of confusing the real issues, it is hard for most people to see that the bottom line is the simple explanation just given. For example, some politicians pose as crusaders against government waste. Beautiful. How can voters help but applaud them? But people forget that waste is but a by-product of the real problem: government spending. To cut down on government waste, you cut down on government spending. And to cut down on government spending, you *cut down on government income* (i.e., direct taxes and inflation taxes).

Another recently popularized issue for ambitious politicians is the drive for a "balanced budget." It sounds great, but once again it leads to the same conclusions. A so-called balanced budget, of and by itself, is meaningless, because all you need to do to balance the budget is raise direct taxes. The government implies that you have only two choices: lower taxes or lower inflation (indirect taxes). No thanks. The alternative they do not bother to discuss is lower direct taxes *and* lower inflation taxes, which *forces* them to cut spending.

Finally, there is the argument that inflating the currency is all right, so long as it does not exceed the country's overall productivity rate. The attitude, more or less, is this: The theft of our ancestors' gold, like the injustice of black slavery, is "a great unchangeable fact." Let's forget about it and concentrate on keeping current inflation of the currency in line with the rate of wealth being produced, thus future prices will tend to rise pretty much in line with the increase in the money supply and no one will be hurt.

Such a stance is taken by many people whom I greatly respect, several of whom have been mentioned in this book. But for me, this is the one piece in the inflation-swindle puzzle that never quite fit. Then it occurred to me: If inflation is really just a hidden tax, somebody has to be paying the inflation tax and somebody has to be receiving it, no matter what the productivity rate is. Once I realized that this fact was immutable, I knew that the hidden tax must in some way be paid by net-tax producers (i.e., those who produce more than they receive from government).

And here's how: If, say, the productivity rate of the nation as a whole increased 3% a year and there was *no increase in the money supply,* then, generally speaking (we can only talk in generalities when dealing with the entire nation, since there are so many variables), prices would *decrease* by 3% a year. Prices *would have to decrease,* because more goods and services would be produced, yet there would be no corresponding increase in the amount of money in circulation.

But, if the money supply also was increased by 3% a year, as advocated by those who believe that an increase in the money supply is okay so long as the increase does not exceed the productivity rate, prices would *not* decrease; they would stay approximately the same. Therefore, net-tax producers (again, those who produce more than they receive from government) would be taxed

through inflation by the amount that prices did *not* drop!
Part of their wealth would be siphoned off through inflation, with the recipients of the inflation tax (net-tax consumers) being the winners—just as they are today on a
larger scale.

While I will certainly agree that inflating the currency
somewhat in line with the productivity rate is better than
inflating it far in *excess* of the productivity rate, the only
difference lies in the *degree* of the redistribution of producer income. *All* inflation (beyond demand receipts
which are 100% redeemable in gold) is taxation. No matter what the productivity and inflation rates are, if you are
a net-tax producer, *you* help pay the bill, which means
that part of your income is given to net-tax consumers.

Of course, none of these facts will ever budge "humanitarian" liberals, who may say in rebuttal: "Okay, so you
have caught on to our schemes. But helping the needy
(i.e., those whom they designate to be 'needy,' such as
civil-service workers making $25,000 to $40,000 a year)
is an end that justifies the means."

But neither will their arbitrary justifications for committing theft change my rebuttal: What good is redistribution of the wealth to anyone if it causes economic chaos,
which in turn results in a loss of freedom? Those who advocate fiscal responsibility and morality are not the ones
who are callous to the needs of the "poor." On the contrary, it is fiscally irresponsible liberals, who cry out for
government to spend unlimited sums of other people's
money on programs they deem to be desirable, who are
callous.

I repeat: What could be worse than being poor *and*
unfree?

Most people, I believe, are finally beginning to realize
that there is no such thing as something for nothing. No
matter how high the tab goes, someone must eventually
pay it. Millions of people have, in fact, been making pay-

ments on the bill for quite some time, and the burden becomes more oppressive each year as direct taxation and inflation-taxation roar out of control. It is possible that you may not live to have to make the ultimate payment—loss of freedom—in which case your children and grandchildren will pay. But, sooner or later, one way or another, the entire bill *will* be paid.

It is only fitting that I leave this chapter on a note from Henry Hazlitt, who for more than half a century has understood all too well exactly what the long-term consequences of politically expedient spending really are. The end result is, indeed, inevitable:

> Doesn't everybody know, in his personal life, that there are all sorts of indulgences delightful at the moment but disastrous in the end? Doesn't every little boy know that if he eats enough candy he will get sick? Doesn't the fellow who gets drunk know that he will wake up next morning with a ghastly stomach and a horrible head? . . . Doesn't the Don Juan know that he is letting himself in for every sort of risk, from blackmail to disease? Finally . . . do not the idler and the spendthrift know, even in the midst of their glorious fling, that they are heading for a future of debt and poverty?[54]

8

Keeping It All in Place

When one considers the daily violations of human rights carried out by government, particularly through its "functions" and its methods for expropriating the wealth needed to pay for these functions, one wonders how the powerholders manage to keep The System intact. What is it that keeps people from rebelling against such massive injustices?

At the outset of Chapter 2, I said that the chief problem for men of power has been the same since the beginning of recorded history: What is the most practical way in which to maintain control over people?

As I also pointed out, democracy, though it has many disadvantages for powerholders, seems to be the most practical way to maintain control, because it gives the illusion of consent. If people can be made to believe that they are free and that the government represents them, the energies of the ruling class do not have to be concentrated on policing measures. In addition, creating the illusion of consent has the advantage of rendering physical uprisings extremely unlikely.

It would be unwise, however, to believe that even in a democracy people could be held in check indefinitely. As the truth about such things as Majority Rule, inflation, taxation, the military draft, and other tyrannical measures began to surface, people eventually would grow hostile in increasing numbers.

Therefore, wise rulers in any democracy must employ backup measures for maintaining control. These tactics range from the subtle in nature to the brutally straightforward. The most subtle of all methods, of course, has already been discussed: monopolistic control of the money system. But beyond the money-system scheme, government uses three additional techniques for seeing to it that The System is never seriously challenged.

LOVE OF SERVITUDE

A person may insist that he lives in a free country, but what good does his loyal statement do him if he is not free to do with his own life as he pleases, despite the fact that he is not interfering with anyone else? Can a person who feels overtaxed, overregulated and overharassed be free?

Sadly, I believe that most of us today do, in fact, believe this contradiction. We believe it because government, while increasing taxes and restrictions on our lives at an ever-accelerating pace, has been telling us for generations that we live in the freest country on earth.

Discussions of freedom have, in fact, become passé—an attitude not new to history. Observed Étienne de la Boétie in the sixteenth century, "It is incredible how as soon as a people becomes subject, it promptly falls into such complete forgetfulness of its freedom that it can hardly be roused to the point of regaining it, obeying so easily and so willingly that one is led to say . . . that this people has not so much lost its liberty as won its enslavement."[55]

The freest people in recorded history undoubtedly were the people of this country just after the American Revolution. Such freedom, however, is easily forgotten, particularly with the passage of long periods of time. The reason that gradual change is desirable from the standpoint of governments is that people are not aware of such change on a day-to-day basis. Many generations have passed since the American Dream was born in 1776, and the libertarians of that era undoubtedly would shed many a tear if they could witness the present-day decay of America.

Creeping totalitarianism is effective because each generation views conditions at any given time as "normal." One must objectively analyze where we began and where we are today in order to have a realistic understanding of what has transpired during a period of two hundred years. The objective of the American Revolutionists was to make men free, to place men *above* government. Today's reality is that government has become firmly entrenched as the omnipotent, omniscient, omnibenevolent guiding force in men's lives.

Not a small part of government's success in achieving its superior position over its citizens can be attributed to its success in teaching them to "love their servitude." Control of men, as Machiavelli pointed out centuries ago, is much easier and far less dangerous if rulers can gain the cooperation of their subjects—i.e., if they can successfully implement mind control—rather than having to rely solely on the use of force.

THE WORD SPREADERS

Adolf Hitler, probably the most successful political propagandist in history, was able to carry out horrifying atrocities against mankind because he possessed an uncanny understanding of how to gain the support of the masses through the twisting of logic and the misrepresentation of facts. Said Hitler in *Mein Kampf*, "The German has no idea how much the people must be misled if the support of the masses is required."

But one cannot mislead millions of people on his own.

Peaceful control of a nation is largely dependent upon the efficiency of the government's propaganda machinery. This entails the effective use of large numbers of "well-informed" individuals—"intellectuals"—who have a vested interest in the power game.

The vested interest that intellectuals have in the success of government is, quite frankly, employment and status. The demands of people in the real world bid up the wages of plumbers, doctors, barbers, carpenters, and the like, but you will never see "intellectuals" listed in the Yellow Pages. There simply is not a great free-market demand for their services.

But as far as government and intellectuals are concerned, theirs is a value-for-value alliance. Government offers the intellectual employment, security and status. And what, in turn, is the chief task of the intellectual? In the simplest of terms, it is to make the masses love their servitude. From government's standpoint, it would be ideal if intellectuals did such a good job at their task that other measures would be unnecessary. Said Aldous Huxley, in his foreword to *Brave New World*:

> A really efficient totalitarian state would be one in which the all-powerful executive of political bosses and their army of managers control a population of slaves who do not have to be coerced, because they love their servitude. To make them love it is the task assigned, in present-day totalitarian states, to ministries of propaganda, newspaper editors and schoolteachers.

To the degree that today's intellectuals parallel Huxley's depiction of efficient control of people, they earn their keep. To the degree that people ask too many questions, complain too much, or cause too many problems, intellectuals are failing to perform their duties well.

Inflation, which is itself a part of the most subtle method of controlling people—control of the monetary system—is a good example of an area in which government intellectuals have done an excellent job. As discussed in detail in the last chapter, almost the entire population of this country has been effectively taught to believe not only in false causes and false cures for inflation, but also that a *result* of inflation (high prices) *is* inflation.

The fact that so many people know so little about the real workings of government is certainly no accident. Government spends billions of dollars of taxpayers' money each year to help its intellectuals create illusions, mysteries and confusion about hundreds of subjects that are important to politicians.

A critical factor in disseminating such propaganda is government's virtually unlimited access to the media. What the president and other top politicians think and say continuously fill the pages of national magazines and daily newspapers. Their faces appear on television screens throughout the land day in and day out. On top of the huge sums government invests in its propaganda programs, such media exposure amounts to untold billions of dollars in free advertising.

Do you think you might succeed in getting your ideas across to people if you were able to appear on television every day and have your views printed daily on the pages of national magazines and local newspapers?

With its use of taxpayer money and its free access to the media, government is in an enviable position to slant the news to its liking. As everyone with the slightest understanding of the business world realizes, figures *do* lie; i.e., they can be made to lie. By giving numbers out of context or by failing to explain certain significant factors properly, subjects like the "unemployment rate," as we have seen, can be presented in such a way as to successfully mislead the public.

The creation of crises is another tool used by government intellectuals to keep people concentrating on anything other than their loss of wealth and freedom. There have been so many excellent books and articles that have exposed phony crises—ranging from the so-called environmental crisis to the so-called energy crisis—that I will not dwell on the point here. I did, however, touch on government causes of the "energy crisis" in Chapter 5, which gives one a good idea of the origin of most other crises with which we are besieged by the media.

Then there are the intellectuals who control the compulsory-education process. There certainly is no moral virtue in compulsory education, so the objective, quite obviously, is to make certain that children grow up thinking the "right way." By the time young adults graduate from high school, it is essential to government aims that they understand that material wealth is evil, that total freedom is an archaic concept, and that equality and security are far more important than liberty. For if children are allowed to learn the truth about such subjects, they will *always* know the truth. And, once the facts are known, it is too late for mind twisting, as Thomas Paine perceptively explained in *Rights of Man:*

Ignorance is of a peculiar nature; once dispelled, it is impossible to re-establish it. It is not originally a thing of itself, but is only the absence of knowledge; and though man may be *kept* ignorant, he cannot be *made* ignorant. . . . It has never been discovered how to make a man *unknow* his knowledge.

The proper teaching of history is especially important to powerholders. "If all records told the same tale—then the lie passed into history and became truth," thought Winston in *Nineteen Eighty-four.* " 'Who controls the past,' ran the Party slogan, 'controls the future: who controls the present controls the past.' "

If one were to study American history in books published in, say, France or England, he might be quite surprised at the disparity between historical "facts" as presented in those books and as they appear in American history books. As an example of how history can be rewritten, think of some of the men who are most revered in our school texts.

Abraham Lincoln, we are taught, fought the Civil War to free the Negro slaves. The truth is that the war was fought primarily because the Southern states, whom the Northern states had continually burdened with stifling tariffs and levies, wanted to secede from the Union. What Lincoln accomplished was to reestablish government's superiority over the individual; i.e., that men had to "belong" to the country whether they wanted to or not. After the North's victory, the issue of the federal government's authority over all people within "its" borders was never again seriously challenged.

The one good thing that did come out of the Civil War was that blacks were given their freedom, but historical documents make it clear that this was not the key issue in the war. Two direct quotes by Lincoln, which, needless to say, are not to be found in public-school texts, make this pretty clear.

In a letter to Horace Greeley in 1862, Lincoln wrote, "My paramount object in this struggle (the Civil War) is to save the union and it is not either to save or destroy slavery. If I could save the union without freeing any slaves, I would do it. If I could save it by freeing all the slaves I would do it; if I could save it by freeing some and leaving others alone, I would also do that."[56]

And in a debate with Stephen Douglas, Lincoln stated, "I am not nor ever have been in favor of bringing about in any way the social and political equality of the white and black races. . . . there must be the position of superior and inferior, and I as much as any other man am in favor of having the superior position assigned to the white race."[57]

Then there was Teddy Roosevelt, another of our "great" presidents. Since the slaves already were free by the time he took office, Roosevelt settled for Indians: "I don't go so far as to think that the only good Indians are dead Indians, but I believe nine out of every ten are, and I shouldn't inquire too closely into the case of the tenth. The most vicious cowboy has more moral principle than the average Indian."[58]

So much for Lincoln; so much for Roosevelt; so much for American "history." "Who controls the past controls the future; who controls the present controls the past."

But the most important function of all for government intellectuals is to teach people either not to think at all ("nothink") or to believe that the truth is the opposite of that which really is true. In *Nineteen Eighty-four*, George Orwell referred to the latter process as "doublethink." Orwell explained this as the ability of a person to maintain two contradictory beliefs in his mind at the same time and to accept both of them without conflict. Doublethink does not involve *saying* the opposite of what one thinks, but *thinking* the opposite of what is true.

The ultimate in doublethink in Orwell's book was the party slogan: "War is peace; freedom is slavery; ignorance is strength." Current events make it clear that many people today literally believe in one or more of the contradictions of this supposedly fictional party slogan.

Americans today are products of several generations of heavy dosages of doublethink. Those who produce goods and services in the market are known as "exploiters," while those who reap the benefits of the producers are known as the "exploited"; those who advocate suppressing individual liberty are called "liberals"; when our country shamefully entered into a political partnership with a regime in China that has killed upwards of 50 million people and holds nearly 1 billion people in bondage, it was celebrated as "a step in defense of peace."

Frederick Douglass, a self-educated slave of the pre-Civil War era, noted the importance of both nothink and doublethink in the maintenance of the plantation system of slavery when he observed that "to make a contented slave, it is necessary to make a thoughtless one (and) to annihilate the power of reason. He must be able to detect no inconsistencies in slavery, he must be made to feel that slavery is right."[59]

And so it goes with government intellectuals. They teach us that Majority Rule is morally valid; that politicians can solve our problems better than we can; that government can do things better, cheaper and more efficiently because of its "mysterious-multiplier" concept; that government interference in the marketplace stimulates free enterprise, prevents unemployment and fights monopolies; that those who oppose government regulations are advocates of disease, poverty and a dirty environment.

Combating Nothink and Doublethink

There is only one known antidote for nothink and doublethink: "straightthink." That is the equivalent of saying that the only cure for drug addiction is the "cold-turkey" method. But it's true. Only the refusal to be intimidated by illogical or irrational thoughts, only the insistence on using one's power to reason, can combat nothink and doublethink.

Too many Americans today have lost the spirit of individualism. As a result of continual admonishment by politicians, the media, intellectuals, and even peers, many people have ceased to use their minds. Conforming to the wishes of an abstract entity known as "society" has become more important to them.

The only way out of such mental enslavement is the use of reason as the *starting point* of every decision; custom, law and tradition must be rejected as a basis of argument. It is impossible to be committed to both truth and conformity at the same time. To seek truth, one must feel free to analyze, to criticize, to question—*to use his own mind*.

It is not easy to practice straightthink when one has been bombarded by nothink and doublethink for years. It is frightening to many people when the things they grew up believing are suddenly exposed in a different light. Our fears, our prejudices, our preconceived ideas and our ingrained adherence to custom and tradition are the biggest obstructions to our understanding and seeking liberty for ourselves and others.

It is virtually impossible for some people to break through these mental obstructions and to take control of their own thought processes. So they go right on believing that the American Dream is in fine shape, that government is inherently good, and that "the world has always had problems." The latter view is especially dangerous, because it totally ignores the evolution of our once nearly free country into a rapidly decaying socialistic society. Making oneself believe that everything is fine is the worst possible example of nothink, and such cooperative refusal to face reality will only accelerate the decaying process. "Facts," says Ayn Rand, "cannot be altered by a wish, but they *can* destroy the wisher."

In today's doublethink atmosphere, seeking and speaking truth can sometimes make one feel very lonely. Government intellectuals have been extremely successful with the use of the "put-down" and the "dismissal." When someone "steps out of line," it is very important that he and his ideas be ridiculed in a popular way.

The put-down and the dismissal are not used just against everyday people. On the contrary, intellectuals do not hesitate to toss aside some of the most outstanding minds in this manner, for these are the minds which pose the greatest threat to mental control of the citizenry.

A good example of this technique involved a friend of mine during his college days. One of his instructors had asked each student to write a report on a philosopher of the student's choosing, and my friend did a critique of Ayn Rand. When he handed in his paper, the instructor told him that it was unacceptable because he "did not consider Ayn Rand to be a philosopher."

The casual dismissal of Ayn Rand as a philosopher by an obscure college professor hardly affects her status in the eyes of the millions of people who have read her works and who believe in the morality of individualism. But it *does* affect her status in the minds of those who either have not read her works or who fear being out of step.

A second example which comes to mind is a recent *New York Times Magazine* article about the brilliant libertarian Harvard professor, Robert Nozick. Nozick is out of step at Harvard, and in the intellectual community in general, because he believes in "antiquated" ideas like individualism and freedom. Although some current philosophers are taking seriously questions raised by Nozick, the article explains that many others simply dismiss his writings, maintaining that he must be "pretending." In his remarkable book, *Anarchy, State and Utopia,* I hardly think Nozick is "pretending," but it is the hope of government intellectuals that such a put-down will render powerful minds like his ineffective when it comes to influencing others to pursue liberty.

If government intellectuals show no qualms about laughing off the ideas of some of the world's great thinkers, it is not hard to see why the average person can be intimidated so easily by the "you-must-be-kidding" attitude of intellectuals. When an everyday libertarian talks about freedom (whether economic or social), the easiest thing for the properly indoctrinated conformist to do is simply to shrug him off as someone who is hopelessly out of touch with the world today. By so doing, of course, the conformist conveniently avoids discussing logic or fact.

"Such ideas are outdated"; "he has oversimplified the problem"; "what would happen if everyone thought that way?" These are typical examples of statements intended to avoid a rational discussion. When someone responds to you in this manner, it is almost always a sure sign that *your* thinking cap is on straight, because it indicates that you have made a logical statement for which he has no logical rebuttal. And if that is the case, do not allow yourself to be thrown off course. Too few people today have the courage to think, as pointed out by Bertrand Russell:

"Men fear thought as they fear nothing else on earth—more than ruin, more even than death. Thought . . . is merciless to privilege, established institutions, and comfortable habits; thought is . . . indifferent to authority, careless of the well-tried wisdom of the ages. Thought looks into the pit of hell and is not afraid."[60]

The Arsenal

The government has a seemingly endless arsenal of subjective, meaningless and/or distorted words and phrases with which it mentally seduces the public. Here, too, it must be admitted that government intellectuals have been extremely successful in their efforts. People accustomed to nothink or doublethink are continual victims. Only those who employ the power to reason can shield themselves from the mental control brought about by these strange words and phrases.

Examples:

—*"The people," "the public," "society,"* etc. These, of course, are abstract terms which refer to large numbers of *individuals*—usually millions of individuals. Wherever I have used these terms in this book, you should assume that I have been referring to large numbers of individuals, recognizing that the wants, needs, desires and personal characteristics of each individual are unique.

When used by government propagandists or doublethinkers, however, the implication is that such terms refer to collective living entities that are capable of thinking, feeling and acting human. Any reference to these terms in such a way as to intimate that they are living entities is, at best, absurd and should be disregarded as having no comprehensible meaning.

—*"Government."* Again, wherever I have referred to government I specifically have been alluding to individuals, namely to those individuals in power; i.e., elected politicians and nonelected bureaucrats. If one thinks of government as a living entity, it tends to take on an aura of sanctity in his mind. And to think of government as a sacred entity is to believe that the *human beings* who comprise it are sacred. To say the least, we know that is not true.

I believe that the subconscious tendency of people to think of government as a living entity is one of the factors which keeps them so passive in the face of government aggression. A violation of your natural rights is not warranted just because it is committed by government— i.e., by those *individuals* who operate under the banner of "government."

—*"Country."* A country is an even more curious abstract entity, because it refers to a land area as well as to individuals. The point about only individuals having human qualities has already been made several times, but what about land? Certainly land is not a living entity. Land cannot think, feel, have desires, or experience emotions.

Therefore, all of the same logic holds true for the term

country that is applicable to terms like "the people," "the public" and "society." Our "country" is not great; nor is it good or bad. Only individuals are great, good or bad. Some *people* in America are great; some are good; some are bad.

——"*Taxation*," "*conscription*" *(the draft)*, "*loophole*," "*windfall*," *inflation*," "*patriotic*," "*apathetic*," "*obligation*," *etc*. These are all words that politicians love to use in a distorted manner, and some of them have been invented specifically to make immoral acts seem respectable.

"Taxation" already has been discussed in detail as a coverup for theft, and "conscription" has been exposed as a way of legitimizing slavery. "Loophole" and "windfall" were pointed out as words which are used to intimidate people who legally try to protect their assets. And the incredible lie that enshrouds the word "inflation" was uncovered in detail.

"Patriotic," "apathetic" and "obligation" are other good examples of words that have been completely distorted over the years through propaganda. One is considered patriotic if he unquestioningly supports his "country." All of our founding fathers, therefore, were *unpatriotic*, because they did not support the government that was in power at that time. Likewise, anyone who challenges the authority of the present-day government to violate human rights is unpatriotic. One can see why it has often been said that one man's anarchist is another man's patriot. Whether or not you are "patriotic" depends not only on the eyes of the beholder, but on the time and place of your actions.

"Apathy" has been popularized by government to refer to virtually any action or nonaction that may not be to its liking. For example, millions of people do not vote because they wish to protest the lack of a real choice of candidates, the unacceptability of all politicians on the ballot, or the workings of The System itself. But government intellectuals and politicians simply refer to such protests as "apathy." "Apathy" is a convenient catchall word used by government officials to shame people into staying in line.

"Obligation" is one of the most interesting words of all, due to the way in which our collectivist evolution has changed its meaning. Technically, an obligation is something one *assumes*. Once you *voluntarily* assume an obligation, then and only then are you responsible for it. Yet politicians, intellectuals and absolute moralists insist on telling people that it is their "obligation" to do things they have never agreed to do.

—*"Duty," "decent," "fair," "justice," etc*. Obviously, all of these words are totally subjective and have different meanings to everyone. Much of the language government uses to control people's minds revolves around combining subjective words like these with other words—often distorted or meaningless words. What you end up with are unintelligible or incoherent phrases like:

—*"Public morals," "public good," "public property," "public justice," "public interest," etc*. Since the public consists of millions of individuals, each person has a different view of that which is moral, good, or in his best interest. So, too, will each individual have a different view of "justice." And "public property" simply refers to property controlled by those people who control government. Such property is available to private individuals only at the discretion of government officials, which means, for all intents and purposes, that it is government officials who really own the property.

—*"Good of society," "well-being of society," "welfare of society," "duty to society," "obligation to society," etc*. Again, society, as an entity, does not exist; society consists of millions of individuals. The well-being and the welfare of each individual in a society is different from that of his neighbor; what is good for him is not necessarily good for others; no one can possibly have a duty to society, because society does not exist as an entity; nor can one have an obligation to a nonexistent entity. (One can be obligated to *specific individuals,* if one *voluntarily assumes* such an obligation.)

—*"Good of the people," "welfare of the people," rights of the people," "the people have chosen," etc.* The "good of the people" and the "welfare of the people" have no meaning for the same reasons that the "good of society" and the "welfare of society" have no meaning. Since "the people" is not a living entity, "the good of the people" translates into that which fulfills the desires of those in power. Neither do "the people," collectively speaking, have rights; only individuals have rights, and each individual's rights are equal to those of every other individual. Such rights are framed in Natural Law and have already been discussed at length.

"The people have chosen" is a meaningless statement for the same basic reason: only individuals can choose. And when this phrase is used to refer to the winner of an election in an effort to imply that the winner has received a "mandate of the people," it is simply a falsehood (as discussed in Chapter 2).

—*"Fair pay," "decent living," "your fair share," "moral duty," etc.* All of these phrases obviously are meaningless since they involve subjective words. Another person's idea of "fair pay," "decent living," his "fair share" and his "moral duty" may be quite different from yours. And you both have a right to your opinions. Neither of you, however, has a right to force your opinions on anyone else.

The ultimate weapons in government's propaganda arsenal take the form of slogans or patriotic statements. These are remarks intended to effect a knee-jerk response from citizens, which means they are intended to produce irrational thought and irrational action. Slogans and statements of this kind, then, rely heavily on nothink and doublethink.

Examples:

—*"And so, my fellow Americans, ask not what your country can do for you, ask what you can do for your country."* This oft-repeated plea by the late John F. Kennedy was brilliantly conceived. I have dissected it in a previous book, but, because it is such a classic example, I feel compelled to repeat the analysis here.

First, the statement refers to that abstract word "country," which in this case is a geographical area in which some 220 million individuals reside. I personally have never asked 220 million people to do anything for me. How can I ask people to do things for me when I do not even know them?

"Ask what you can do for your country?" Does this mean asking each of the 220 million individuals within the geographical area known as the U.S.A. what you can do for him? Does it include the millions of murderers, rapists, robbers and others who are guilty of aggression? If it does not include all 220 million Americans, then which people does it include? In reality, Kennedy's statement really was encouraging people to ask what they could do for government, meaning *those people who control the country*.

Restated in translated form, then, it becomes: "Ask not what those in power can do for you; ask what you can do for those in power." Had the statement been made in this kind of straightforward manner, without the use of abstract and misleading terms, it is doubtful that people would have responded so positively. Which is exactly why governments have compiled large arsenals of mind-twisters such as this.

—*"Love it or leave it."* People who use this very intimidating slogan imply that somehow they own the country and that you remain here only at their discretion. (In that case, perhaps the only people who might have a valid right to make such a demand are American Indians.) Translated, a person using this slogan really is saying that if you do not agree with his views on any number of issues, you have no right to live in the United States.

In other words, you have no right to dissent—the exact opposite of the principle upon which our country was built.

Must a person love everything about a country to have the right to remain in it? There are many things I love about the geographical area known as the United States of America; likewise, there are many people who live within that area whom I love. I have no desire to leave.

But there are also many things that concern me. One of the things I dislike most is the fact that other people, particularly members of government, forcibly attempt to interfere with my life and impose their moral standards on me. I would like to see this type of aggression brought to an end and all men allowed to live their lives as they please, so long as they do not commit aggression against others.

My feeling is that if anyone does not believe in the right of men to be free, then perhaps it is *he* who does not "love it." If someone does not like living in a country where people still have a right to voice their dissent, then it seems to me that it is he who should be looking for a new country. Perhaps he is the one who should "love it or leave it!"

—*"All power to the people."* This abstract phrase has become very popular worldwide in recent years. We have already discussed the fact that there is no such living entity as "the people." The problem, therefore, is that no one is ever sure who "the people" are. Am I a people? Are you a people?

Again, the translation is pretty obvious. Anyone who shouts this irrational battle cry is really saying, "All power to those individuals whom *I* deem to be 'the people.' " And, as revolutions throughout history have shown—including recent revolutions in Iran, Ethiopia, Cambodia and many other countries—"the people" always turn out to be the handful of individuals who led the revolution.

If it were to be taken seriously, "all power to the people" would have to mean each person's having power over his own life, which certainly would be proper. What it really means to most of those who use it, however, is that some people desire power over the lives of others.

The Frills

While intellectually inspired propaganda, twisted and confusing words, and intimidating slogans are government's main mental weapons for maintaining peaceful control of the masses, there are other kinds of actions it employs in an effort to appeal to the emotions of citizens.

One of these is the "ceremony." This method has been used effectively in every known civilization throughout history. It is a call to one's emotions, which means an appeal to set aside one's reasoning power. Nonetheless, the time-tested effectiveness of the ceremony cannot be disputed. Says Eric Hoffer:

"When faith and the power to persuade or coerce are gone, make-believe lingers on. There is no doubt that in staging its processions, parades, rituals and ceremonials, a mass movement touches a responsive chord in every heart. Even the most sober-minded are carried away by the sight of an impressive mass spectacle."[61]

In this light, it was rather depressing to watch government spend billions of dollars to "celebrate" the bicentennial of the United States a few years ago. What were we celebrating, the fact that our once libertarian society had evolved into a welfare state in two hundred years? That a country once comprised of rugged individualists who wanted only to be left alone to pursue their own happiness had evolved into a socialistic society? That the experiment of our ancestors—the attempt to make men superior to government—had failed, and that government once again was in control of men's lives?

People who thrilled to the glamour of the Bicentennial Celebration reacted in the precise manner desired by government. The spectacle of the year-long celebration took most people's minds off the fact that the American Dream was on its last legs. To me, the Bicentennial Celebration was like a rowdy funeral procession. The eloquent words and actions of all those responsible for it were a cruel hoax on the American people. It was the ultimate in doublethink: the celebration of the loss of freedom.

Finally, there is "tradition." The appeal to people to do things only because they have been done before is again an appeal to dispense with one's reasoning power. When people go along with actions just because they are steeped in "tradition," they place a mysterious divinity on the passage of time which puts it above morality. The unquestioned acceptance of such immoral actions as the draft, compulsory education and taxation are prime examples. Says Will Durant:

"Time sanctifies everything; even the most arrant theft, in the hands of the robber's grandchildren, becomes sacred and inviolable property. Every state begins in compulsion; but the habits of obedience become the content of conscience, and soon every citizen thrills with loyalty to the flag."[62]

It is truly incredible how an immoral action gains an air of respectability with the passage of time. No one remembers that the Queen of England's ancestors were barbarians who conquered that land through savage violence. If one is to follow blindly the traditions of one's government, no matter how useless or immoral such traditions may be, then murder, theft or enslavement can be justified by the mere argument that such actions have been previously acceptable.

To build patriotic and unquestioned loyalty in the mind of every citizen—to make him love his servitude—is the most desirable method of control for any government. Our government has been especially effective at this, making slow but continuous strides toward the ultimate: total control of people through total control of the mind. Whether this ultimate aim can ever be achieved is a question pondered by Erich Fromm: "Can human nature be changed in such a way that man will forget his longing for freedom, for dignity, for integrity, for love—that is to say, can man forget that he is human?"

STRUCTURE OF SERVITUDE

At present it is unrealistic to believe that every citizen will cooperate with government's wishes, no matter how cleverly the tools of propaganda are used by the power-holders. Therefore, behind the mental control of any population, there must be a firm structure of law. The more effective the manipulation of people's thought processes, however, the less government must rely on laws to keep its system of rule in place.

But the law is an essential tool of control, and can be used rapaciously when necessary. As Will and Ariel Durant put it, "Animals eat one another without qualm; civilized men consume one another by due process of law." The dependence on a legal structure to place forcible limits on the freedom of men is part and parcel of every government's overall system of control.

Since all governments, including democracies, insist that citizens obey their laws, all governments are, to that extent, authoritarian; i.e., they demand unquestioning submission to authority.

Most libertarians agree that laws which protect individuals from unprovoked force and fraud are justifiable; unfortunately, however, the vast majority of existing laws have nothing whatsoever to do with protection of lives and property. Most laws, as already discussed, do just the opposite; i.e., they *validate* the use of force against citizens. Victimless-crime laws, such as those discussed in Chapter 6, are prime examples of this.

Today, in addition to the continual campaigns on the part of absolute moralists to pass still more laws to restrict still further the freedom of citizens, there are also many "countercrusades" to "legalize" various acts that are currently outlawed. The significance of the latter illustrates just how twisted the original concept of freedom has become. If men truly were free, why would things have to be legalized? Free men have the right to do anything they please so long as they are not violating the rights of others. Natural rights do not have to be granted. If government is inclined to legalize anything, it should legalize freedom!

THE OBSTRUCTION

It is amazing how many people do not know the difference between the Declaration of Independence and the Constitution—or even that there is a difference. The Declaration of Independence was, in effect, the birth of the American Dream. It was approved by the Continental Congress in Philadelphia on July 4, 1776.

The Declaration of Independence was *not* a set of laws and did not establish or authorize the formation of a new government. On the contrary, this document, in effect, announced that men were superior to government and that the existing government had no moral right to rule them.

The Declaration of Independence was indeed an historic document, a radical experiment in freedom which stated, among other things, that men are endowed with "certain unalienable rights," including "life, liberty, and the pursuit of happiness"; that governments derive "their just powers from the consent of the governed"; and that "whenever any form of government becomes destructive of these ends, it is the right of the people to alter or to abolish it."

While it is true that the Declaration of Independence also stated that men have the *right* "to institute new government," it did not say that men were *compelled* to form or be ruled by a new government. The Declaration of Independence was by far the boldest statement in history on the issue of individual freedom. It clearly was a temporary obstruction for those who aspired to control the lives of others.

THE STRUCTURE

So from July 4, 1776, the people of this country lived under circumstances rarely, if ever, experienced in the recorded history of man: a virtual absence of centralized control over the lives of individuals. This glorious fling of near-total freedom lasted for almost thirteen years, until the "passage" of a set of man-made rules called "The Constitution of the United States."

We have been told since we were children that "the beauty of the Constitution lies in its flexibility." Doublethink. What "flexibility" really means is that those in power can keep changing the rules to suit themselves simply by creating something known as an "amendment."

Amendments burden citizens with new laws (virtually always in violation of their natural rights) or nullify rights guaranteed in the original Constitution. Not only do men not have the right to grant natural rights to other men (because all men already possess such rights at birth), but what the "flexibility" of the Constitution really means is that any rights arbitrarily "granted" by its original authors can be withdrawn at any time by current power-holders.

A perfect example of just how "beautiful" the flexibility of the Constitution can be was the passage of the Sixteenth Amendment, which became law on March 15, 1913. As discussed in Chapter 7, this amendment made it "legal" for government to use force to take various percentages of people's incomes, such percentages to be subject to change at any time at the sole discretion of those in power.

In addition, the Sixteenth Amendment nullified a guarantee made in the original Constitution. Article I, Section IX, Clause IV stated that no tax could be levied "unless in proportion to the census," meaning that no one could be taxed a greater amount than any other person. (This reference to taxes, of course, was not a reference to income taxes; taxes on income were unheard of at that time.) But the Sixteenth Amendment simply washed away this guarantee by stating the opposite: that Congress *could* tax people "without regard to any census."

Such flexibility is beautiful all right—from the standpoint of politicians. When one recalls that it was also in 1913 that government took total control of the money system, through passage of the Federal Reserve Act, it must be admitted that 1913 was a *very* good year for government. These two actions legalized theft on a grand scale and paved the way for future government "functions" which would help to perpetuate The System.

As if the power to amend the Constitution were not bad enough, government itself also has the sole right to *interpret* the Constitution. And virtually every Article and Amendment *needs* interpreting, because they are notoriously vague. Men—government men—decide what every word in the Constitution means.

Finally, there is the so-called elastic clause of the Constitution, inconspicuously hidden away in Article I, Section VIII, Clause XVIII. This is the clause that, in effect, renders all "rights" granted under the Constitution meaningless; the word *flexible* would be a drastic understatement here. The "elastic clause" gives government the right to "make all laws which shall be necessary and proper for carrying into execution the foregoing powers, and all other powers vested by this Constitution in the Government of the United States, or in any department or office thereof."

Translation: Government has the right to do anything!

It is interesting to note that, while the law is the structure that stands behind mental control of the populace, it is that same mental control which in turn is instrumental in getting people to obey the law. Through years of conditioning, people have been trained to accept the law as a given; the idea is to induce individuals to use the law as a starting point—a premise—regarding all questions of morality.

This, of course, is completely backwards. One does not prove that a law is moral simply by stating that it *is* a law. Laws *can* be moral; they can also be immoral—and usually are. The important thing is to realize that laws have no relationship to morality. For example, Article IV, Section II, Clause III of the Constitution not only condoned slavery, but made it *illegal* not to turn in a runaway slave. If one were to insist on connecting morality with the law, then he would have to be willing to state that, at least prior to 1865, slavery was moral.

But to a person who believes in Natural Law, all laws which legalize theft, enslavement or any other form of forcible interference in the life of *any* human being—no matter in what terms such laws may be couched and no matter what the purported justifications of such laws may be—are immoral. The reality, therefore, is that most laws—federal, state and local—are immoral.

Politicians preach about respecting the law, but I must go along with Thoreau, who said, "It is not desirable to cultivate a respect for the law, so much as for the right." Unfortunately, laws are but dictums forced upon people to assure that servitude has a structure. Tyranny can be decorated with impressive-sounding legal language, but that does not change the fact that it is tyranny.

The few laws which actually do protect men from aggression are morally valid. But the true purpose of *most* laws is to protect *government* from the threat of men becoming free. Notwithstanding this reality, a pragmatic person realizes that if one were to challenge every immoral law, he would soon be in jail—or dead.

No matter how much libertarian purists may protest to the contrary, the fact is that you can do nothing to enhance the cause of freedom—neither your own freedom nor the freedom of others—if you are locked up. The legal system, rightly or wrongly, is what gives structure to our servitude. No government can afford to be without a set of laws, no matter how meaningless or immoral such laws may be.

Therefore, while one should do everything within his power to respect the natural rights of others, he should proceed with caution when it comes to matters of law.

FORCE OF SERVITUDE

At last we get to the bottom line of control, as expressed so candidly by one of the more famous mass murderers in history, Mao Tse-tung: "Political power grows out of the barrel of a gun." These are probably the only words Mao ever spoke with which I agree, but it is sad to have to admit that the statement is a true fact of life.

Gunpower is the argument that never fails!

Without the threat of force behind the structure of the

law, there would always be some people who would refuse to obey those in power. The intellectual rhetoric, the
slogans, the ceremonies, and all the rest of the mental
games government plays are effective; the sanctity of the
law is pretty much accepted; but, in the end—and prefer-
ably far in the background—it is government's willingness
to use force, when necessary, that ensures *absolute* control of citizens.

Obviously it is unwise for powerholders to flaunt their
gunpower. As noted, the most practical (and safest)
method of control is to concentrate on the mental approach. But reality dictates that there must be laws behind mental control and there must be brute force behind
laws. As Machiavelli pointed out, "You cannot have good
laws without good arms."

In order for government force to be effective, one
group must have an absolute monopoly on its use. At the
outset of Chapter 2, I pointed out that one of the two
characteristics common to all governments—whether they
be democracies or dictatorships—is an institutionalized
way of controlling people, backed up by a monopoly on
the use of force. As John Hospers explains it, if there are
two entities competing for the use of force within a nation, then that country is in a state of civil war.

Needless to say, if you really were a free person, no
one, including government representatives, could use force
against you. To the extent that government uses force for
any reason other than to protect individuals from aggression, such force is immoral and is in violation of
Natural Law. And since Natural Law is violated not only
by the use of force, but by the threat of force, *all* political
action (other than that intended to protect individuals
from aggression) is immoral; that is so because all political action carries with it the threat of force.

The fact that men still use force to control the lives of
other men is the most uncivilized aspect of our twentieth-

century civilization. But it is a reality that has always existed and is not likely to go away, for it is the ultimate assurance that The System will not be challenged.

Force is the last resort for keeping it all in place—for ensuring control of the people should all else fail.

9

Taking Back America

The time has come. The citizens of this country either must draw the line and take America back from the politicians who now control it or they must be prepared to relinquish forever their remaining claims on liberty.

By "taking back America," I am not implying that the geographical area of the U.S.A. should belong to everyone in common; that type of unintelligible nonsense is for the collectivist-minded liberals who have helped to raise government to its current omnipotent position.

By "taking back America," I mean nothing short of *restoring the American Dream*. This means each individual's regaining his right to his life, his liberty and his pursuit of happiness. It is time for Big Brother to get out of our lives—to let go of the reins and allow us to control our own destinies. Self-responsibility was and is an integral part of the American Dream.

The fundamental concept of our founding fathers was that people have a natural right to sovereignty over their own lives and that governments have no right to interfere with that sovereignty. In that respect, the Declaration of Independence, as a document, was unique in human history. For the first time, men were saying that they were above government, that governments derive "their just powers from the consent of the governed."

"American Government," said Rose Wilder Lane, "is not an Authority; it has no control over individuals and no responsibility for their affairs. American Government is a permission which free individuals grant to certain men to use force in certain necessary and strictly limited ways; a permission which Americans can always withdraw from American Government."[63]

Government, therefore, has nothing whatsoever to do with the American Dream. On the contrary, it is government that has succeeded in nearly destroying that dream. The American Dream is a way of life that can be experienced only by free individuals.

It is important to understand that the American Dream has nothing to do with a "country." The American Dream has to do with the freedom of people to pursue their own happiness without interference from others. It could have originated anywhere in the world, but, fortunately for us, its birth occurred in an area referred to as the United States of America.

Therefore, when I say I love America, my statement should be more clearly defined. It is true that I like much of the natural beauty of our country, as well as the climates in many of its areas. But what loving America really means to me is loving the American Dream. It means loving freedom and individualism. It means admiring all of the millions of people who have contributed both to the birth of the American Dream and to its furtherance. It means admiring all people living today, both in America and throughout the world, who passionately believe in the cause of human freedom. These people cannot be distinguished by race, religious belief, nationality, occupation or sex. They can be distinguished only by their common belief that liberty must be accorded the highest of all values.

What I do not love is the fact that another concept has challenged, and nearly destroyed, the American Dream. The proponents of the "welfare state," or collectivist society, have succeeded in making millions of people believe that the American Dream is "outdated." Nothing could be further from the truth; an idea as basic as freedom can never be outdated. On the contrary, I would see the limitation of the power of man over man as a sign of progress. The reality is that the American Dream was barely in its infancy when its destruction began.

In truth, it is the firmly controlled society (i.e., the totalitarian-ruled society) that is outdated; it has been around since the beginning of recorded time. Indeed, it is rare to find a government at any time in history, anywhere in the world, that was not a monarchy or other kind of dictatorship. The attempt to make men free was almost unheard of until 1776.

In handling my personal affairs, a basic rule of mine is to stick with things that have worked for me in the past (assuming that they also stand the test of logic). This strategy has rarely failed me. When I look at the history of the United States, I ask myself what has worked and what has not worked. Our history has made it very clear that freedom and self-responsibility—i.e., a lack of government intervention and restraint—have worked.

How do I know this? For the simple reason that, from the moment we undertook our bold experiment in freedom, people began to pour into our country by the millions in search of the American Dream. It was the Industrial-Revolution reasoning all over again: people do not travel thousands of miles across oceans, at great risk and expense, leaving familiar surroundings behind, to settle in a new country where the situation is not much better than that which they left. The truth about American "poverty" before the onset of Big Government is that, by comparison to what people left behind in their homelands, America was a dream come true. Most of all, America was the dream of freedom come true.

People are mistaken who believe that before the advent of Big Government, the American Dream was not available to the masses. The American Dream meant the *freedom* to pursue a better life, and it was that freedom which inspired millions of people to cross the oceans to get to America. Those millions of immigrants were not looking for government handouts; they were looking for *opportunity*. The American Dream gave them that opportunity.

What has *not* worked is government intervention. The early generations in this country laid the foundation for the greatest advances in the history of mankind—both technological and socioeconomic—*prior* to the Federal Reserve Act (the key to inflation), the Sixteenth Amendment (the institution of income taxes), the New Deal and the Great Society. All of the latter have helped lead to the destruction of a way of life that was so magnificent that people from all over the world yearned to share in it.

We *do* live in the greatest and freest country on earth. But it is much less great and much less free than it was. The question is, do we love living here enough to do something about preserving what is left of that greatness and freedom, enough to try to restore them to their original status?

Those who call others unpatriotic or negative because they point out the realities of our decaying structure have it backwards. It is they who are unpatriotic, for it is they who apparently do not love freedom enough to do something about restoring it.

For example, a typical reaction of a blind "patriot" might be to feel that I should be thankful for living in a country where I am allowed to write books such as this one. Should I? I think not. For if I sincerely believe that human freedom is a natural state, then it follows that it is my natural right to express my ideas openly. I think it would be improper, as well as contradictory, for me to be thankful to others for allowing me to do something that it is my inherent right to do.

I am, however, glad that I do not live in a country that

would *not* allow me to write this book. And therein lies an important point. I am not writing this book because I think that the United States has the *worst* form of government in the world. If anything, I am writing it for the opposite reason—the fact that we probably still *are* the freest country on earth, but that I am concerned that we are moving ever more rapidly in the direction of other liberty-starved nations around the globe. I am writing it because I believe that our government, like all governments throughout history, is winning its long-standing tender offer to its citizens: "security" in exchange for freedom.

In *The Federalist Papers,* James Madison warned, "In framing a government which is to be administered by men over men, the great difficulty lies in this: you must first enable the government to control the governed; and in the next place oblige it to control itself."

Madison's warnings were not heeded. The government did not, and does not, "control itself." "Government by the people" now means that government can take a substantial amount of your income, can evict you from your home if you refuse to pay the "real-estate taxes" it establishes, can close the doors to your business if you do not do as it tells you (including handing over a large percentage of your profits), can print worthless "dollars" to help others compete with your hard-earned dollars for the goods and services available in the marketplace, can dictate what prices you must charge for your products and what you must pay your employees, can tell you what you can and cannot put into your own body, and can interfere with your private sexual behavior, to name but a few examples.

"Government by the people" has come to mean *government by those in power*.

It took many millennia before man was ready to make his way out of the jungle and onto the savannah. But once the Agrarian Revolution began, his life became one of rapid change. The Agrarian Revolution brought with it the advent of government, and, except for a few brief moments in history, men of power have been in control ever since.

The biggest setback to governmental control over men was the American Revolution. Within less than one hundred and fifty years, however, the government of this country had begun to assert firm control over Americans. While democracy was perhaps the best form of government ever devised, once The System became firmly entrenched it was only a matter of time before powerholders contrived a way to manipulate it to their advantage. The key to The System became Majority Rule, engineered through the power of The Vote. As early as 1857, Thomas Macaulay, the British historian, predicted what the inevitable results of The System would be:

The day will come when (in the United States) a multitude of people will choose the legislature. Is it possible to doubt what sort of a legislature will be chosen? On the one side is a statesman preaching patience, respect for rights, strict observance of public faith. On the other is a demagogue ranting about the tyranny of capitalism and usurers and asking why anybody should be permitted to drink champagne and to ride in a carriage while thousands of honest people are in want of necessaries. Which of the candidates is likely to be preferred by a workman? . . . When Society has entered on this downward progress, either civilization or liberty must perish. Either some Caesar or Napoleon will seize the reins of government with a strong hand, or your Republic will be as fearfully plundered and laid waste by barbarians in the twentieth century as the Roman Empire in the fifth; with this difference, that the Huns and vandals who ravaged the Roman Empire came from without, and that your Huns and vandals will have been engendered within your country, by yoru own institutions.[64]

Macaulay's powers of prophecy were incredibly accurate. Our democracy has destroyed itself through an excess of democracy. Majority Rule has evolved into a free-for-all stampede of citizens appealing to politicians to give them more of the plunder. On the horizon is chaos, and just beyond is totalitarian rule.

It is time to face the reality that man no longer shapes government to his liking; government shapes man to *its* liking, via the clever use of The Vote. *Atlas Shrugged, Brave New World* and *Nineteen Eighty-four* can no longer be lightly tossed aside as fantasies. These books were *prophecies,* and the prophecies are becoming true before our very eyes. Indeed, many of the "fantasies" in books like these not only have come to pass, but are now accepted as a normal way of life.

Today one feels the ether of these books in the air. Rational people know that there is something wrong. There is tension and uncertainty. There is ill will. There is fear. Eric Hoffer observes that "the feeling of doom is stronger now. There is a widespread feeling that our economic system and our civilization are nearing their end. In the 1930s we still had values, ideals, hopes, illusions, certitudes. In the 1970s many people see life drained of meaning, and there is hardly a certitude left."[65]

The excitement of living seems to have deserted us. The spirit of adventure and the willingness to take risks are gone. Our once cherished Stoic virtues have been abandoned. We have allowed the powerholders to steal from us the joy of life itself. Two hundred years of government-inspired nothink and doublethink have desecrated the American Dream.

Now the question is, can it be restored?

REALITY

The starting point for resolving any problem is reality. If one is to solve a problem, or at least improve upon it, he must acknowledge what he is up against. There are many unpleasant realities which stand in the way of restoring the American Dream, and, quite frankly, they have always tended to make me pessimistic. Regardless of any pessimism they may cause, however, they cannot be ignored if we are to have any hope at all of taking back America.

First, of course, is the reality that there have always been and always will be men who aspire to power over others. To make matters worse, the envious nature and absolute morality of a great many people fuel this yearning for power. People who desire to see the happiness and success of those more fortunate than they destroyed, or who want to impose their moral standards on their neighbors, are a politician's dream. Along with the other expedient desires of virtually all citizens, these two ugly desires in particular are able to tyrannize peace-loving men through the mechanism of The Vote.

Because of these realities, it is probably unrealistic to believe that men can ever be completely free, i.e., literally free of all government control.

We should also face the reality that "democracy" is a power scheme which few men will ever understand. If it operated strictly on the basis of safeguarding the rights of individuals, democracy probably would work very well. But in its twentieth-century version, it is something quite different. It not only gives the illusion of consent of the people, it also creates the illusion (through short-term benefits) of helping the "poor." But it is doubtful that the "poor" can be made to understand, at least until it is far too late, that they are only being used as pawns.

Another reality of no minor consequence is that most people living today have grown up in an era of increasingly collectivist thinking. They understand neither the realities of collectivism nor that there is a far superior alternative to it. Never having experienced the freedom of the early 1900's, let alone the freedom of our founding fathers, they have no way of realizing—especially in view of the well-planned nothink and doublethink teachings of our public schools—that what they are experiencing is not freedom.

Then there are those who insist on hiding their heads in the sand and merely tossing it all aside with the attitude that "the world has always had problems." Such people often point to the fact that we survived the Great Depression with flying colors. But, as John Hospers detailed in an article in *Reason* magazine, these people avoid many sobering realities. For one thing, the federal deficit, in 1929, was minuscule by today's standards; today it is an economic lodestone around the neck of every citizen. In 1929, the dollar still had substantial gold backing; today our currency is nothing but paper. Prior to the Great Depression, the free lunch was practically unknown; today government handouts and other government functions have destroyed our incentive and consequently our productive capacity, and people have come to expect them.

I could go on, but I believe the point has been made. The hard realities that stand between freedom lovers and the restoration of the American Dream are considerable in both number and size. Given these realities, some people have even opted to "escape"—to leave the United States. But there is a sobering reality attached to that solution too: today there is virtually no place on earth to which a man may escape to be free. No matter where you go, there will be a government in control. And most, if not all of them, will be worse than our own government—at least for now.

Given the slim chances of finding a better place in which to live, I believe that the best hope for the American Dream is to try to bring it back to America.

SOLUTIONS

Unfortunately, as every adult is well aware, there are no perfect solutions in this world; solutions are created by men, and men are imperfect creatures. I stated from the outset that this book made no pretense of being an end-all-be-all, and I hold to that. I do, however, believe that the situation can be improved; perhaps this is a naiveté I will outgrow with age.

I would like you to think of the suggestions I offer in this final chapter as sparks. It is my hope that they will ignite enthusiasm and creativity in other advocates of human freedom and that those people, in turn, will devise more and better ideas for recapturing liberty.

Before I put the first word of this book on paper, I realized that when one attempts to make people conscious of realities, he is all but assured of being written off by many as a "prophet of doom." On the other hand, if one writes only in idealistic terms, few rational people will take him seriously.

In trying to come up with solutions, my objective has been to link *realism* and *idealism*. In other words, given the *realities* of our situation, what is the most *practical* action we can take to begin to approach the dream of a free society?

This translates into the following question: How can we best deal with the unpleasant realities *which now exist* in such a way as to best improve our long-term well-being and that of future generations?

The answer, I am sad to say, is that practicality dictates that we cannot adhere to strict libertarianism—at least initially. Intellectually, I shall always adhere to pure libertarianism. But from the standpoint of practical solutions, of bringing about libertarian *change* rather than libertarian *discussion*, I feel it is a grave mistake to refuse to take reality into consideration in attacking the problems that exist in the real world of today. Whether a totally free society is ever possible is an academic question at this time; *taking the first step toward it is not.*

Like my Agrarian-Revolution ancestors, I myself am not positive that civilization can exist without some form of government. That is a hard confession for a libertarian to make, but perhaps I have not evolved far enough in my thinking (and in my belief in mankind) to envision a civilized society, in the twentieth century, totally devoid of any form of government.

For those who believe in freedom, but who share my apprehensions about a governmentless society, the original contradiction remains: that in order to preserve freedom, freedom must be restricted. While on the one hand we acknowledge the need for protection from forcible interference by others, the reality is that the mere existence of government *is* forcible interference.

The crucial question, then, is where does one draw the line between individual independence and "social control?" How does one define exactly what constitutes "forcible interference?" Is pollution of the air (including noise pollution, for example) forcible interference? The law of nonaggression is a good guide, but admittedly many questions about freedom are subjective enough to cause problems. Even in a totally libertarian world there would still be the problem of what to do when one man's freedom allegedly interferes with that of another man.

Is democracy the best solution we can come up with in an attempt to be free in a civilized world? At present, it appears to be (although many hardcore libertarians believe that a world with no government at all would work very well). To concede that democracy is probably the best system that has been created until now, however, does not rule out the possibility of a better solution at some future date. Our minds should always be open to this possibility if we are sincere about our desire to improve our own well-being and that of all mankind.

But until that better solution comes along, I believe we would be wise to try to maximize the present system. And maximizing the system means *minimizing* the problem: government. It means acting on the motto, "that government is best which governs least."

What a nightmarish predicament for a libertarian to find himself in. By conceding even minimal powers to government, he is conceding that some rights of some men must be violated. This is so because government, in order to perform *any* function, must expropriate assets from others.

(The pure libertarian's solution to this dilemma, of course, is to make taxation and government control voluntary and to recognize the right of every individual to self-rule; i.e., if anyone does not wish to subscribe to government "protection," he should be left alone to fend for himself. Morally speaking, what right does "the majority" have to force him to come under government rule? If democratic government is truly "by consent of the governed," then it would seem that anyone wishing not to be governed should be allowed to go his own way. For purposes of our discussion, however, I will disregard this point, since it opens areas of debate which, for proper presentation, would require far more space than we have here.)

Early in this book I said that if a person claims to understand human freedom, yet insists on certain exceptions to it, he either is admitting that he is advocating the violation of Natural Law or he is demonstrating that he does not really grasp the concept of human freedom. It is important for me to emphasize, therefore, that I am *not* advocating the violation of Natural Law when I concede minimal functions to government. On the contrary, I am advocating that government control of individuals' lives be reduced as much as possible and as quickly as is practical. I am advocating a maximum return to freedom.

While from a philosophical standpoint it may be despicable to agree to "compromise," I would argue that to decrease current violations of Natural Law by 99% is not a bad near-term goal. That accomplished, we can then concentrate on how best to handle the remaining 1%— i.e., the remaining government functions—on a wholly consensual basis without the need for government coercion.

Nevertheless, so long as that 1% exists, the same questions will continue to haunt us: Whose rights shall be violated? To what extent? Who shall decide? The hope that these questions can be resolved in a manner that is reasonably satisfactory to us rests on an assumption that I made at the outset of this book: that most men and women, when armed with truth, will act honestly and decently; that most men and women are basically good, but are misled; that most men and women, once they understand the facts, will act in good faith.

If these assumptions are erroneous, then it is doubtful that *any* solution will work.

WHAT WON'T WORK

Before discussing a number of steps which I believe, if taken, can help to restore liberty in this country, it would be instructive to examine a few things that *won't* work. Too often when people are eager for solutions, they plunge in recklessly and take the same kind of expedient action that has caused the very problems with which we are now confronted. As Bernard Baruch, the great wizard of Wall Street, pointed out, rushing around and taking action just for the sake of action usually proves nonproductive:

> Mankind has always sought to substitute energy for reason, as if running faster will give one a better sense of direction. Periodically, we should stop and ask ourselves if our efforts are focused upon the crux of the problem— the things that must be settled if there is to be a manageable solution—or if we are expending our energies on side issues which cannot yield a decision, no matter what their outcome.[66]

Some examples of things that *won't* work:

—*Either listening to, or dishing out, meaningless "patriotic" rhetoric, whether in the form of slogans, admonishing statements, or appeals to custom and tradition.* None of this "patriotic" gibberish will do one thing to change the realities of where we now stand.

You are not indebted to "government" (which means politicians) for allowing you to exercise some of your remaining natural rights. You were born with these rights, and government can take them away from you only through the use of force. Said Rose Wilder Lane:

> If Americans ever forget that American Government is not permitted to restrain or coerce any peaceful individual without his free consent, if Americans ever regard their use of their natural liberty as granted to them by the men in Washington or in the capitals of the States, then this third attempt (the American Revolution) to establish the exercise of human rights on earth is ended. . . .
>
> Everything that an American values, his property, his home, his life, his children's future, depends upon his keeping clear in his mind the revolutionary basis of this Republic.
>
> This revolutionary basis is recognition of the fact that human rights are natural rights, born in every human being with his life, and inseparable from his life; *not*

*rights and freedoms that can be granted by any power
on earth.*[67]

Self-proclaimed patriots profess a love of "country";
libertarians profess a love of human freedom.

—*Continuing to listen to half-cocked, short-term solutions served up by vote-conscious politicians.* We have
had our fill of these since Roosevelt and his New Deal.
When people's emotions run high, they are apt to do exactly the wrong thing: follow a charismatic leader who offers easy solutions. This means short-term patching,
which only causes things to get worse.

Each president serves up a new batch of "solutions,"
which he feels will strengthen his voter appeal. Jimmy
Carter's selection included such things as dumping free-
enterprise trading partner Taiwan for the criminal dictatorship in Mainland China, blackmailing businessmen
with "voluntary" wage-and-price controls that were anything but voluntary, and admonishing Israel for not hurry-
ing to conclude a peace treaty with Egypt so that his
ratings might go up in the polls.

It is time to start ignoring the political "solutions" that
have actually been the *cause* of our problems. Powerholders should no longer have your ear when they offer
mumbo-jumbo explanations of inflation, decry the need to
"protect the public morals," or espouse the evils of
profits.

To paraphrase Voltaire, men will stop committing
atrocities when men stop believing absurdities.

—*Looking to government for solutions to your problems.* Government cannot solve your problems because
government *is* the problem. When people proclaim that
"there ought to be a law" to correct what they deem to be
a "social injustice," they are advocating the use of government force to make others conform to their desires of
moral beliefs.

Government force is something we should strive to minimize. The world is full of problems and purported injustices. If you use your efforts to try to solve these problems through the use of government force (i.e., the passage of laws), you are *increasing* the problems. If you mind your own business and concentrate on your own freedom and self-sufficiency, you are contributing to the solution.

Compassion is a good thing; charity is a good thing; concern is a good thing. Force is *not* a good thing. The question is not whether man loves his fellowman enough to insist on "helping" him. The survival question for mankind is whether man loves his fellowman enough to leave him alone! Your neighbor has the right to be left alone to live his life as he pleases.

—*Getting hung up on the question of equality.* Guaranteed security and equality conflict with freedom. As Will and Ariel Durant have said, "when one prevails the other dies." Efforts toward forcible equality have gained momentum over the past fifty years, which is exactly why freedom has been dying. The American Dream gives all men equal *rights*; it does not call for *making* all men equal.

—*Wasting your time arguing with irrational people— people who believe that something for nothing is possible, that theft is justified by a "worthwhile" end, or that government is a living, omnipotent, omnibenevolent entity that can solve everyone's problems.* You do not have enough time to improve your well-being, enhance the cause of liberty, and also function as a flyswatter.

WHAT YOU CAN DO WITHOUT BECOMING A CRUSADER

Many people do not have the inclination to get involved in movements or crusades, because they believe that they are a waste of time. I generally agree with such a view. But you *can* help to take back America, and thereby regain much of your individual freedom, without becoming involved in group action. You can make major contributions to restoring the American Dream without becoming a crusader.

There are several ways in which this can be accomplished:

—*Most important, be consistent on the issue of human freedom.* In dealing with others, *always* adhere to the philosophy of nonaggression. I stated in Chapter 1 of this book that the initial premise for the philosophy of libertarianism is that each man owns his own life and therefore has the right to do anything he wishes with his life, so long as he does not use force or fraud against others. I termed this concept Natural Law.

I also emphasized that liberty must be given a higher value than *all* other objectives, and that one may not, with integrity, abandon his belief in the supremacy of liberty on an emotional whim. This means rejecting *any* action that involves aggression against others, no matter how worthy you may believe the objective to be.

This unrelenting commitment to liberty requires an understanding of, and belief in, the inseparable connection between freedom and property rights. To take a man's property, regardless of the justification, is a violation of his human freedom. You should refuse to be a part of any such action in every area possible (meaning in areas other than those in which government's use of force, or the threat of such force, leaves you no alternative).

Being adamantly in favor of liberty does not mean that you are insensitive to the needs of others, so do not allow anyone to intimidate you with such accusations. Attempting to solve the needs of the "poor" by the use of force against others is an immoral action and will only succeed in creating bigger problems.

You may wish to contribute to charity voluntarily, and

it is certainly your right to do so. Indeed, one of the things which would emerge from a restoration of the American Dream would be an increase in voluntary charity. When people are free to keep what they earn, a spirit of charity is much more likely to prevail.

—*Wage a personal battle against any traces of envy that may have a hold on you*. This is a negative emotion which not only is counterproductive to your attempts to improve your own well-being, but also has been very instrumental in the destruction of the American Dream. Dispense with any notion you may have that your neighbor's material success is somehow a loss to you.

Your success is totally dependent upon your own efforts. The opportunity to become as rich as one desired was an integral, subconscious thread that ran through the concept of the American Dream. As previously stated, America cannot afford *not* to have rich people, for they are the very backbone of productivity, employment, and a better life for all, with or without their enormous charitable contributions.

—*Demystify and desanctify government, both in your thinking and in your conversations with others*. This necessitates developing the habit of challenging basic assumptions. For example, while your peers may wish to debate which government projects or services are a waste of tax dollars or the extent to which people should be taxed, you should have the courage to challenge the basic premise, i.e., to point out that, regardless of the purposes for which certain people seem to believe certain funds should be used, *all* taxation is immoral because all taxation is theft.

Also, stop thinking of government as a living entity, and certainly do not be in awe of it. "Government" is a name given to millions of individuals, and the individuals who most exemplify what government stands for are power-hungry politicians whose expedient actions are based on The Vote. You are not being disloyal or unpatriotic when you do not go along with their every wish. If our system truly were "government of and by the people," then politicians would have to do as *you* say; if they did not, then it is *they* who would be guilty of being disloyal and unpatriotic.

Almost without fail, the long-term results of government actions are the exact opposite of what they are purported to be. Among the scores of examples covered in this book, perfect illustrations of this are how minimum-wage laws cause unemployment, how wage-and-price controls cause *higher* prices, and how licensing laws make it virtually impossible for those at the bottom of the economic ladder to start a business.

Above all, reject government's use of the "mysterious-multiplier" concept. As noted, that "concept" is a sham.

If you develop a true understanding of the myths about government and make the real facts known to others in your normal day-to-day conversations, you will be making an important contribution to the cause of liberty without being involved in a crusade.

—*Never go out of your way to cooperate with the government.* Where possible, avoid situations that would involve your becoming entangled with government in any way. Some people, due either to intimidating patriotic rhetoric or to the erroneous belief that government is all-good, all-knowing and/or all-powerful, mistakenly go out of their way to make it easier for government to interfere in their lives.

Going above and beyond the call of duty when it comes to refusing to take legitimate tax deductions is a good example of this type of error. Neither should government influence your decisions regarding foods, vitamins and other substances you wish to take into your own body, or decisions regarding sexual matters or any other area which comes under the heading of victimless-crime laws. You are not morally obligated to cooperate with government's audacious attempts to interfere in your private life, although, for practical reasons, you do have an obligation to yourself to be discreet.

It goes without saying that investing in government "securities" would be the biggest of all mistakes in cooperating with government violations of freedom. First of all, the money raised from the sale of such securities is used to support government functions, almost all of which entail aggression toward others. Second, such securities can only be paid off through the sale of new securities, and this glorified Ponzi Scheme could very easily collapse in the not-too-distant future. In that event, government would simply resort to the same action it took with regard to its gold-warehouse receipts: refuse to pay them.

—*Making an unwavering commitment to become fiercely independent and individualistic*. The restoration of the American Dream is the restoration of self-responsibility. Self-actualization is an exhilarating experience which government cannot "hand out" to someone. By minding your own store—by being independent and individualistic—you can make a great contribution to freedom simply because you will be eliminating yourself as a part of the problem. Thoreau believed that "living one's own life to the full is the best means of helping one's fellow man." I totally agree.

The Stoic virtues—individualism, self-control, self-responsibility and respect for private property—which made the American Dream come true for millions of people, are in direct contrast to the desire for guaranteed security and dependence on government. "The price of individual liberty," said Rose Wilder Lane, "is individual responsibility and insecurity. . . . When common men were slaves and serfs, they obeyed and they were fed, but they died by thousands in plagues and famines. Free men paid for their freedom by leaving that false and illusory security."⁶⁸

The only way that you, as an individual, can ever hope to be free—at least in mind and spirit, if not in body—is to know that you have earned everything you have received. And that brings us to the next point—one of the toughest to adhere to, but perhaps the most important of all.

—*When at all possible, neither ask for nor accept government favors, handouts or benefits of any kind.* While the realities of monopoly and coercion leave you no choice but to use some government services (roads, libraries, postal system, etc.), you should demonstrate your independence, individuality and self-esteem by refusing to participate in the theft of other people's property wherever possible. Nothing can be more devastating to vote-conscious politicians than to have their free-lunch offers refused.

Remember, in the final analysis it is the voters who are responsible for deficit spending and inflation, because it is their Expediency Factors which encourage politicians to take politically expedient actions. The government problem is therefore perpetuated by the fact that most citizens continue to clamor for their "share"—and more.

If you would rather be part of the solution than part of the problem, you should ask only one thing of government: to be left alone! Every individual who stops asking for and accepting handouts lessens government's motivations to steal.

The question that comes to mind, of course, is who will take the first step? Who will be the first to give up his free ride, while millions of others are still benefiting from the theft? The answer is *you*. If just every person who reads this book would start to refuse government benefits, a small ripple would begin to be felt. And if every person who reads this book would state his feelings to friends and acquaintances, it could cause a substantial ripple.

The cycle must be broken: politicians make politically expedient promises to get elected, violate the rights of citizens in order to carry out those promises, borrow money (which cannot be repaid) and inflate the currency (to pay for promises that cannot be covered by direct taxation and borrowing)—all of which help to destroy incentive and demoralize the public. The public in turn calls for government controls on business in response to politicians who mislead them as to the real source of their problems. The final effect of all this is to destroy production and employment.

The first step toward breaking this cycle is for you, the expediency-minded voter, to stop being fooled by short-term benefits designed only to capture votes. Start thinking long-term, which means being concerned about economic collapse and loss of freedom.

Forget about what has been stolen from you in the past and what is being stolen from you right now. If one were to insist that government reimburse him for every dollar it has taken from him, he could use that as an excuse to keep accepting government benefits forever. It is true that you will have to stand by and watch others get the benefit of your stolen dollars, but if individualism and self-responsibility can be popularized once more, that situation could improve each year. The point is, there has to be a first step; otherwise we shall all take the *last step*—together—in the near future.

You may feel that this is totally unfair, and, in theory, you are absolutely right. Perhaps, for example, you have paid heavily to enable others to receive Social-Security payments and you are looking forward to an early retirement loaded with "free" benefits. But the point I am trying to make—indeed, a central point of this book—is this: If our something-for-nothing fantasy does not soon end, there may not *be* any benefits for you when your time comes; indeed, there may not be any retirement for you at all!

If the economy continues on its present course, it must self-destruct, meaning not only that you will still be working long after the time you had planned to retire, but that you will be working at a job that government chooses for you, during the working hours it dictates to you, and for the wages it decides to pay you.

Everyone who receives a government check of any kind—which includes most Americans—is contributing to the destruction of America. This includes welfare checks, subsidy checks, government payroll checks, or any other kind of government check.

This is what I believe every citizen today should ask himself: Is my pension, my welfare check, my subsidy, my government salary—is my piece of the government pie—worth it to me if it means my children will live in a police state, a police state brought on by the financial collapse of America? Is it worth it to me if such a collapse and ensuing totalitarian rule occur during *my own lifetime?*

If you now work for the government, the biggest contribution you can make to America is to quit your job and find work in the private sector. If you are responsible and conscientious, the marketplace is full of opportunities for you. And when you put your efforts into private industry, you will be producing wealth—i.e., products and services that people *want*, not services they are *forced* to take.

Likewise, *if you are in a financial position to do so,* notify the government that you wish to forfeit Social Security and all other benefits which may be due you. Every action of this kind helps to contribute to the solution, without the need to become involved in any group movement.

Speaking for myself, I want no favors or benefits of any

kind from government, no matter how much government takes from me by force. I do not want Social Security; I do not want subsidies; and I certainly do not want government "protecting" me from myself, whether such presumptuous "protection" involves foods, medications or safety devices. I decline government "help" in all these areas, maintaining a staunch conviction that I am quite capable of making all decisions regarding my own wellbeing.

We must all grow up. We must become wary of anyone—especially the politician—who implies that people can live without producing. Government favors, services and handouts of all kinds involve theft, and the proceeds of such theft must be refused whenever and wherever circumstances permit us to do so. *Intellectually,* the morality of theft must be refuted at *all times.*

—*Do not think of yourself as part of a group.* Groups are grist for the politician's mill. By aligning yourself with others on the basis of sex, race, religion, profession, or on any other basis, you play right into the hands of vote seekers. The result is the creation of voting "blocs"—labor against business, blacks against whites, "rich" against "poor," men against women, and so on— blocs to which politicians can make expedient promises. Grouping is an Expediency-Factor trap laid by government.

If you are a black, a Mexican-American, a senior citizen, or a member of any "minority," refuse to allow government to use you as a political pawn. Politicians are not your friends; they use you to win elections. You have as valid a right to be individualistic as any other American. Government can use force against people, but it has no magical power to change their emotions. Self-respect and the respect of others must be earned; these are things government cannot give to anyone.

Think of yourself as an individual. For society to be free, *individuals* must be free!

—*Ignore self-styled "consumer advocates" and other publicity-hungry crusaders who have set themselves up as civilian protectors of the public.* Nader types have helped to accelerate government intervention and have thereby contributed greatly to the destruction of our economy. Neither Ralph Nader nor any other self-styled crusader has any right to speak on my behalf or yours; let people like this find other ways to assuage their egos.

If I am dissatisfied with a product or service, I am quite capable of complaining to the company from whom I purchased it. If the company refuses to give me satisfaction, I have the option either of not dealing with that company in the future or of taking the dispute to court (charging either fraud or a violation of an implied contractual obligation).

People must become highly suspicious of overzealous, publicity-hungry consumer and environmental advocates before it is too late.

—*If you are a businessman, stop running to government for special favors, monopoly protection, price fixing, and other forms of intervention.* The effects of such action have already been discussed at length. If you take part in its perpetuation, you are contributing to the problem; if you refuse to be a party to such government intervention, you are contributing to the solution.

In addition, stop appeasing free-enterprise antagonists. Have the courage to stand up for and openly defend the system that played a major role in making the American Dream a reality.

—*Take a rational, well-thought-out approach to the question of voting.* Because of the Four Great Political Realities mentioned in Chapter 2, coupled with the fact that voting seems to represent nothing but a validation of

The System, there is a very serious question as to the morality of the act of voting.

It certainly is not moral to commit aggression against others; yet when you vote for a candidate, you are voting to put someone in a position to rule the lives of your fellowmen—men who either do not want that candidate to rule them or do not want *anyone* to rule them. And if it is an issue you are voting for or against, you are usually voting to interfere with the lives of those who are on the opposite side of such an issue.

Another moral consideration is whether you are voting for someone because you genuinely favor his governing you or because you are adhering to the time-honored approach of most voters—voting for the "lesser of two evils."

Suppose that Candidate A, by your standards, is unfit for public office; likewise, you feel that Candidate B is unqualified to represent you. Is it still your patriotic duty to vote for one of these two men? Should you obediently cast your vote for the "lesser of two evils"—an election ritual that has been performed by untold millions—and cast your vote for *someone*?

As Sy Leon has explained, those who adhere to this philosophy ignore one important moral reality: *The lesser of two evils is still evil!*

Every time you vote for someone whom you consider to be the lesser of two evils, you cast a vote not for someone whom you genuinely desire to have represent you, but for despair. It is an admission on your part that you cannot fight The System—which may be true, but that does not mean you must contribute to its perpetuation.

The person who votes for a candidate simply because he is not as bad as the other candidate is the one who is apathetic; he is symbolically throwing in the towel via his ballot. He is, in effect, encouraging a politician whom he considers to be evil to believe that he represents "the people."

Those who persist in clinging to the old cliché about "not being able to change the system unless you participate" are missing the whole point: it doesn't matter who wins! History has proven that participation has absolutely nothing whatsoever to do with change. The Demopublican Party has it rigged from the outset.

These are the 1970's; we have come a long way since men first believed that the sun revolved around the earth. Now it is time that we grew up and faced the reality that government does not represent us. Candidates are elected by an elite group of men and women who have managed to finesse their way through the political maze that leads to the inner circle of the establishment. The lesser-of-two-evils voting philosophy merely validates the right of government to perpetuate this ruse.

In view of the realities of The System, does a nonvoter really "get what he deserves?" Hardly. Since he has, in effect, voted in favor of not being ruled, what he really believes is to be left alone. Nonetheless, politicians maintain that if you do not vote, you have no right to complain. They tell you that you are apathetic. That is like telling a man he is apathetic if he refuses to choose between having either his TV set or his watch stolen. It is absurd to conclude that because such a man refuses to "vote" on which crime should be committed against him, he "deserves it" when one of the two items is stolen. If the ballot does not provide you with a choice to your liking, how else can you exercise your so-called freedom of choice except by not voting?

You have a natural right to say no to anything. And when you decline to vote, you are saying no to *all* the candidates. When someone chastises you for not voting, isn't he really saying that you have no *right* to exercise a "no" vote?

The truth is that the person who refuses to vote (for moral and/or intellectual reasons) shows far more love of his country, and far more courage, than the lesser-of-two-evils robot. Instead of simply falling into line, such a dissenter is, in effect, saying, "I refuse to go along with illogical rhetoric; I refuse to be intimidated by patriotic slogans; I refuse to be coerced by promises of 'getting what I deserve' should I not exercise my 'right' to vote; I refuse to be deceived into believing that I have a free choice."

The average citizen, intent on doing the moral thing, does not realize that there is an alternative open to him aside from voting for one of two candidates of whom he disapproves. He can cast a vote of dissent, thus communicating to government that he opposes *both* candidates and does not wish to have either one represent him.

Massive nonvoting could conceivably put an end, once and for all, to the dangerous illusion that "the people have chosen." If nonvoters (the *real* silent majority) gained enough support, it is conceivable that politicians might adopt libertarian reforms to appease such a massive nonvoting majority.

To say the least, it certainly would be difficult for a winning candidate who received 5% of the votes of eligible voters to claim to have a "mandate of the people." And it would be very unconvincing to try to accuse 80% or 90% of the population of being "apathetic."

Yet one must never forget the reality that politicians have no shame. With nonvoters already piling up an overwhelming majority of nearly two to one over the "winner" of each presidential election, politicians still refuse to acknowledge the discontent of the majority and simply pass off nonvoters as "apathetic."

Whether or not to vote is something you must decide for yourself. But you should consider all aspects very seriously, not only from an intellectual standpoint, but from the standpoints of morality and practicality. If you do lean toward voting, you certainly should at least consider an alternative to the Demopublican Party. The only party I know of that offers a platform consistent with Natural Law, and is therefore respectful of the rights of *every* individual, is the Libertarian Party.

Let me first make it clear that to be a libertarian and to act like a libertarian does not require that one join the Libertarian Party. Libertarianism is the belief that every man should have sole dominion over his own life and property and that no one has the right to use force against him unless he himself is guilty of aggressing on the rights of others. Therefore, if you believe in the American Dream, you already are a libertarian—even if you have been calling yourself a Republican, Democrat or nonvoter.

The most disconcerting thing about the Libertarian Party is that it *is* a political party. While the party platform (a copy of which I strongly urge you to read) clearly spells out across-the-board freedom for *everyone*, much more so than even the Declaration of Independence, one cannot escape the Four Great Political Realities, particularly the fact that a politician must lie in order to get elected and, once elected, must commit aggression to make good on as many campaign promises as possible.

If Libertarian-Party leaders are serious about their total-freedom philosophy, the practical question is, how will they ever get a presidential candidate elected on a platform that does *not* promise short-term, something-for-nothing solutions to expediency-minded voters? (In view of this seemingly insurmountable obstacle, it is somewhat amazing that they already have succeeded in gaining one seat in the Alaska House of Representatives. Perhaps some people *are* beginning to understand the situation?)

There is no question that the Libertarian Party offers a distinct alternative to the Demopublican Party. So-called conservatives traditionally have favored economic freedom, but have always wanted to draw lines where civil liberties are concerned. So-called liberals traditionally have campaigned for personal freedom, but have favored restraints on economic freedom. In other words, both are inconsistent on the issue of liberty.

It is only the true libertarian who does not pose a contradiction, because he favors personal *and* economic freedom. This means *no* compromise when it comes to freedom.

I once asked John Hospers, the Libertarian Party's first presidential candidate (1972), if the realities of The System would not eventually corrupt Libertarian office holders even if the Party did succeed in gaining the presidency. His answer was very straightforward and practical. He said that indeed that was a possibility, but that it might take fifty or a hundred years for the Party to become as corrupt as the Republicans and Democrats. In the meantime, not only would the people of this country enjoy fifty to a hundred years of drastically increased freedom and prosperity, but they would be buying considerable additional time in which to come up with alternatives to our present system before it collapses. I thought that was a very honest answer and certainly a worthwhile reason for Libertarian-Party members to continue to pursue their goal of gaining the presidency.

But it's a long, uphill climb. The Demopublicans, through "election laws," managed to keep the Libertarian Party off the ballot in eighteen states in the 1976 presidential election. In addition, of course, Libertarian-Party candidates were deprived of equal media time, Secret-Service protection, and campaign funds that are made available to Demopublican candidates out of the government kitty.

On the other hand, when you realize that the Libertarian Party has operated under these handicaps, the fact that it garnered 1.25 million votes nationwide in the 1978 elections is nothing short of a sensational accomplishment. I cannot help but wonder how much closer the citizens of this country would be to taking back America had John Hospers been elected to the presidency in 1972 or Roger MacBride in 1976.

As I said, however, the voting decision is yours, and it should not be taken lightly. Consider all factors, then make your own decision.

I could list many other ways in which you could help to restore the American Dream without becoming a crusader, but those already offered should more than suffice to get you started in the right direction. Using the concept of Natural Law as a guide, I am sure you can expand on the list quite easily.

I leave you with this warning: remember that the government is armed and dangerous and therefore has the means to change the rules of the game at any time. It does, in fact, do so continually. That puts you, me and everyone else at a decided disadvantage, no matter how much we wish to help the cause of freedom. Government can change anything, and everything, overnight, simply by passing a new law.

There is nothing you can do about this except to be mentally prepared for the unexpected, so that when it occurs it does not shatter your hopes and enthusiasm.

MAJOR SOLUTIONS ON A POLITICAL LEVEL

If you are inclined to become more "involved," i.e., to help bring about change on a scale that goes beyond making sure that your own day-to-day actions are consistent with the ideals of freedom, there are many ways you can contribute. Since most of the laws now in existence are violations of human rights, campaigning for the repeal of almost all of them would be worthwhile.

An important note of caution: Do not get lulled into

trying to make everyone in our society financially "equal." That is precisely the wrong direction—the direction that has been taken by expediency-minded politicians for years. To restore the American Dream, the objective must be to get back to a system whereby everyone has an equal *opportunity* to improve his well-being—an equal opportunity to pursue his life, liberty and happiness, without interference from others.

Our overall objective should be a drastic diminishing of the power of man over man. That can only mean maximization of liberty, which, as previously stated, translates into *minimizing* government and government functions.

The individual must again become all-important. Minimizing government means coming as close as possible to cutting it back to its "legitimate" functions, as soon as is practical. Once again, at most, these functions are:

1) Providing protection for the lives and property of citizens.

2) Providing a system of arbitrating contractual disputes.

3) Providing for a so-called national defense.

On one point all libertarians and all advocates of human freedom are united: it is *not* government's function to "help people fulfill their desires." Such help translates into a fueling of Expediency Factors and inevitable violations of individual rights. In short, the more government is minimized, the more it becomes government "of the people, by the people, and for the people."

There are several ways in which minimization of government can be accomplished:

—*All office holders, especially the president, should serve only one term.* This one step would remove a great deal of corruption from The System. While it may be true that politicians would still have to lie in order to get elected, at least they would not feel as obligated to deliver on their promises of aggression once in office. In other words, politicians might have to promise to violate the rights of certain people in order to get votes, but, realizing that they would not be running for reelection, some may have enough integrity not to follow through and actually commit the promised violations.

When I say "one term," I am talking about one term for an entire lifetime—never again to run for office. Let's do away with the lifetime, professional politician.

Some people might argue that this does not give politicians time to develop their political skills, but that is *exactly* what I am advocating an end to! Political "skills" are what give politicians the expertise to manipulate us for their benefit, particularly for the purpose of getting reelected. The professional politician should become a creature of the past. All politicians should be required to return to the real world and earn a living just like everyone else.

—*Taxes of all kinds should be phased out as swiftly as is practical*. While taxation is, plain and simple, theft, this is where practicality comes in. Even if the libertarian's dream of an immediate end to all taxation were to come true, the reality is that it would cause chaos and violent revolution. Further, it would be unfair to the millions of people who have grown up not realizing that living off the government dole is immoral.

The taxation burden was brought about in a gradual manner, and I believe that it should be phased out in the same way. Perhaps a twenty-five-year plan for cutting back on income taxes, at the rate of 4% a year, would be realistic. The ultimate objective, of course, should be to repeal the Sixteenth Amendment so that government would never again have the right to tax people's incomes. Eventually, only voluntary user charges on government services might remain as a way to cover government's minimal expenditures.

The "inflation tax," of course, should be repealed immediately, in toto—meaning that government should not be allowed to print new money at all, except to replace money that is damaged or worn out. If there are no budget deficits, there is no need to print money. As previously explained, if production increased without a corresponding increase in the money supply, prices would simply drop; each dollar would be worth more, because there would be fewer of them.

There is no other way to deal with inflation. So-called hedging against inflation creates a society of speculators and further weakens production. As Henry Hazlitt has cautioned, "there is no safe hedge against inflation except to stop it." Longer term, after people have had a chance to see what wonders a decrease in the printing of money can bring, the goal should be to get government completely out of the money business, whence it came. This means repealing the legal tender laws and abolishing the engine of the inflation fraud—the Federal Reserve System.

—The redistribution-of-the-wealth functions of government should be phased out, which means cutting government spending to the bone. This, of course, is the corollary to phasing out taxes. Government spending would simply decline at the same rate as the decline in taxes.

Within a matter of a few years, this cutback would begin to turn our whole economy around. Those at the low end of the economic ladder would start to see the benefits within a short time, because, of course, it is they who are hurt most by government spending and taxation. The worse the economy, the worse it is for the "poor." Most of these people, however, have had no way of understanding the facts behind this truth, so they keep right on voting for redistribution-of-the-wealth programs.

These less fortunate people do not understand the inherent contradiction in the welfare-state philosophy, a contradiction which must inevitably lead to collapse: to have wealth to redistribute, you need a high level of production; redistribution programs, however, destroy incentive and productivity, so there is less and less to redistribute.

While some programs, such as welfare and unemployment compensation, should be phased out over shorter periods of time, others, particularly the Social-Security fraud, should be phased out over much longer periods. Because a great majority of citizens have been victims of the Social-Security swindle, the fairest approach would be to decrease benefits over, say, a fifty-year period, so that people who have been counting on Social Security for their retired years would not be left out in the cold.

In other words, people becoming eligible for Social Security during the first year that the plan went into effect would receive 100% of the originally promised benefits; people eligible the next year would receive only 98%; those eligible the third year would receive 96%; and so on.

—*Government services, and thus government employees, should be gradually eliminated.* Again, it would be important here to make the phaseout period reasonable enough so that government employees could be absorbed into the civilian work force. Employees who have been at their jobs twenty or thirty years obviously should not be thrown out of work. In most cases, such employees have innocently invested their lives in government-job security, with perfectly good intentions.

The smoothest way to effect a transition would be over a long period of time, with those who have been on government payrolls the least number of years being released first. As older employees die off, their jobs should simply be eliminated. Eventually, what we would end up with would be more people gainfully employed in the private sector, producing the goods and services consumers want; for reasons that have been repeated many times, this makes for a healthy economy and improves everyone's well-being.

Long term, there would still be postmen, firemen and other kinds of "civil servants," except they would no longer be civil servants; they would be legitimate private employees performing the same functions as before, only better, less expensively and more efficiently than in the old government-employment days.

—*The laws of supply and demand should be allowed to operate freely.* That can only be accomplished by abolishing virtually all governmental regulatory agencies and repealing virtually all laws regulating business. Among laws that should be repealed *immediately* are minimum-wage laws, so-called antitrust and antimonopoly laws (which, in fact, *protect* monopolies), fair-pricing laws and rent-control laws. It goes without saying that all business subsidies of any kind should be outlawed.

All regulatory agencies should, at the very least, be eliminated over a period of one to ten years, but the most useless and harmful ones should be dismantled at once so that business can get back to producing wealth, increasing employment and making life better for everyone.

Among the agencies that should be abolished immediately are the SEC, ICC, CAB, FCC and FTC. Originally I had planned to include the Environmental Protection Agency and the Occupational Safety and Health Administration in this list of agencies to be immediately abolished, but, on reflection, I feel they should be dismantled over a period of two to three years. This would give those who have legitimate concerns regarding worker safety and the quality of our environment confidence that the heavy hand of government is not needed to safeguard these areas. I wish to make it clear, however, that I believe the EPA and OSHA to be among the most destructive of governmental agencies; because they cripple productivity, they actually *endanger* the lives of citizens.

—Along this same line, so-called consumer advocates, environmentalists, and other self-proclaimed protectors of the people should be held civilly and criminally liable for their actions. If such people use coercion or force to interfere with the freedom of others, including the freedom of businessmen, they should be vigorously prosecuted. And, needless to say, they should not be handed "government funds" to carry out their egomaniacal crusades. They, too, should have to work for a living, or suffer the consequences of unemployment.

—Most government property and businesses should be sold off. Theoretically, government has no right to own land or to operate businesses under the ruse of "public ownership." Public ownership simply means that those in power control certain property. Incredibly, however, federal, state and local government combined owns 42% of the 2.2 billion acres of land in this country.

As Lysander Spooner pointed out a century ago, for government to claim that it owns vast tracts of land lying between the Atlantic and Pacific Oceans is absurd. Government is supposed to be in the business of protecting the lives and property of individuals. Where and how did it get into the land business?

By selling off most of its land, buildings and businesses, government would be in a position to pay off the entire national debt and probably have billions of dollars left over to rebate to citizens. As a bonus, the absurd notion of "public property" would cease to exist, which would eliminate whole areas of argument that would never even arise if there were no such thing as a "public place."

—All victimless-crime laws should be repealed at once, and all people imprisoned for violations of such "crimes" should immediately be granted a full pardon. These include not only the traditional victimless-crime laws, but also the rarely discussed victimless-crime laws relating to

such things as the draft, compulsory education, busing and affirmative action.

—*All laws which invade the privacy of individuals should be repealed, and certainly no new laws to make such invasion easier for government should be enacted.*

The millions of files government now holds on citizens—files which contain material of a strictly private nature—should be destroyed. As other agencies are abolished and laws are repealed, so too should the FBI and CIA be phased out. It sounds great to ramble on about how these agencies protect our lives from domestic and foreign threats, but the reality is that they spend most of their time snooping on *us.*

Obviously, by the time you read this book, both agencies will be working overtime compiling files on my personal life. Anyone who suggests an improvement in The System or a move in the direction of freedom is immediately looked upon as a "conspirator." As Sy Leon says, " 'conspiracy' . . . means to talk with others about defending yourself against politicians."

—*Our ludicrous and counterproductive interference in the affairs of other nations, including foreign aid, should immediately be brought to a halt.* I purposely avoided discussing foreign policy in this book, primarily because it, too, is a book unto itself. But the mess of our so-called foreign policy has gotten so out of hand that it would be inappropriate not to at least mention it here.

First, along with the decline of other moral virtues, groveling has been the dominant characteristic of our foreign policy for years. We grovel at the feet of Third-World Nations who demand that we give them handouts under the threat of allying themselves with Russia (the absurdity being that, in most cases, the countries to whom we knuckle under end up going to Russia for more handouts anyway).

"To be a liberal American today," says Irving Kristol,

"is to be infused with instant guilt . . . especially toward poor and distant nations to whom we have never done any harm." The Western World, and the United States in particular, has gradually become the blackmail victim of underdeveloped countries. Much of this has been motivated by our politicians' irrational desire to race around the globe competing with Russia for allies. Had all the billions of taxpayer dollars we gave away bought us the friendship and goodwill of people in other countries, perhaps one could make a practical argument (though not a moral one) that it was worthwhile.

But the reality—and the coup de grace—is that all of our "aid" and meddling have only succeeded in causing us to be *hated* by most of the world. Our continued interventionist actions in the face of such hate are the actions of a panicked nation (meaning panicked politicians). Our strength from within is decaying, so we comb the earth trying to buy support to reassure ourselves.

The same panic and lack of character is reflected in our policy of continuing to enter into political partnerships with bloody, totalitarian regimes. Playing the China card was a disgrace to every freedom-loving American. For Leonard Woodcock, chief of the U.S. liaison office in Peking, to refer to it as marking "a new era in our relations that will contribute to the well-being of both countries and of all mankind" is shameless "doublespeak" (language intended to induce doublethink) even for a politician.

Hogwash. It marked a new era that will contribute to the coffers of Coca-Cola, United Airlines and the other American companies who began a wild stampede for their share of the 900-million-people pie of China. I am in favor of complete freedom of trade between companies and people throughout the world, but not under the umbrella of political partnerships between governments.

It is doublespeak when politicians say that by restoring

"diplomatic relations" with grotesque regimes like that of Mainland China we are taking a step toward "understanding" them. Who *wants* to understand criminals?

Some day, perhaps when it is too late, American politicians will realize that attempting to further the cause of peace by making political deals with criminals is doublethink. For us to sit in the United Nations and negotiate with the inhumane dictatorships of Cuba, Russia, Ethiopia, Vietnam, North Korea, and many others is tantamount to the warden of a prison sitting down and negotiating with hardcore convicts. The leaders of these nations have murdered millions of their own citizens and hold those still alive in absolute bondage. We should withdraw from the United Nations immediately and demand that its headquarters be removed from our soil.

We do not need to spread our shaky dollars around the world frantically begging for friends. We do not need to make political agreements with inhumane dictatorships in order to feel safe. Instead of flooding foreign countries with armaments and free handouts in an effort to buy goodwill, what we should do is set a *domestic* example for the rest of the world. Indeed, that is exactly what we did in bygone days when immigrants came by the millions to share in the American Dream. And those immigrants should still be allowed to come here.

Why do so many Americans fear immigrants? All of us or our ancestors were immigrants at one time or another. And, ironically, newly arrived immigrants are the people most endowed with the American spirit, because they are thankful for the opportunity to work at any job they desire and for any wage they wish to accept; they are thankful for the *freedom* to do as they please. Increased immigration would be a shot in the arm to the American Dream, not the hindrance that so many fear.

—*We should always keep more ambitious goals in mind for the long term, goals for decreasing the size of government and increasing the importance and liberty of the individual.* Perhaps some day a freedom lover will figure out a way to maintain an orderly society without the tyranny of Majority Rule. That is a worthwhile goal for young libertarians at universities to be thinking about—how to make people completely free from the desires of the majority.

Another long-term, ambitious goal is the attainment of the world's first totally laissez-faire business environment. While it is hard to imagine such freedom at this time, who knows what the future holds if we can ever take back America from the powerholders and allow individuals to be free to pursue their own well-being? Even if we should never attain a pure laissez-faire society, every step toward it is still a step closer to freedom and to a better way of life for everyone.

And, of course, the ultimate long-term goal: complete elimination of government. That is the premier question for young libertarian scholars: Can civilization and order prevail without at least a skeletal form of government to protect men from aggression? Perhaps the dream of a governmentless society is as unrealistic as Karl Marx's dream of a society where everything would belong to "the people" in common. But who knows? Perhaps we have not evolved far enough. Said Thoreau, " 'That government is best which governs not at all;' and when men are prepared for it, that will be the kind of government which they will have."

You and I will not live to see a nation that is totally devoid of government, but it is possible that we may live to see an America in which government is relegated to the role of protecting our lives and property—in the words of John Hospers, an America in which we would scarcely be aware of the existence of government.

RESTORING THE AMERICAN DREAM

Is it too late? Is The System too entrenched to permit the rescue of the bold experiment undertaken by our libertarian founders in Philadelphia in 1776? Is the world so wrought with problems that our only alternatives are world control or world destruction?

If there is to be any hope for the world, I believe that Americans must restore the American Dream. As America has declined over the past decades, the rest of the world has declined along with it. I do not think that this has been a coincidence. I believe that America once represented a shining hope for all mankind—the living proof that freedom was attainable. As that hope has diminished, so too have the aspirations of enslaved peoples throughout the world.

If the devastating cycle of politically expedient promises/government-function spending/direct taxation and inflation is not halted and then drastically reduced, attempts to use free enterprise as the scapegoat will accelerate. And as taxation and regulation of business increase, motivation to produce will die, leading inevitably to a nationalization of industry; that is the step which will take America from the decaying stage to the death stage. It happened in Greece; it happened in Rome; it happened in every civilization that tried to provide the free lunch for its citizens and then blamed businessmen for its financial collapse.

If we are to stop the momentum of repeating the errors of past civilizations, the people of this country must come to understand that the free lunch is an illusion; they must come to understand that if they do not give up the free lunch voluntarily, they ultimately will lose it, and everything else, through government force.

As I began to write this final chapter, I received a piece

of literature in the mail which most people would have thrown in the wastebasket. But I kept it, because this seemingly unimportant piece of junk mail epitomized the twisted moral standards so prevalent today. It was an advertisement for a book entitled *Encyclopedia of U.S. Government Benefits,* and I reprint here some of the advertising copy:

"Here at last is *the only complete guide to government payments and services ever published.* You will find . . . how to get Social Security and Medicare benefits, scholarships and loans, a government mortgage . . . what are the eligibility requirements for all benefits; and much more."

In other words, it was a guide on how to outmaneuver your neighbor for a bigger share of the stolen goods!

The choice is ours. We can keep our Expediency Factors in high gear, thus cutting off our left arm and ignoring the fact that we are, in the process, killing our right arm as well. Or we can use our power to reason, begin thinking long term, and start living like civilized men of goodwill.

One of the biggest roadblocks to restoring the American Dream is that each succeeding generation has grown up under increasing government intervention and restraint, thus being conditioned to accept the welfare state and government control as normal.

When freedom and free-enterprise advocates of the 1930's tried to warn our parents and grandparents that FDR's folly of false prosperity would be paid for by their children and grandchildren, apparently not many of them took heed. Most were caught up in blind patriotism and thought of FDR as a patron saint. But their patriotism was misguided. They were patriotic to politicians—to men of power—instead of to the cause of liberty. Shall we continue to make the same mistake and finish off the job of destruction for future generations?

I was greatly disturbed by a conversation I had a while

back with Sy Leon, the always objective, pure libertarian. I said to him, "Just think, Sy, at the rate we're going, people living in the United States fifty years from now will be virtual slaves of a totalitarian regime. Isn't that depressing?"

In response, Sy said (and I paraphrase here) that fifty years ago there were people sitting around a room just like we were, talking about the same thing. The tyranny they envisioned has turned out to be far worse, but the average person today does not think of it as tyranny, because he has grown accustomed to this way of life. Therefore, even though people in this country probably will be living under pure totalitarianism fifty years from now, they will have learned to cope with it and will not think of it as being as bad as we do.

What a horrible thought! It was right out of *Brave New World:* Mustapha Mond assuring the Savage that eight-ninths of the people were happier "below the water line." In other words, what one doesn't know won't hurt him. The point is that if a person grows up never having experienced freedom, he has nothing to which he may compare his way of life.

I think about this often as I watch the people of this country hooked on their "somas"—NFL football, jogging, TV sitcoms, and a general attitude of letting the good times roll. Their minds are so tuned to enjoying their false prosperity that their general response to our current crisis is, "I just can't believe things are as bad as some of these doomsayers claim; the world has always had problems, but the government has a way of working things out."

But they are wrong. The world has never before been confronted with the problems of today, except on a smaller scale in places like Greece and Rome, and in those cases things did *not* work out! Those civilizations died. And it is absolutely impossible for things to "work out" for us unless William Simon's statement can become a reality: "I am confident that the American people would demand massive reforms *if they understood the situation*."

OUR BEST HOPE

To understand our real plight and what needs to be done, people—young people in particular—must be taught. Unless a massive dissemination of truth and fact occurs, most people will continue *not* to understand the situation. And that means they will continue to make the situation worse.

The majority of people in this country certainly will never read this book, nor any other book which sets forth the realities of government. That is why I believe that the real hope for America lies in educating the young. And since government-controlled primary and secondary schools certainly are not going to teach children the truth, that means that in the early years the job must be done by parents.

Since the main hope of saving our country really boils down to home education, I was until recently extremely pessimistic about the future. After all, if parents do not understand the situation, how are they to teach their children? But, as I said in my prefacing remarks to this book, little rays of hope are beginning to appear.

Recently, a woman by the name of Linda Timmons wrote a "letter" to the *Los Angeles Times* which again made me wonder if it is not possible that people *are* beginning to understand the situation. Her writing so moved me that I feel it appropriate to reprint her letter here in its entirety. If Ms. Timmons' evolution toward truth is representative of a sizable portion of our population, then perhaps there is good reason to hold out hope for restoring the American Dream.

I've got the paycheck blues again, and it made me start thinking about America, land of the free.

I had always interpreted that phrase to mean I was free to live my life the way I chose. I believed I had the right to make all decisions affecting my life as long as I didn't harm anyone or break any laws. I believed that the laws were there to protect me, and that people who broke them were criminals.

These concepts always sounded fine to me. I was sure I could live a happy, productive life within their framework, because I knew I was an honest, conscientious person responsible for my actions. I was proud to be an American.

I lived with this fantasy until I was 19 years old. That was when my husband received his draft notice, on our first wedding anniversary. Within days, the boy I had loved since I was 13 was gone. The government, which made the laws to "protect" me, said that he had to go where it sent him, and that he had to do what it ordered. If he didn't, he would be a criminal and could go to jail. And so they sent him to Vietnam. They risked his life without his consent. I didn't understand.

My husband came back safely after 11 months, and was honorably discharged from the service. We started a family, saved our money and bought a small house in Hermosa Beach, where we'd grown up. We were careful not to get into debt. Each year the property taxes on our small house increased; in 1976 they doubled, and then last year they doubled again. We couldn't afford the $2,400 that the government wanted—but this was our home, this was the town where we grew up. What were we to do? The government, which made laws to protect us, said that we had to pay if we wanted to stay. I didn't understand.

Proposition 13 lowered our property taxes, so that we could keep our home. But now the court is suggesting that soon my children may not be able to attend the school at the end of our street; they might have to ride a schoolbus for up to 40 minutes each way, to go to school in someone else's town. We chose to live in this town because we grew up here. It is a small community, with lots of involved citizens. We wanted our children to have pride in their neighborhood, and in its school. The government, which makes rules to protect us, says that this is not important; something called integration (not education) is more important.

Receiving what's left after taxes of my first few paychecks of 1979 has prompted me to reflect on my life. I believe that I finally understand: I am not free at all; it is the government that's free to do what it wants. The laws are not designed to protect my family and me; they are designed to protect the government. And we, the people, support this system with our money, our children —our very lives. If we don't, we risk breaking the law.

Yes, now I understand, and I am not so sure how I feel anymore about being an honest, conscientious person responsible for my actions. America, land of the free —it rings hollow. I'm still proud to be an American, and I wouldn't want to live anywhere else, but I am not as naive as I once was.

At the college level, there has been an increase in the number of libertarian instructors, some of the more prominent being John Hospers, Thomas Sowell, Murray Rothbard, Milton Friedman and Robert Nozick. Instructors of this quality are making young men and women think again—young people who have been brought up in a collectivist, wealth-is-evil, theft-is-moral society. They have inspired students to challenge the logic and morality of heretofore unchallenged assumptions. Though this libertarian renaissance is in its early stages, the results have been encouraging. I find more and more young people rejecting the notion that it is all right to violate people's rights so long as it is for a "worthwhile" cause.

The first thing youngsters must understand is the morality inherent in Natural Law. Once understood, freedom and free enterprise automatically fall into place. They must learn that property rights and human rights cannot be separated. They must learn that capitalism has not failed; that what has failed is our mixed economy—i.e., government intervention in the economy. They also must learn that the gold standard did not fail; that it was government's immoral and irresponsible inflating of the currency that failed.

They must learn that forced equality means a loss of freedom, and that in all countries where it has been attempted, the citizens have experienced only equal misery. They must learn that socialist countries have been totally unsuccessful in their attempts to improve the well-being of their populations and that, in the end (and usually in the beginning), they come running to the United States, which still has enough excess wealth to help bail them out, despite the battered condition of the American Dream.

And they must learn the destructive ramifications of the equation:

Expediency Factors + The Vote = Government Functions

Once this is understood, they will also understand that it is "Government Functions" that must be drastically reduced, for it is that part of the equation that spells loss of liberty.

TIME IS RUNNING OUT

Perhaps the American Dream will never again flourish on this planet. Perhaps its next appearance will occur in a world in a far-off galaxy unknown to us. If so, you and I certainly will not be part of it. The nearest star in space lies 30 trillion miles beyond Pluto and most stars in our own galaxy are a thousand times more distant. For you and me, the picture is pretty clear: we either restore the American Dream, right here and now, or we most certainly will never live to experience it again.

And to restore it, we have to recapture the spirit that exemplified it—the spirit of individualism, of self-reliance, of risk taking—the spirit described by Rose Wilder Lane in *Give Me Liberty:*

It was the Americans who lived and kept their fighting spirit through the hard and bitter times that followed every surge of prosperity, it was men and women who cared enough for their own personal freedom to take the risks of self-reliance and starve if they could not feed themselves, who created our country, the free country, the richest and the happiest country in the world.

Time is running out on the United States and other Western democracies. Freedom and equality cannot coexist. We have tried it and, like others before us who attempted it, the results have been disastrous. It is time for you and me to decide how badly we want the free lunch. If we continue to pursue it, then we cannot expect to live in a free society.

It is time to face the reality that the party is over. "Letting the good times roll" is a fantasy of our false-prosperity past. For nearly fifty years we have acted like naughty, irresponsible children, grabbing things without permission. The sooner we admit our errors and begin accepting our punishment, the sooner we can get back to enjoying the freedom that has escaped us. Either we pay for our false prosperity voluntarily or we will pay for it through government force. And, without question, all future generations will pay for it.

The final turning point in the decay of the American Dream was the "Great Society." The Great Society represented false prosperity, which is possible only through slavery. The American Dream represents *true* prosperity, which is possible only through freedom. The heart of the American Dream is freedom; the lifeblood is free enterprise.

A free man is someone not under the control or power of another. A free man is free to govern himself. I do not want to relate to you as a competitor for government favors. I want to relate to you as a neighbor, acting in goodwill. I want to relate to you as a free man.

Freedom or free lunch—which will it be? Ultimately, freedom must be achieved or it must be forever lost in the pursuit.

Notes

Chapter 1

1. Will and Ariel Durant, *The Lessons of History* (New York: Simon and Schuster, 1968), p. 20.

Chapter 2

2. Sy Leon, with Diane Hunter, *None of the Above: The Lesser of Two Evils . . . Is Evil* (Santa Ana, California: Fabian Publishing Company, 1976), pp. 204–205.

3. Jim Davidson, "Why Voting Isn't Necessarily the Most Patriotic Act You Can Perform," *Playgirl* (November 1976), p. 18.

4. Will Durant, *The Story of Philosophy: The Lives and Opinions of the Great Philosophers of the Western World* (New York: Simon and Schuster, 1961), p. 20.

5. Ibid., p. 20.

6. Leon, *None of the Above*, p. 170.

Chapter 3

7. Henry Hazlitt, *Economics in One Lesson* (New York: Harper & Brothers Publishers, 1946), p. 171.

8. Milton Friedman, *Capitalism and Freedom* (Chicago: The University of Chicago Press, 1962), p. 15.

9. Rose Wilder Lane, *Give Me Liberty* (Mansfield, Missouri: Laura Ingalls Wilder-Rose Wilder Lane Home Association, reprinted by *Libertarian Review*, 1977), p. 4.

10. John Hospers, "A Free America," *Reason* (May 1978), p. 34.

Chapter 4

11. S.I. Hayakawa, "Mr. Hayakawa Goes to Washington," *Harper's* (January 1978), p. 39.

12. Walter E. Grinder, Introduction to *Our Enemy, the State*, by Albert Jay Nock (New York: Tree Life Editions, 1973), p. xviii.

13. Durant and Durant, *Lessons of History*, p. 72.

14. "Fundamentals of Liberty; Lesson 41: Protection—II," p. 6. ["Fundamentals of Liberty" is a home-study course developed under the direction of Robert LeFevre by Rampart College.]

15. Henry Hazlitt, *The Conquest of Poverty* (New Rochelle, New York: Arlington House, Publishers, 1973), p. 115.

16. Hayakawa, "Mr. Hayakawa Goes to Washington," p. 42.

17. James Brown, "Newsman Paul Harvey—He Reigns on His Parade," *Los Angeles Times*, Calendar (8 October 1978), p. 3.

18. "Fundamentals of Liberty; Lesson 22: Prices and Employment—II," p. 7.

19. Milton Friedman, "Humphrey-Hawkins," *Newsweek* (2 August 1976), p. 55.

20. Milton Friedman, "Tax Shenanigans," *Newsweek* (19 December 1977), p. 55.

21. "Trends," *Reason* (October 1975), p. 36.

22. Robert Poole, Jr., "Fighting Fires for Profit," *Reason* (May 1976), p. 7.

23. "Teachers Flunk IQ Test in Dallas," *Los Angeles Times* (19 July 1978), Part I, p. 13.

24. Phil Kerby, "Era of Limits—Even for Taxpayers," *Los Angeles Times* (4 January 1979), Part II, p. 1.

25. John Hospers, "The Two Classes: Producers and Parasites," *Reason* (September 1975), p. 13.

26. Hayakawa, "Mr. Hayakawa Goes to Washington," pp. 42–43.

27. Will Durant, *Our Oriental Heritage* (New York: Simon and Schuster, 1954), footnote p. 19.

Chapter 5

28. "Deflating Paperwork," *The Wall Street Journal* (12 February 1979), p. 18.

29. William E. Simon, *A Time for Truth* (New York: McGraw-Hill Book Company, Reader's Digest Press, 1978), p. 92.

30. Robert A. Rosenblatt, "Disillusioned, 2 Bureaucrats Return to Real World," *Los Angeles Times* (24 December 1978), Part VII, p. 1.

31. Ronald J. Ostrow, "Bell Calls Bureaucracy Threat to Nation," *Los Angeles Times* (26 January 1979), Part I, p. 4.

32. "Fundamentals of Liberty; Lesson 18: Competition and Monopoly," p. 5.

33. Robert A. Rosenblatt, "Fruehauf's Chief Calls FTC 'Anti-Business,'" *Los Angeles Times* (6 September 1974), Part III, p. 16.

34. Simon, *Time for Truth*, p. 83.

35. Milton Mueller, "Affirmative Action: Quota to End All Quotas?" *The Libertarian Review* (January 1979), p. 38.

Chapter 6

36. Roger L. MacBride, *A New Dawn for America: The Libertarian Challenge* (Ottawa, Illinois: Green Hill Publishers, 1976), p. 77.

37. Fred M. Hechinger, "Schoolyard Blues: The Decline of Public Education," *Saturday Review* (20 January 1979), p. 20.

38. Anne Wortham, "Individualism: For Whites Only?" *Reason* (February 1979), p. 33.

39. Thomas Sowell, "Are Quotas Good for Blacks?" *Commentary* (June 1978), footnote p. 40.

40. Murray N. Rothbard, *For a New Liberty* (New York: Macmillan Publishing Co., 1973), p .116.

41. Robert Sherrill, "How to Dupe the Snoopers," *The New York Times Book Review* (18 February 1979), p. 13. Mr. Sherrill's information has been taken from Robert Ellis Smith's *Privacy: How to Protect What's Left of It.*

Chapter 7

42. "In His Own Words: Ex-Treasury Secretary William Simon Fears That the Economy Hasn't Got a Prayer," *People* (16 October 1978), p. 72.

43. "The Tax Mess," *Newsweek* (10 April 1978), p. 71.

44. Morgan Maxfield, with James Gwartney, *1929 Revisited: An Economic Handbook for the Turbulent Seventies* (Kansas City; Missouri: National Youth Foundation, 1977), p. 48.

45. "In His Own Words: William Simon," p. 72.

46. Jim Davidson, "Tired of Being Pushed Around Every April 15? Punch out the IRS!" *Playboy* (April 1976), pp. 84 and 86.

47. Sanford L. Jacobs, "Tax-Refusal Experts Will Tell You

How, For Just a Small Fee," *The Wall Street Journal* (26 March 1979), pp. 1 and 35.

48. Melvyn B. Krauss, "The Swedish Tax Revolt," *The Wall Street Journal* (1 February 1979), p. 18.

49. Hazlitt, *Economics in One Lesson*, p. 182.

50. "Fundamentals of Liberty; Lesson 27: Banking," p. 6.

51. Christopher Drew, "Doomsayers Still See Economic Collapse Looming Despite Dollar's Big Recovery," *The Wall Street Journal* (6 November 1978), p. 6.

52. Henry Hazlitt, *The Inflation Crisis, And How to Resolve It* (New Rochelle, New York: Arlington House, Publishers, 1978), p. 76.

53. Ibid, pp. 57 and 121.

54. Hazlitt, *Economics in One Lesson*, p. 4.

Chapter 8

55. Étienne de la Boétie, *The Politics of Obedience: The Discourse of Voluntary Servitude*, translated by Harry Kurz (Montreal, Canada: Black Rose Books, 1975), p. 60.

56. Vermont Royster, "1979: The Year of Testing," *The Wall Street Journal* (3 January 1979), p. 12.

57. Robert Froman, *Racism* (New York: Delacorte Press, 1972), pp. 53–54.

58. Lewis H. Carlson and George A. Colburn, *In Their Place: White America Defines Her Minorities, 1850–1890* (New York: John Wiley & Sons, 1972), p. 1.

59. Wortham, "Individualism," p. 31.

60. Giles St. Aubyn, *The Art of Argument* (Buchanan, New York: Emerson Books, 1962), p. 28.

61. Eric Hoffer, *The True Believer* (New York: Harper & Row, Publishers, 1951), p. 67.

62. Durant, *Our Oriental Heritage*, p. 24.

Chapter 9

63. Rose Wilder Lane, *The Discovery of Freedom: Man's Struggle Against Authority*, Foreword by Robert LeFevre, Introduction by Roger Lea MacBride (New York: Arno Press and The New York Times, 1972), p. 190.

64. Hospers, "Free America," p. 33.

65. Eric Hoffer, *Before the Sabbath* (New York: Harper & Row, Publishers, 1979), p. 53.

66. Maxfield, *1929 Revisited*, p. 155.

67. Lane, *Discovery of Freedom*, pp. 189–190.

68. Lane, *Give Me Liberty*, pp. 21 and 44.

Bibliography

Adams, James Ring. "Coping with Proposition 13." *The Wall Street Journal*, 10 October 1978.

"A Growing Penalty." *Los Angeles Times*, 4 May 1979.

"As U.S. Citizen, You Owe $4,807." *Los Angeles Times*, 23 January 1979.

Auerbach, Alexander. "Agencies That Got Unlisted Numbers." *Los Angeles Times*, 16 June 1976.

Bartlett, Bruce. "Why Government Will Never Stop Inflation." *The Libertarian Review*, March 1979.

Boyd, Marjorie. "Pensions: The Five Trillion Dollar Scandal." *The Washington Monthly*, February 1978.

Boyd, Marjorie. "What's Wrong with the Civil Service: Inflated Grades." *The Washington Monthly*, April 1977.

Brown, James. "Newsman Paul Harvey—He Reigns on His Parade." *Los Angeles Times*, 8 October 1978.

Capitalism and the Historians. Edited and with an Introduction by F.A. Hayek. Chicago: The University of Chicago Press, Phoenix Books, 1963.

Carlson, Lewis H., and Colburn, George A. *In Their Place: White America Defines Her Minorities, 1850–1890*. New York: John Wiley & Sons, 1972.

"Carter and Key Economic Aides Carry Inflation War to U.S. Bureaucracy Itself." *The Wall Street Journal*, 14 November 1978.

"Carter Sees Government Inefficiency as Threat." *Los Angeles Times*, 25 March 1979.

Chandler, Russell. "Mormons Run Own Welfare System." *Los Angeles Times*, 19 November 1977.

Chapman, Stephen J. "What's Wrong with the Civil Service: Inflated Pay." *The Washington Monthly*, April 1977.

"China Fallout." *The Wall Street Journal*, 31 January 1979.

Conine, Ernest. "Fighting Overregulation Is 'In.'" *Los Angeles Times*, 6 November 1978.

Davidson, Jim. "Tired of Being Pushed Around Every April 15? Punch Out the IRS!" *Playboy*, April 1976.

Davidson, Jim. "Why Voting Isn't Necessarily the Most Patriotic Act You Can Perform." *Playgirl*, November 1976.

Davis, William. *It's No Sin to Be Rich: A Defense of Capitalism*. Nashville, Tennessee: Thomas Nelson, Publishers, 1976.

"Deflating Paperwork." *The Wall Street Journal*, 12 February 1979.

Dickson, Paul. *The Official Rules*. New York: Delacorte Press, 1978.

Drew, Christopher. "Doomsayers Still See Economic Collapse Looming Despite Dollar's Big Recovery." *The Wall Street Journal*, 6 November 1978.

Durant, Will. *Our Oriental Heritage*. New York: Simon and Schuster, 1954.

Durant, Will. *The Story of Philosophy: The Lives and Opinions of the Great Philosophers of the Western World*. New York: Simon and Schuster, 1961.

Durant, Will and Ariel. *The Lessons of History*. New York: Simon and Schuster, 1968.

Eaton, William J. "Corporate Profits Up 26%; Held Inflation Catastrophe." *Los Angeles Times*, 21 March 1979.

Eaton, William J. "Paperwork Cost Put at Billions." *Los Angeles Times*, 22 November 1978.

"83% in Poll Favor Basing College Hiring on Ability." *Los Angeles Times*, 1 May 1977.

Emerson, Ralph Waldo. *Essays, Poems, Addresses*. Roslyn, New York: Walter J. Black, 1941.

Federalist Papers, The: A Collection of Essays Written in Support of the Constitution of the United States. From the original text of Alexander Hamilton, James Madison and John Hay. Selected and Edited by Roy P. Fairfield. Second Edition. Garden City, New York: Doubleday & Company, Anchor Books, 1966.

Friedman, Milton. *Capitalism and Freedom*. Chicago: The University of Chicago Press, 1962.

Friedman, Milton. "Humphrey-Hawkins." *Newsweek*, 2 August 1976.

Friedman, Milton. "Tax Shenanigans." *Newsweek*, 19 December 1977.

Froman, Robert. *Racism.* New York: Delacorte Press, 1972.

Fromm, Erich. *The Heart of Man.* New York: Harper & Row, Publishers, Perennial Liberty, 1971.

"Fundamentals of Liberty." A home-study course in two volumes developed under the direction of Robert LeFevre by Rampart College.

Girard, Penny. "Western Union U.S. Telegraph Monopoly Ends." *Los Angeles Times,* 26 January 1979.

Graham, Bradley. "Slumping Productivity Reaches Critical Point, but Some Find Reason for Hope." *Los Angeles Times,* 4 December 1978.

Hayakawa, S.I. "Mr. Hayakawa Goes to Washington." *Harper's,* January 1978.

Hazlett, Thomas W. "Reason Interview: William E. Simon." *Reason,* February 1978.

Hazlitt, Henry. *The Congress of Poverty.* New Rochelle, New York: Arlington House, Publishers, 1973.

Hazlitt, Henry. *Economics in One Lesson.* New York: Harper & Brothers Publishers, 1946.

Hazlitt, Henry. *The Inflation Crisis, And How to Resolve It.* New Rochelle, New York: Arlington House, Publishers, 1978.

Hechinger, Fred M. "Schoolyard Blues: The Decline of Public Education." *Saturday Review,* 20 January 1979.

Hoffer, Eric. *Before the Sabbath.* New York: Harper & Row, Publishers, 1979.

Hoffer, Eric. *The True Believer.* New York: Harper & Row, Publishers, 1951.

Hoffer, William. "Who's Regulating the Regulators?" *TWA Ambassador,* June 1976.

"Hollywood House Haunts Him Still." *Los Angeles Times,* 8 December 1976.

Hospers, John. "A Free America." *Reason.* May 1978.

Hospers, John. *Libertarianism: A Political Philosophy for Tomorrow.* Santa Barbara, California: Reason Press, 1971.

Hospers, John. "The Two Classes: Producers and Parasites." *Reason.* September 1975.

Huxley, Aldous. *Brave New World.* New York: Harper & Row, Publishers, Perennial Classic, 1969.

"Illegals, The." *Times,* 16 October 1978.

"Inflation Victims: Paychecks Bigger—Buying Power Less." *Los Angeles Times,* 13 October 1978.

"In His Own Words: Ex-Treasury Secretary William Simon Fears

That the Economy Hasn't Got a Prayer." *People*, 16 October 1978.

Jacobs, Sanford L. "Tax-Refusal Experts Will Tell You How, For Just a Small Fee." *The Wall Street Journal*, 20 March 1979.

Jastrow, Robert. *Until the Sun Dies*. New York: W.W. Norton & Company, 1977.

Johnson, Paul. *A History of Christianity*. New York: Atheneum, 1977.

Katz, Howard S. *The Paper Aristocracy*. New York: Books in Focus, 1976.

Kerby, Phil. "Era of Limits—Even for Taxpayers." *Los Angeles Times*, 4 January 1979.

Krauss, Melvyn B. "The Swedish Tax Revolt." *The Wall Street Journal*, 1 February 1979.

Kristol, Irving. "Foreign Policy: End of an Era." *The Wall Street Journal*, 18 January 1979.

La Boétie, Étienne de. *The Politics of Obedience: The Discourse of Voluntary Servitude*. Translated by Harry Kurz, Montreal, Canada: Black Rose Books, 1975.

Lambro, Donald. *The Federal Rathole*. New York: Arlington House, Publishers, 1975.

Lane, Rose Wilder. *The Discovery of Freedom: Man's Struggle Against Authority*. Foreword by Robert LeFevre. Introduction by Roger Lea MacBride. New York: Arno Press and The New York Times, 1972.

Lane, Rose Wilder. *Give Me Liberty*. Mansfield, Missouri: Laura Ingalls Wilder-Rose Wilder Lane Home Association. Reprinted by *Libertarian Review*, 1977.

Leon, Sy, with Hunter, Diane. *None of the Above: The Lesser of Two Evils . . . Is Evil*. Santa Ana, California: Fabian Publishing Company, 1976.

MacBride, Roger L. *A New Dawn for America: The Libertarian Challenge*. Ottawa, Illinois: Green Hill Publishers, 1976.

Malabre, Alfred A., Jr. "Money Supply's Outpacing Economic Growth Is the Real Culprit in Inflation, Analysts Say." *The Wall Street Journal*, 27 December 1978.

Mann, Jack. "The Presidency and Political Poetry." Reprinted from *The Washington Post*, 25 January 1976.

Maxfield, Morgan, with Gwartney, James. *1929 Revisited: An Economic Handbook for the Turbulent Seventies*. Kansas City, Missouri: National Youth Foundation, 1977.

Mill, John Stuart. "On Liberty." Taken from *Man and the State:*

The Political Philosophers. Edited by Saxe Commins and Robert N. Linscott. New York: Random House, 1947.

Montemayor, Robert. "Family Defies Ban, Gets Boy Laetrile in Mexico." *Los Angeles Times*, 27 January 1979.

"Mother's Plea to Teach Child Denied." *Los Angeles Times*, 12 December 1978.

Nelson, Bryce. "In Washington, Influence Is Up for Grabs." *Los Angeles Times*, 29 December 1978.

Nelson, Bryce. "Washington: Life of Luxury a Capital Idea." *Los Angeles Times*, 25 November 1978.

Nock, Albert Jay. *Our Enemy, the State.* With an Introduction by Walter E. Grinder. New York: Tree Life Editions, 1973.

Norval, Morgan. "Why We Need Guns." *Reason*, October 1975.

Oliver, Myrna. "Illiterate Contractor Enjoined by Court." *Los Angeles Times*, 23 June 1976.

Orwell, George. *Nineteen Eighty-four.* New York: Harcourt, Brace & World, 1940.

Orwell, George. *Nineteen Eighty-four.* With an Afterward by Erich Fromm. New York: The New American Liberty, A Signet Classic, 1961.

Ostrow, Ronald J. "Ban on Corporate Mergers Studied." *Los Angeles Times*, 26 January 1979.

Paine, Thomas. *Rights of Man.* Edited and with an Introduction by Henry Collins. Baltimore: Penguin Books, A Penguin Classic, 1969.

"Playboy's Interview with Ayn Rand." Reprinted from *Playboy* by The Objectivist, Inc., 1964.

Poole, Robert, Jr. "Fighting Fires for Profit." *Reason*, May 1976.

Poole Robert, Jr. "Milestones." *Reason*, January 1979.

Rand, Ayn. *The Virtue of Selfishness.* New York: The New American Liberty, Signet Books, 1964.

"Review & Outlook: Spending, Transfers and Poverty." *The Wall Street Journal*, 13 October 1978.

Rosenblatt, Robert A. "Disillusioned, 2 Bureaucrats Return to Real World." *Los Angeles Times*, 24 December 1978.

Rosenblatt, Robert A. "Fruehauf's Chief Calls FTC 'Anti-Business.'" *Los Angeles Times*, 6 September 1974.

Rothbard, Murray N. *For a New Liberty.* New York: Macmillan Publishing Co., 1973.

Rothbard, Murray N. *The Case for a 100 Percent Gold Dollar.* Washington, D.C.: Libertarian Review Press, 1974.

Rothbard, Murray N. *What Has Government Done to Our Money?* Novato, California: Libertarian Publishers. 1978.

Royster, Vermont. "1979: The Year of Testing." *The Wall Street Journal.* 3 January 1979.

Russell, Bertrand. *Why I Am Not a Christian.* New York: Simon and Schuster, A Touchstone Book, 1957.

St. Aubyn, Giles. *The Art of Argument.* Buchanan, New York: Emerson Books, 1962.

Secter, Bob. "Polygamist's Tragedy: He Wanted to Be Left Alone." *Los Angeles Times*, 5 February 1979.

Secter, Bob. "Prop. 13 Fever Vanishes After Short Siege in Illinois." *Los Angeles Times*, 1 December 1978.

Shaw, Gaylord. "10 Million Dropouts to Join Nonvoters." *Los Angeles Times*, 5 September 1976.

Sherrill, Robert. "How to Dupe the Snoopers." *The New York Times Book Review*, 18 February 1979.

Silk, Leonard, *Economics in Plain English: All You Need to Know About Economics—In Language Anyone Can Understand.* New York: Simon and Schuster, 1978.

Simon, William E. *A Time for Truth.* New York: McGraw-Hill Book Company, Reader's Digest Press, 1978.

Smith, Adam (George Jerome Goodman). "Maybe I Am Easily Scared: Energy and Superinflation." *The Atlantic Monthly*, December 1978.

Smith, Roger. "Despite Taxpayer Revolt, Most Will Pay More in '79." *Los Angeles Times*, 31 December 1978.

"Sound and Fury Over Taxes." *Time*, 19 June 1978.

Sowell, Thomas. "Are Quotas Good for Blacks?" *Commentary*, June 1978.

Spooner, Lysander. "Natural Law, Or The Science of Justice." Reprinted from *Libertarian Forum*, September 1974.

Spooner, Lysander. *No Treason: The Constitution of No Authority* and *A Letter to Thomas F. Bayard.* Libertarian Broadsides, no. 5. With Introductions, Annotations and a New Afterword by James J. Martin. Colorado Springs, Colorado: Ralph Myles Publisher, 1973.

"Taiwan: Shock and Fury." *Time*, 25 December 1978.

"Tax Mess, The." *Newsweek*, 10 April 1978.

"Teachers Flunk IQ Test in Dallas." *Los Angeles Times*, 19 July 1978.

Thoreau, Henry David. *Walden* and *On the Duty of Civil Diso-*

bedience. New York: Harper & Row, Publishers, A Harper Classic, 1965.

Timmons, L. "Singing the Blues About the Red, White and Blue." *Los Angeles Times,* 22 February 1979.

"Trends." *Reason,* October 1975.

"Trends: Airline Deregulation This Year?" *Reason,* May 1977.

"Troubled by '78 Economy? Wait'll '79." *Los Angeles Times,* 2 January 1979.

"Welfare: A Surprising Test." *Newsweek,* 27 November 1978.

Wortham, Anne. "Individualism: For Whites Only?" *Reason,* February 1979.

Index

Activists, Hollywood, 106–107, 201

Affirmative-action laws, 220–225

Agrarian Revolution, 40–41, 83, 321

Agricultural, development of, 41–42

Airlines, deregulation of, 20, 194

Alcoa Aluminum, 193

Aliens, illegal, 84, 141

American Revolution, 43, 61, 321

Antitrust laws, 188–196

Asimov, Isaac, 26–27, 203

Atlas Shrugged, 18, 322

Australia, 62–63

Authoritarianism, 46

Banking, 261–263

Baruch, Bernard, 328

Bell, Griffin B., 183

Black Hair/Blond Hair Theory, 51

Bonds, U.S. Treasury, 252–253, 335

Brave New World, 19, 25, 322, 359

Browne, Harry, 21

Budget, federal, 238, 284–285

Bureaucrats, 156–165, 182–184

Business regulation, 177, 211–212; cost of, 178–180

Busing, 226

Caesar Augustus, 171–174

Capitalism, 77–95

Carter, Jimmy, 58, 59, 107, 135–136, 248, 251, 280–281, 330

Charity, 166–170

China, 38, 101, 103, 105, 106–108, 175, 330, 354–355

Civil Aeronautics Board, 194, 351

Civil War, 294–295

Commentary, 221

Communism, 78; real, 101–109; theoretical, 95–100

Competition, free-market, 89, 90–91, 192–193

Conscription, 218

Constitution of the United States, 23, 122, 175, 260–261, 308–313

Consumer price index, 23, 268

"Consumer-protection" laws, 197–200, 227–228, 340, 351

Cranston, Alan, 160

Cuba, 38, 101, 103, 175, 355

Davidson, Jim, 53, 57

Declaration of Independence, 124, 309–310, 316

Deficit, federal, 249–253

Deficit spending, 249–253, 272–273; pre-election, 251

Definition Game, 36

Democracy, 45–70, 323–324, 326

Democrats, 68

Demopublican Party, 60–62, 68, 344

Depression, economic, 76–77

Depression, Great, 85–86, 117, 242, 324

Disabled, caring for the, 165–171

Discrimination, reverse, 220–225

Doublethink, 295–296

Douglass, Frederick, 296

Draft, military, 218

Drugs, laws governing use of, 233–235

Durant, Will, 20, 23, 57, 68, 123, 174, 307, 331; and Ariel, 36, 123, 308, 331

Economics, 72–77; definition of, 73; and freedom, 72; laws of, 74–76, 77

Economists, 73, 125

Economy, collapse of U.S., 76, 252, 277–279, 337–338

Education, compulsory, 153–154, 219–220

Emerson, Ralph Waldo, 175

Eminent domain, 226–227

Energy, 201–204, 206–207; nuclear, 201–203

Environmental Protection Agency, 200–205, 351

Environmental regulation, 200–205

Equality: under communism, 101–102; versus freedom, 32, 123–125, 331

Ethiopia, 38, 103, 306, 355

Expediency Factor, 39, 64–70

"Fair-pricing" laws, 186, 207–208

False prosperity, 76–77, 253

Federal Communications Commission, 190, 195–196, 351

Federal Reserve Act, 86, 262–263, 311, 319

Federal Trade Commission, 195, 351

Fire protection, 152–153

Food and Drug Administration, 29, 199

Force, government use of, 36–37, 313–315, 331

Ford, Gerald, 21, 204, 251, 280

Foreign policy, 353–355

Freedom, 18, 332–333; as an outdated concept, 37–38; definitions of, 35–38; and economics, 72; versus equality, 32, 123–125; restriction of, 37, 42, 63, 326–327

Friedman, Milton, 43, 94, 143, 146, 181, 362

Fromm, Erich, 67, 308

"Fundamentals of Liberty," 34, 129, 140, 192, 193

Gambling laws, 231–232

Garbage collection, 151–153

Goebbels' Law, 256

Gold, 256–266; standard, 263–266; warehouses, 259–260

Government: birth of, 40–42; characteristics of, 45, 69; co-operation with, 334–335; cost of modern, 238; employees, 156–165; employee pension plans, 162–163; use of force by, 36–37, 313–315, 330–331; legitimate functions of, 42–43, 115, 347; modern functions of, 114, 118–119, 120–122; handouts, accepting, 336–339; propaganda, 290–293; property, 352

Government services, 148–154, 350–351; mandatory subscription to, 149, 154–156

Grouping, political, 65, 339–340

Gun control, 228–230

Hayakawa, S.I., 121–122, 136, 140, 172–173, 182, 211

Hazlitt, Henry, 19, 21, 130, 187, 254, 255, 277, 279, 287, 349

History, American, 293–295

Hitler, Adolf, 35, 46, 104, 256, 277, 290

Hoffer, Eric, 94, 105, 134, 306, 322

Hospers, John, 165, 173, 210, 249, 255, 314, 324, 345, 346, 356, 362

Huxley, Aldous, 25–26, 61, 133, 291

Illusory Deregulation Theory, 206

Immigration, 355

Income, guaranteed, 135–136

Industrialization, 78–79

Industrial Revolution, 78–79, 81, 82–84

Inequality, 123–125

Inflation, 253–287, 291–292, 348–349; definition of, 266–268; German, 255–256, 277–278

Intellectuals, 22–24, 290–299

Internal Revenue Service, 241, 245–246

Interstate Commerce Commission, 194–195, 351

Johnson, Lyndon, 175, 242, 250–251

Johnson, Paul, 256

Kahn, Alfred E., 279

Kennedy, Edward, 191, 255

Kennedy, John F., 58, 305

Keynes, John Maynard, 112, 113

Kingitis, 69

King, Martin Luther, Jr., 222–223

Kristol, Irving, 353

La Boétie, Étienne de, 289

Labor, division of, 78–79

Labor faking, 134–135

Labor Theory, 98–100

Laissez-faire, 79–80

Laker Airlines, 189–190

Lane, Rose Wilder, 102, 103,

137, 316–317, 329–330, 335–336, 363–364

Law: force of, 313–314; morality as basis of, 214–215; morality of, 312–313; religion as basis of, 214

Leon, Sy, 47, 63, 69–70, 120, 341, 353, 359

Libertarian: definition of, 18, 30–35, 344–345

Libertarianism, 30–35, 344–345

Libertarian Party, 20, 61–62, 344–345

Libertarian Review, The, 225

Lincoln, Abraham, 294–295

Lobbyists, 65, 184–185

Macauley, Thomas, 321–322

MacBride, Roger, 62, 346

Madison, James, 320

Majority Rule, 48–55, 321–322

Man, nature of, 38–40

Marx, Karl, 103, 109, 113–114, 123, 260, 356

Maxfield, Morgan, 250–251, 269

Mill, John Stuart, 21, 215–216

Minimum-wage laws, 117, 207–208

Minting, 259–261

Money, 256–266; definition of, 74; types of, 257–258

Monopolies, 188–196

Morality: as basis of law, 214–215; versus needs and desires, 126–129

Mueller, Milton, 225

"Mysterious-multiplier" concept, 111, 128, 271, 334

Natural Law, 29–35, 327–328

"Needs and desires," 31; versus morality, 126–129

New Deal, 117, 319, 330

New York City, 161–162

Nineteen Eighty-four, 19, 43–44, 293–295, 322

Nixon, Richard, 21, 182

Nock, Albert Jay, 173

Nonvoting, 20, 57–64, 342–346

Norval, Morgan, 230

"Nothingism," 109

Nothink, 295, 296

Nozick, Robert, 298, 362

Occam's Razor Principle, 24

Occupational Safety and Health Administration, 199–200, 351

"On Liberty," 215–216

Orwell, George, 43, 104, 123, 295

Ownership, common, 95–97

Ownership, true tests of, 34, 98

Paine, Thomas, 293

Pensions, government-employee, 162–163

Plato, 57, 68

Political Realities, The Four Great, 56–57

Politicoholism, 69–70

Ponzi Scheme, 146, 251–252

"Poor," caring for the, 165–171

Pornography laws, 232

Postal Service, U.S., 151

Poverty: as a political issue, 132, 159–160

Power, lust for, 39–40, 43–44

Price gouging, 87–90
Privacy, 236–237, 353
Profits, 87–90, 279
Property: common, 96–97; protection of, 41–43; rights, 32–34, 226–227
Proposition 13, 20, 132, 154–156, 206, 246–247
"Public place," definition of, 235

Quick-as-Hell Full-Employment Theory, 140
Quotas for hiring and college admission, 220-225

Rand, Ayn, 18, 31, 75, 183, 297–298
Reason, 137, 173, 222, 230
Recession, economic, 76
Regulatory Mousetrap Theory, 183
Religion, as basis of law, 214
Rent controls, 206
Republicans, 68
Reverse discrimination, 220–225
Rights: equal, 32, 124–125, 331; natural, 32; property, 32–34
"Robber Barons," 84–85, 95
Roman Empire, 171–175, 321
Roosevelt, Franklin D., 116–117, 172, 175, 242–243, 330, 358
Roosevelt, Theodore, 295
Rothbard, Murray, 19–20, 154, 171, 232, 254, 362
Russell, Bertrand, 299

Russia, 38, 46, 62, 101–108, 123, 175, 355

Securities and Exchange Commission, 197–198, 351
Servitude, involuntary, 218
Servitude, love of, 289–308
Sexual behavior, laws governing, 232–233
Simon, William E., 20–22, 25, 94, 137, 161, 176, 182, 184, 204, 211, 359
Sixteenth Amendment, 86, 242, 311, 319, 348
Slavery, 49–50, 312
Slogans, patriotic, 299–307, 329–330
Smith, Adam, 21, 81–82
"Smith, Adam," (George Jerome Goodman), 255
Smoking, 234–235
Socialism, 102–114
Social Security, 116, 145–147, 247, 251–252, 338–339, 350
Solzhenitsyn, Alexander, 105–106
Sowell, Thomas, 221–224, 362
Spooner, Lysander, 49, 64, 167, 246
Straightthink, 296–307
Subsidies: business, 186–188; farm, 117, 188
Suicide, 235–236
Supply and demand, law of, 74–75, 90, 351
Sweden, 109, 248
System, two-party, 60–62
Systems, economic, 78

Taiwan, 108, 330

Tariffs, 186–187, 243

Taxation, 239–249, 348–349; evasion of, 245–246; through inflation, 272, 349; protecting against, 245–246; "soak-the-rich" policy of, 117, 130, 242

Tax-Cut Illusion Theory, 247

Tax revolt, loss-of-incentive, 247–248

Taxes, types of, 243–244

Thoreau, Henry David, 57, 66, 312, 356

Time for Truth, A, 20–22, 94, 204

To-hell-with-itism, 18–19

Totalitarianism, 45–46, 47–48, 114

Transfer payments, 111, 121, 138–156

Unemployment, 139–145, 207–209

United Nations, 355

Usury laws, 231

Victimless-crime laws, 216–236, 352

Von Hoffman, Nicholas, 63

Vote, The, 55–57, 110–112, 323

Voting, 55–69, 340–346

Wage-and-price controls, 205–207, 279–280

Washington, D.C., 65, 160, 185

Washington Monthly, The, 161, 162

Wealth: definition of, 74, 257; production of, 74–76; redistribution of, 120–176, 349–350; surplus, 74–76; ways to obtain, 134

Welfare, 121, 130, 159–160

Woodcock, Leonard, 354

"Worker-safety" laws, 197–200

Wortham, Anne, 222, 223

Zoning laws, 230–231